ID0699688

THE BRUTAL TRUTH ABOUT ASIAN BRANDING

And How to Break the Vicious Cycle

THE BRUTAL TRUTH ABOUT ABOUT ASIAN BRANDING

And How to Break the Vicious Cycle

Joseph Baladi

WILEY

John Wiley & Sons (Asia) Pte. Ltd.

Other Wiley Editorial Offices
John Wiley & Sons, 111 River Street, Hoboken, NJ 07030, USA
John Wiley & Sons, The Atrium, Southern Gate, Chichester, West Sussex, P019 8SQ,
    United Kingdom
John Wiley & Sons (Canada) Ltd., 5353 Dundas Street West, Suite 400, Toronto, Ontario,
    M9B 6HB, Canada
John Wiley & Sons Australia Ltd., 42 McDougall Street, Milton, Queensland 4064,
    Australia
Wiley-VCH, Boschstrasse 12, D-69469 Weinheim, Germany

Library of Congress Cataloging-in-Publication Data
ISBN 978–0–470–82647–8 (Hardback)
ISBN 978–0–470–82649-2 (ePDF)
ISBN 978–0–470–82648-5 (Mobi)
ISBN 978–0–470–82650–8 (ePub)

Typeset in 10/13 Sabon Roman by MPS Limited, a Macmillan Company
Printed in Singapore by Saik Wah Press Pte. Ltd.

To my mother and father, who sacrificed so that I might find opportunity.

CONTENTS

INTRODUCTION

While the development and growth of much of Asia over the past two decades has been nothing short of spectacular, much of this has come not from the emergence and contribution of *great* Asian brands, but in spite of their absence. In fact, with the notable exception of one or two brands, a very persuasive argument can be made that no great Asian brands (excluding Japanese brands, as explained in Chapter 2) exist—at least not as measured by consumer surveys in Asian capital cities, where Western brands are preferred by eight out of ten Asian consumers.

Asian brands continue to languish as a result of lack of differentiation, innovation, and consistency. In a 2009 *Newsweek* cover story (the headline for which inferred that there are as yet no Chinese global brands), Premier Wen Jiabao was reported to have called for China "to create companies that can innovate and churn out 'brand-name export products'—meaning companies with reputations for quality, innovation, and service so strong that customers are willing to pay a premium for their products."[1] Currently, Asian consumers are willing to pay a premium only for the likes of Apple, BMW, Omega, and similar Western brands that provide not only the security of implicit guaranteed quality, but also the unique emotional dimensions that create personal and bonding resonance.

The inability of Asian brands to graduate from good to great has been a particularly pernicious and persistent obstacle to companies across the region in their efforts to move up the value chain and provide brands of desire. A big part of that problem is the inability—and in some cases, unwillingness—of brand owners to face the reality of rapidly changing market and consumer landscapes precisely at a time that demands creativity and innovativeness.

That a problem with Asian brands even exists will be contested by those who argue that economic power is shifting from the West to Asia—and to China, in particular. Putting aside the argument that much of the economic power that is underwriting this paradigm shift comes from business-to-business (B2B) activity, rather than from the creation of compelling consumer brands, it is almost certain that a transition of power and influence to the East has commenced. Chapter 1 of this book questions what form that shift will take, and how sustainable it might prove to be. At the heart of the issue is the question: Will that momentous transition remain purely economic, or will it also be cultural?

The vehicle that delivered the cultural impact of the "American Century" (i.e. the 20th century) was the great American brand. Brands such as Levi's, Colgate, Pampers, and Mustang offered ever-improving functional attributes that delivered on product purpose, combined with emotional cues that went on to inspire and define generations of global consumers. The obvious question that emerges is: How effective (how cultural) will be the current transition of the world order from West to East in the absence of great Asian brands?

Chapter 2 attempts to answer this question by exploring five key reasons for the lack of development of Asian brands in general, and great Asian brands in particular. A central theme of that chapter, and indeed of the entire book, is the behavior, attitudes, and roles of Asian chief executive officers (CEOs) in regards to the branding process.

"THE GOVERNMENT KNOWS BEST"

Soon after I arrived in Singapore in 2002, I joined the tail end of a nine-month nation-branding project headed by a very senior government official. The brand positioning statement had been crafted and was making the rounds of ministers and other important government officials for their comments. I began to feel very troubled when the requests to rewrite and revise the statement kept coming in. When I explained to the head official why it was unwise to fundamentally change a positioning that had been crafted as a result of nine months of research, analysis, and workshops, she replied: "The government knows best." Her certainty and conviction were absolute, and it was obvious from her expression that she wouldn't budge from her position. I was stunned.

I have since witnessed that same mentality play out in the private sector across Asia, where—instead of the government—it is the CEO who knows best. The traditional hierarchical management structure that still characterizes most Asian companies has impeded, in some measure, the creation and sustainability of competitive advantage. Where the CEO rules absolutely, creativity and innovation falter. Where the CEO considers himself an oracle of knowledge, very few dare to question, contradict, or even offer an opinion. Where the CEO seeks validation, most will rush to agree with him and offer reassurance. Where brand is the catalyst and branding the process that determines the very flavor of a company, most Asian CEOs are settling for vanilla.

These ingrained attitudes of CEOs are, then, a major impediment to effecting management change; however, another important contributor to the slow development of Asian brands is, simply, CEOs' lack of knowledge about how the process of branding works and how pervasive it needs to be in the DNA of the organization. This situation is made even more complicated when CEOs *don't know what they don't know*. In as much as brand and branding are concerned, the existence of this "condition" creates a ripple effect that can grow to momentous proportions. The consequences for the organization are widespread, both internally and in terms of its external relationships with consumers and customers. This powerful chain reaction can manifest itself either positively or negatively. In other words, branding within the organization can literally be all about vicious or virtual cycles.

Better appreciation of the strengths and benefits of a robust branding infrastructure starts with a better understanding of key fundamental constructs. Chapter 3 provides an introduction to strategic platforms that are indispensable to managers about to embark on branding initiatives or programs within their companies.

For those companies actively considering branding projects, Chapter 4 identifies two essential pre-branding steps that are entirely strategic in nature: formulation of the company's business strategy and guiding principles. Given their importance, it is extraordinary how often they are misunderstood, underutilized, or simply ignored.

Chapter 5 identifies and discusses eight essential brand strategy drivers. Though not exhaustive, these drivers are the critical pillars that support all companies. They represent the building blocks that collectively contribute to the formation of strong and relevant brands. Because everything in branding is connected, the absence of even one of these elements will seriously undermine the structural integrity of any brand-building program.

Chapter 6 examines the phases of a typical "full-bodied" strategy-driven, brand development methodology. An understanding of the process and each of these phases provides the CEO and his or her team with one invaluable skill: the ability to properly assess branding project proposals. Proposals define the direction of the project. They must, therefore, reflect the correct and optimum scope items, as well as address the specific needs or circumstances of the company. Beyond providing decision makers with a more effective platform from which to make decisions, they will also be better equipped to estimate the realistic costs required to complete the project.

While this book is devoted mostly to revealing the systemic weaknesses that undermine the emergence of strong Asian global brands and provides a comprehensive road map for overcoming these, Chapter 7 goes a step further and discusses a common Achilles heel endemic to many Asian companies: implementation. In reality, branding projects consist of two stages. The first is the brand development process; the second is implementation. Without implementation, any effort companies make to review, revise, or change their positioning will be for naught. This chapter also makes the point that it is equally important that the brand promise delivers to another key stakeholder: the company's own employees.

The Brutal Truth About Asian Branding aims to reveal the reality of Asian branding—warts and all, and to provide a prescriptive road map that will align Asian brands with what they are destined to become: great and defining. Chapter 8 argues that, although presently largely dormant, there *is* greatness in Asian brands; and that the near future will be characterized by major change and will be championed by a phalanx of exceptional Asian leaders who are willing to experiment and challenge the conventional. These first of many will lead by example and demonstrate, through the success of their own companies, the kind of heights Asian brands are capable of reaching.

It is only by first identifying what is wrong, that the process of building great brands can begin in earnest. Currently, branding efforts by Asian companies are largely a haphazard, hit-or-miss affair. This is preventing Asian brand development from reaching critical mass. What is needed to successfully effect change is executive education coupled with courage (to do things differently). The goal of this book is to shine a light on the current face of Asian branding so that CEOs can see it clearly and objectively, and thereby make informed choices about where to go from here.

While Asia's current crop of CEOs are part of the problem that is holding back the development of great Asian brands, there are exceptions—maverick leaders who are materializing in individual markets and demonstrating that new thinking can deliver spectacular successes. These trailblazers will emerge as important catalysts for change.

There is spectacular greatness locked up in Asian brands. Empty talk and misconceptions will not unlock their promise. Only brutal truth will.

NOTE

1. Craig Simons, "Name a Global Brand that is Chinese. Can't Do It? Here's Why," *Newsweek*, July 27, 2009.

I

A TIME OF PROFOUND CHANGE

"America's financial strength helped it export its entertainment and culture. Now an emerging 400 million-strong Indian consumer market, as well as an economically vibrant Asia, is shifting consumer power to the region. It's now our time to make our culture the prime culture of the world. The time for Bollywood is now."

Bollywood producer, Shehar Kapur[1]

THE OLD WORLD ORDER

I was born in the second half of the 20th century. I spent the first 10 years of my life in Brazil—what was then, and to some degree remains today, a developing (if not an emerging) country. Although I was only young when my family and I departed, I have clear memories—of sights, smells, and sounds—of that early childhood. I was profoundly influenced by Brazil's culture.

I spent the next 10 years in Australia: culturally a place that, in the 1970s, was on a different planet from Brazil. Even seeing it through the eyes of a child, the differences were startling; however, I could also see the similarities. Those similarities, I would later realize, formed the foundation of an overarching universal culture that was as much part of the Australian experience as it was of the Brazilian one, and much of the rest of the world. That culture was Western. The television shows we watched, the movies we went to see, the music I heard in the background as a child and later chose to listen to as an adult, the literature that was read to me and which I later read for myself, the clothes I wore, as well as the things that I eventually grew to believe were "right" or appropriate, were all heavily influenced by the West, and especially by America. I didn't know it then, but I was living in the "American Century," when the world took its cue for almost everything from that country.

How that came to be is the result of a combination of a multitude of factors, starting with the largesse of the Marshall Plan following the end of the Second World War and extending into the decades that followed through the sheer ingenuity, energy, enthusiasm, and mentality of American leadership, American business, and the American people. This is not to say that a master plan existed, or that there was some sort of engineered or premeditated Western or American altruism that fueled the effort that mended and rebuilt the world in the latter part of the 20th century. But as we look back through the lens of history, the facts do provide abundant evidence that the culture and values that America championed were, by and large, embraced by people all over the world.

> The single, most profound thing American businessmen figured out a long time ago was that brands fundamentally *define* people.

The genius of the strategy lay in communicating American culture and values through American brands. The single, most profound thing American businessmen figured out a long time ago was that brands fundamentally define people. In the living rooms of Paris, the slums of Bombay, and the souks of Lebanon, people watched *I Love Lucy*, drank Coke, and wore Levi's. These brands represented, and at the same time reflected, the liberating values of America: the opportunity to work and succeed, and to enjoy life in a manner that was somewhat heroic. That message was communicated through Hollywood, through popular song-writers and performers, and through the example of numerous ordinary individuals who were "making it"—those who attained the so-called American Dream. Though created and exported by Americans, what made this dream successful was its universal appeal.

For much of the 20th century, great numbers of people the world over aspired to that same dream. During that time, American "brands"—from products and services such as Colgate and Hertz, to iconic figures such as Elvis Presley, Martin Luther King, and JFK—came to define the lives of millions of people around the world, and in the process, defined the world itself. Observed French foreign minister Hubert Vedrine: "The United States of America dominates in all arenas: the economic, technological, military, monetary, linguistic (and) cultural one. There has never been anything like it."[2] What came into being in the second half of the last century was a paradigm of life created in the image of America.

What makes a paradigm powerful is how it completely conditions one to interpret and accept the "life" we are presented with as the life we are intended to live. In other words, paradigms convert the surrounding reality into a normative reality. The world that America shaped became reality, and it extended over so many years that a good portion of the world's population—up until recently—simply accepted it as *the* reality. Over this period and in spite of the Cold War, and notwithstanding the loud complaints and resistance by more parochial cultures (the French, for example), a new world order settled in. It was Western, English speaking, and decidedly American.

Though many may plausibly argue today that the American world order is faltering, no sufficiently powerful alternative order has emerged to replace it. So, while not everything that comes out of the United States today is automatically embraced by the rest of the world, as might have been the case in the past, America still remains the main "frame of reference" for many—however criticized and maligned it may be. But the writing seems to be on the wall. Big changes are afoot. As Singapore's Professor Kishore Mahbubani observed: "Once upon a time the world was in love with America. And America loved the world too. It was a magical love affair, with America acting as a shining beacon of freedom and prosperity for billions around the world. That love affair is over. The unique circumstances which created it can never be replicated again."[3] Whether Mahbubani's conclusion will prove to be accurate will depend as much on what America does, as on what develops in Asia, in the immediate and near-term future.

THE NEW WORLD ORDER

While America's overall influence is unlikely to decline in a dramatic or precipitous manner, its economic pre-eminence is likely to be surpassed by China, which has demonstrated both the will and the capability to

"'China is like a new sun in the solar system,' pulling the balance
of world power back toward the East. . ."

Clyde Prestowitz, quoting a "top Singapore official"

translate its size, population, and resources into world influence. Indeed, the idea that the 21st century will be the "China Century" has already generated worldwide currency.

But what, exactly, does "surpass" mean? To many people, it refers to China's economic growth, or GDP (or both), outstripping that of America. And there exists a very good basis for that argument. The massive Chinese economic take-off that began with economic liberalization in 1978 under Deng Xiaoping has delivered extraordinary dividends for the country, and in the process has changed how companies do business and consumers buy—both in and (especially) outside of China. Since 1978, China's GDP has quadrupled, and today its economy is the world's sixth largest.

While technology has changed the way ordinary people around the world communicate and how business is conducted, it is globalization that has changed forever the way we live and the way we think. This phenomenon has particularly impacted China, changing the lives of millions of its people as well as the populations of neighboring countries. The process has made China increasingly confident and assertive. Increasingly accessible world markets, coupled with the significant relaxation of government regulations and interference, have enabled local entrepreneurs, government-managed companies ("state-owned enterprises," or SOEs), and incoming Western multinational companies to leverage the masses of low-cost, working-class citizens who are keen to flee their poverty-ridden destinies and manufacture virtually everything the world wants and needs. That China has become the world's factory is an undisputed fact. That this is beginning to realign the axis of business influence from the West to the East, and specifically China, is also, many would argue, a fact. The power and pre-eminence that Asia as a whole, and China in particular, has created has put in place an inexorable and inevitable shift that in mere decades from now (or possibly less) will have this region outperforming every other part of the world in economic terms. And even China's harshest critics, who argue that its "business model"—a combination of low-end, low-quality manufacturing capabilities made possible by an unlimited supply of low-paid, low-skilled workers—is unsustainable, are showing signs of reconsidering their stance.

The reality of China today goes far beyond the stereotypes with which it is often associated. Cheap labor, while important, is not the only engine driving the Chinese economy. What is increasingly characterizing Chinese companies is their skill in driving down operating costs through higher levels of efficiency. Furthermore, China doesn't just manufacture low-tech products. Over the past 10 years, Chinese companies have stunned the world with a dual strategy of home-grown and highly developed high-tech companies manufacturing everything from sophisticated consumer electronics to complex and complicated computer and biotech technologies, and acquiring established first-tier (and in some cases, iconic) Western companies—complete with intellectual property (IP) and proprietary technology. (The Lenovo purchase of the IBM PC division was certainly the most celebrated of such acquisitions.) Lastly, the major human resource (HR) investment China is making in the fields of engineering and applied sciences—fields increasingly being depleted of talented people in the West—is contributing to higher levels of technological development, allowing Chinese manufacturing to move up the chain and make increasingly more sophisticated products.

So, it is in terms of economic prowess that China (whose economy is expected to exceed that of the United States by 2020)[4] will be an even greater force to be reckoned with in the years ahead and will reshape the global business landscape. But, to date, it is this factor alone that is, by and large, contributing to the "China Century" appellation. As consequential as economic power is, it is nowhere near as spectacular as the idea of a world order paradigm shift of the American type, which influenced the fabric of global life during the latter half of the 20th century.

> Will China's ascent translate into sufficient momentum to change the world order as we know it?

So, the question emerges: Will China's ascent translate into sufficient momentum to change the world order as we know it? Expressed differently: Will masses of people around the world eventually release their grip on familiar, reliable, inspirational, and aspirational America and tentatively reach out to emerging, dynamic, and unpredictable China? Will China begin—at some point during this century—to influence people around the world very much like America has done (and continues to do)?

American leadership was influenced and inspired by two connected beliefs. The first belief was that, given its pre-eminence in the world, the United States had a responsibility to lead. Former US president Bill

Clinton declared in 1996: "Because we remain the world's indispensable nation, we must act and we must lead." His secretary of state, Madeleine Albright, went a step further when she inferred that leadership conferred the responsibility of proactive behavior: "We must be more than audience, more even than actors; we must be the authors of the history of our age."[5] The second belief was that "helping the rest of the world get rich is good for America."[6] This idea contributed directly to the rise and rapid spread of globalization.

If China is to fulfill the promise of the China Century, it seems inevitable that it, too, must adopt a similar leadership philosophy— at least in part. The cultural and historical evidence, however, suggests that China may not be capable of taking exactly the same route. To those holding power in China, the idea of proactive leadership will need to be, by circumstantial necessity, far more self-serving than altruistic: that what is good for China strengthens China first (before the rest of the world). Secondly, in the absence of a liberal democracy, China's economic engine is being fueled by a disconcerting strain of Chinese nationalism: what Josef Joffe, in his book *Überpower*, describes as "humiliation at the hands of foreign powers near and far (stretching) backwards for centuries (that is resulting in) a generous dollop of Social Darwinism, the conviction that one's race or nation must prevail over lesser ones."[7]

If this nationalism translates into a bellicose political posture, China will be incapable of capitalizing on its strong economic power to take on the world's number one role. The honeymoon it is currently enjoying with the populations of countries around the world—including those of Europe and the United States—will sour if they sense the emergence of an imperialistic agenda. Moreover, a dispassionate approach to leadership that excludes the role of doing good (for the world) will not only alienate non-Chinese populations, but will also filter down into the business sector and embed itself as an expression of management philosophy that could well encourage Chinese companies to pursue profit at the expense of virtually everything else. Where profit is the overriding goal and effectively becomes a company's guiding principle, "greatness" is guaranteed *not* to happen. What is also likely not to happen is the emergence of great Chinese brands—those brands that are capable of having an emotional impact on Chinese and other consumers around the world.

In an Ernst & Young "new global reality" report that analyzed the impact of globalization on business, one analyst observed that "the new (world) order might feel more like a multi-dimensional balancing act: how to make your company resilient to shocks but flexible enough to

Source: Newsweek, July 27, 2009.

grasp new opportunities." In that same report, Professor Donald Sull of the London Business School explained that this amounted to an "essential balance between absorption and agility. The former allows firms to weather shocks with a protected core market, diversified cash flow, a strong brand or long-term customer contracts; while agility is essential for spotting and exploiting new opportunities."[8]

Two key words stand out on the "absorption" side of the equation: strong brand(s). While Chinese and other emerging market companies are demonstrating strong agility capabilities, they are struggling to create the safety buffers they will need if they are to weather the "shock" of increasingly sophisticated consumer expectations. Many will discover that there is arguably little value in moving lightning fast if, in the process, they end up missing the point. And the point revolves entirely around the emotional cues that brands must have in order to enter and stay within the orbit of consumers' lives. The longer it takes

Chinese brand owners to recognize this fact, the longer it will take for Chinese brands to emerge as *bona fide* global brands.

> Right now, Asians, including the more affluent mainland Chinese, are doing what most of the rest of the world is doing: They are buying Western and Japanese brands.

Without great Chinese brands, no paradigm shift will take place. Without a Chinese Nike, or a Chinese Apple, or a Chinese Starbucks, or a Chinese Brad Pitt, or a Chinese Universal Studios, or a Chinese Bon Jovi, and even a Chinese Oprah—that the world, and not just China and the rest of Asia, recognizes—the China Century will be a hollow label unworthy of comparison to the American Century. Why? Because all of the above are brands, and real economic power is driven by consumer spending. Right now, Asians, including the more affluent mainland Chinese, are doing what most of the rest of the world is doing: They are buying Western and Japanese brands.

THE REST OF ASIA

"The world is trying to keep up with Asia, more than ever . . . siguro (maybe) you can say it with a little bit of arrogance, the future is here. . ."

Ria Puangco, strategic planner, Grey Group

For China to redefine the world order, it will likely need to align its efforts strategically with the equally vigorous efforts of most of its neighboring Asian countries, including India. This "team effort" will likely result in the future being more accurately described as the "Asian/ Chinese Century" or perhaps just the "Asian Century."

Over the past century, the Asian business mentality (with the exception of that of post-war Japan) was best characterized as one of following, rather than leading. During this period, very little in the way of creative or innovative milestones emerged from the region. This is perhaps not surprising, as much of Asia during those 100 or so years suffered from the multiple burdens of colonial exploitation, despotic (or outright incompetent) leaders, chronic local economic mismanagement and corruption, rampant inflation, war, and periodic natural disasters. Economically speaking, for decade after decade, much of Asia was a "basket-case."

Yet, the massive property developments that are visibly reshaping and transforming most of Asia's capital cities, and the ubiquitous signs of middle- and upper-class affluence, are today obscuring the fact that Asia was once a profoundly troubled region. It is, nevertheless, extraordinary how many young Asians—from Singapore to Shanghai and from Bombay to Bangkok—are completely, even blissfully, ignorant of their immediate past. There is an almost universal assumption that affluence, modernity, and comfort were always more-or-less a part of everyday life. Observes an elderly Singaporean: "Young people will never understand how we feel. . . (They didn't see) the squalor. I came from a poor family and even though school fees were just $3, my parents struggled to pay them."[9] The region's transition (across many, if not all, countries)—from helpless to independent, supplicant to generous donor, unskilled to well-trained, and borrower to lender—has been dramatic. The Asia of today bears little resemblance to the Asia of merely two decades ago.

Generally, dramatic, rapid change is catalyst driven. Asia owes its transformation to three important catalysts: (1) the technology revolution, (2) globalization, and (3) the ascent of China. Some argue that a fourth catalyst also deserves recognition—the ascent of India. The individual impacts, as well as the confluence, of these three (or four) major developments have been the main drivers that have enabled many Asian countries to transition from a region of Third World strugglers to leading First World power economies.

Today, much of the region can legitimately boast of developments and accomplishments that are beginning to elude those of some parts of the Western world. These include: the existence of strong product quality, very well-educated and competent workforces, solid and powerful financial sources, endless research and development (R&D) capabilities, a passion for technology, growing infrastructure in most countries, and the development of free trade agreements throughout the region. Rounding out all of these—or, as some would claim, creating all of these—is the contribution of what might be loosely labeled as "Asian values," which infuse Asians with everything from personal discipline to a solid work ethic. End product: Asia has come a long way, indeed.

And the process is ongoing. Asia is generating ever more energy and momentum as it powers through with aggressive scale and scope to earn not only the admiration of people, companies, and countries around the world, but also a consensus that its efforts are inexorably reshaping this present century into an image of itself.

TOLL-GATES AND VISION

As impressive as this powerful Asian vehicle of energy and ambition appears to be, it will eventually slow down even as it passes what amounts to its first "toll-gate" (one of several that lie ahead). This first toll-gate can also be equated to "phase 1" in what is a multi-phase journey that will deliver the Asian/Chinese Century. The great growth of the late 1980s, the 1990s, and the early years of this century was, to a large degree, reflective of the opportunities created by the three interconnected catalysts mentioned earlier (i.e., technology, globalization, and the ascent of China). At the risk of oversimplifying, where success, growth, and affluence occurred, it was almost inevitable.

Much of this process was fueled by an opportunistic business model—that of the "trader"—in next-to-ideal (and unlikely to be repeated) circumstances. Things were made, and then were sold when the right opportunities presented themselves. In this way, tens of thousands of individuals built their wealth in all corners of Asia. Some individuals still operate in this manner, but they are becoming fewer as the model becomes unsustainable—mostly because the same catalysts that created the circumstances for that type of growth have also provided the climate for aggressive competition.

All Asian companies are now struggling with effectively differentiating themselves in a sea of unrelenting competition.

And it is with competition and its effects that the region enters "phase 2"—what lies beyond the first toll-gate. This phase is all about going up the value chain. While the region comprises countries and companies at very different stages of development, the lead countries—the "Asian Tigers" of South Korea, Singapore, Taiwan, and Hong Kong—have successfully built solid infrastructures that have enabled them to manufacture goods efficiently and deliver high-quality services. *All* Asian companies are now struggling with effectively differentiating themselves in a sea of unrelenting competition. What this really means is that they are struggling to break the code needed to build great brands—brands that are unique, relevant, and compelling. Phase 2 will be all about building brands. This catalyst alone will largely facilitate the essential move up the value chain.

To date, in their efforts to build brands Asian CEOs have been singularly unsuccessful. Brand building is proving to be challenging to decision makers in Asia for a variety of reasons (see Chapter 2), but particularly because it is conceptual in nature. Asian CEOs are notorious for investing only in what they can see and feel. What is "invisible" is often underestimated and ignored. The likelihood of this mindset changing will depend on the kind of political and business leadership that evolves in China and the rest of Asia. If it remains self-centered and self-serving, the massive growth of the past two decades will not be sustainable. Asian businesses will begin to encounter changing expectations of consumers, who are demanding not just higher-quality products, but, increasingly, that they deliver emotional relevance. Unless Asian businesses are able to develop genuine relationships between their brands and consumers—in Asia, as well as around the world—they will fail to move up the value chain.

The first toll-gate has been successfully crossed. What lies beyond is a hill (some would say a mountain) that will provide a litmus test to those empowered to make change: the politicians and business leaders—and perhaps not in that order. Much of the change needed to transform China and the rest of Asia lies ensconced within the conceptual idea of the "brand." As this book will go on to explain, the "Asian brand" is capable of greatness. That greatness will contribute in a very large part to the formation of the Asian/Chinese Century. The road ahead is paved with the need to change thinking and practices. Those individuals who have the vision to see beyond the hill and demonstrate the will to cross each and every toll-gate will create great companies that influence and impact society in very positive, responsible, and, importantly, transformative ways. In today's world, this is evolving as the leading-edge role of business, and it is where the future of Asian business lies.

NOTES

1. Clyde Prestowitz, *Three Billion New Capitalists* (Basic Books, 2005), p. 233, quoting Sumathi Bala, "Bollywood Dreams Going Global," *Financial Times*, August 28, 2004, p. W6.
2. Josef Joffe, *Überpower: The Imperial Temptation of America* (Norton, 2006), p. 28.
3. Kishore Mahbubani, "Economist Debate on Brand America, Against the Motion," *The Economist*, February 2009.

4. David Shambaugh, "The Road to Prosperity," *Time*, September 28, 2009, p. 15.
5. Joffe, *Überpower*, *op. cit.*, pp. 37–38.
6. Prestowitz, *Three Billion New Capitalists*, *op. cit.*, p. 2.
7. Joffe, *Überpower*, *op. cit.*, p. 200.
8. *Redrawing the Map: Globalization and the Changing World of Business* (Ernst & Young, 2009).
9. Esther Ng, "From all Walks of Life, They Came to Pay their Respects," *Today*, May 21, 2010, p. 3.

2

FIVE REASONS WHY THERE ARE VERY FEW GREAT ASIAN BRANDS

With Asia's ever-increasing share of world GDP and expanding levels of exports to the West, one might be excused for wondering why branding in Asia continues to be an area poorly understood by Asian managers and badly executed by Asian companies. Not withstanding the plethora of award. programs celebrating every business discipline under the sun (including branding), as well as branding practitioners who continue to sell the mythical success stories of ever more powerful Asian brands, the reality is that Asian brands across the board are continuing to exhibit weak vital signs. Despite significant industry education, as well as major investments by government agencies to enhance the overall understanding of branding practices so as to strengthen Asian brands, very little traction has taken place over the years. Figure 2.1A provides a snapshot of the Singapore branding experience tracked over a period of five years from the point of view of the press. General conclusion: Branding is either misunderstood or simply ignored. The experience in other nearby markets such as Malaysia (see Figure 2.1B), Indonesia, and Thailand, as well as— significantly—mainland China, has been very similar.

When we refer to "Asian" brands, we are referring to all non-Japanese Asian brands. This will no doubt surprise and perplex some readers. Japan is indeed part of Asia. But Japanese brands began developing a full generation before the rest of Asia got going, and most of their more visible and well-known global marques are at a very different point along the evolutionary development curve. To include Japanese brands in the overall Asian branding calculus would dilute the present reality and misleadingly suggest that *all* Asian brands are performing well when they manifestly are not. The goal should be to

Figure 2.1A The Singapore branding experience from the viewpoint of the press

"Of the 100 companies surveyed, about half view branding as short-term blitzes to bump up sales rather than a long-term holistic strategy to build the name and reputation of the firm." *The Straits Times,* April 6, 2003	"(Most SMEs) don't appreciate the value of good branding and marketing.... the typical SME is too focused on immediate returns and undertakes short-term sales-driven activities..." *The Straits Times,* May 24, 2005	"Speak to almost any small or medium enterprise and they would most likely tell you that the proportion of their annual budget allocated for branding is unsubstantial, if anything at all." *TODAY,* September 20, 2008

Figure 2.1B The Malaysian branding experience from the viewpoint of the press

"Most Malaysian companies are not spending enough in brandbuilding and development (stated) Minister of International Trade and Industry Datuk Seri Rafidah Aziz. She said local companies need to rethink their approach to branding or lose out in the current competitive market...." *New Straits Times,* February 7, 2004	"Datuk Seri Ong Tee Keat, transport minister in Malaysia, stated that despite being aware about the benefits of branding and marketing, most local firms in Malaysia fail to take its advantage." *Article Alley,* December 23, 2009	"...there are significant gaps in branding knowledge and understanding amongst many Malaysian SME companies. The majority seems to perceive brand building purely as a cost and do not see the importance of branding as a valuable asset which needs to be invested in." *MARKETING-Interactive,* March 12, 2010

make things clearer, not more opaque. For all practical purposes, strong Japanese brands are more appropriately categorized alongside successful Western brands. And for that reason, they are excluded from this discussion.

In terms of non-Japanese Asian brands, one could argue that—save for one or two—there exist virtually no great Asian brands. Even Asians themselves, when asked what brands they prefer, or aspire to own, will name Western brands such as Coke, Nike, Apple, BMW, Armani, and GAP. With the notable exception of two non-Japanese brands (Samsung and SIA), Asian brands are rarely, if ever, nominated. This fact has been constantly borne out by surveys over the past 10 years. To underscore this point, the *BusinessWeek/Interbrand* annual study of the world's top 100 brands has, for years, showcased almost exclusively only Western/Japanese brands in the top 50. *The Straits Times* reported as much: "Indeed, the government trade agency (International Enterprise

Singapore) highlighted the fact that Asian brands were conspicuously absent in a ranking of the top 100 global brands done in 2001 by Interbrand and *Business Week* magazine."[1] Some six years later, the 2007 survey was no different. The sole exception that year was Samsung, which came in at number 21. Findings from surveys conducted within the region itself confirmed the trend. The "Top 1000 Asia-Pacific Brands" survey conducted by *Media* magazine and sponsored by the *Wall Street Journal* identified only two non-Japanese Asian brands in the top 10 (Samsung and LG). Even more worrisome is that only three more brands were identified in the top 50.[2]

What defines a so-called great Asian brand? What separates a great brand from the merely good brand? And is that important?

What defines a so-called great Asian brand? What separates a great brand from the merely good brand? And is that important? In his book, *Good to Great*, Jim Collins explains that "good is the enemy of great." He argues that the very presence or achievement of good deters the pursuit of great. He also makes another more intrusive point: "Greatness is not a function of circumstance. Greatness, it turns out, is largely a matter of conscious choice."[3]

Collins's point is perhaps even more valid in Asia than in the United States. Here a wholesale presence of good brands is frustrating the emergence of great brands, although this notion will get a lot of push-back from Asian marketers across the region. Proud Indians will argue passionately that India has many big, successful brands, some of which outperform their foreign competitors. Brands such as Tata, Jet Airways, and Kingfisher are household names that generate strong levels of trust and local pride. Koreans will point to Amore Pacific, Face Shop, Jinro, and Jeju Air as examples of Korean brands denoting quality, luxury, and entrepreneurship. In Taiwan, innovative brands such as HTC, Acer, and Asustek all but dominate their categories. And even in emerging countries such as Vietnam, local marketers cite brands like Vinamilk, Vietcombank, BIDV, and Q-Mobile as examples of ever-increasing branding traction.

Most of these brands boast strong levels of local awareness, as well as big consumer franchises in their own countries. But with very few exceptions, they have failed to generate sufficient escape velocity to replicate their success in substantive measures outside of their home markets. Even brands such as HTC and Acer—long viewed as poster boys for the successful transition from OEM (original equipment manufacturer) to OBM (original brand manufacturer)—are finding that gaining real, sustainable traction as consumer brands is difficult and elusive. All these brands are "good" brands. To mostly local customer franchises, they are seen as reliable, trustworthy, even desirable. Away from home, while some struggle to generate awareness, they mostly fail to excite and uplift consumers or at the very least create enduring emotional relationships with them. Having said this, it is equally important to recognize that it is these very same brands that represent the region's best candidates for "great" brand status. They are all sitting on one side of the fence, and it is within their control to step over to the other side.

Asia has yet to create Asian signature brands with global credentials. But what makes the region palpably exciting is the abundance of good brands ready to move up to the next level. They are marking time, but developing the ability to change that and surge forward won't happen automatically. It will require willpower.

Even if this is true; even if the region is mostly about merely good and not great brands—does it matter? I believe the reason it matters is that the merely good Asian brands will not provide the vehicle that will deliver the Asian/Chinese Century and, with it, the anticipated change in the world order. If this historical transition matters, then it will require that Asian CEOs make many conscious and difficult choices in the times ahead.

The question of whether it matters is largely rhetorical. It matters a great deal for another reason. As explained in Chapter 1, the world today is more complex, more sophisticated, and changing faster than ever before. The more salient point is that this kind of change will not only continue, but will do so in an exponential manner. In terms of information, the "noise" that this process will create will be deafening. Countless messages, claims and counter-claims, promises, assurances, and predictions from millions of sources will overwhelm the landscape of everyday life and test the capability of individuals to make sense of all the stimuli, and separate what matters from what does not, so as to make sensible choices and decisions. This is the world that we and future generations face.

From a geo-political perspective, Asian governments will continue to invest in building strong Asian companies because they will increasingly emerge as the "face" of Asia to Asians themselves, as well as to the outside world.

The role of brands will continue to evolve, becoming even more important than at present. As Chapter 3 explains, brands are not limited to the products and services that people buy, and go far beyond the perimeters of business and commerce. Brands provide identity and meaning—to products, services, people, religions, and ideologies. As such, they are a form of shorthand that enables instant comprehension, reassurance, and trust in an increasingly cacophonic environment. From a business perspective, strong brands that communicate clear and compelling messages will be critically important in an environment characterized by increasingly voracious competition. From a geo-political perspective, Asian governments will continue to invest in building strong Asian companies because they will increasingly emerge as the "face" of Asia to Asians themselves, as well as to the outside world. Recognition of the importance of going beyond merely strong brands to great Asian brands will only increase— and more rapidly in those markets where decision makers adopt it as a matter of conscious choice instead of belatedly reacting to developments.

> There is a fundamental disconnect between the expected emergence of the anticipated so-called Asian/Chinese Century and the idea that it can be fueled by Western brands.

There is a fundamental disconnect between the expected emergence of the anticipated so-called Asian/Chinese Century and the idea that it can be fueled by Western brands. In reality, of course, this cannot happen. Either Western brands will continue to dominate, reducing the Asian/ Chinese Century concept to hype, or great Asian brands will rise to prominence. The general consensus is that a robust and genuine Asian/ Chinese Century is pretty much a done deal; that it is going to happen. This can only mean that great Asian brands will also need to be developed. But for this to take place, the stubborn resistance to change that has characterized recent decades will need to be replaced by a profound, tectonic shift in business practices, mentality, and culture. The longer it takes for Asia to create great brands, the longer it will take for the region to achieve its potential—or, some say, its destiny.

And while it may sound a little bombastic to say that great Asian brands will not just facilitate the economic rise of a whole region, but will also be a leading catalyst of world order change, consider that the governments of Singapore, Malaysia, Taiwan, and Hong Kong, among others, have created specific task forces with a mandate to create world-beating company and product brands. Malaysia has arguably made the loudest song and dance, with successive prime ministers agreeing to be patrons of multiple "Malaysia" brand excellence-related organizations. In that country, the Malaysia External Trade Development Corporation (MATRADE) was established in 1993, with the mission to "develop and promote Malaysia's exports to the world."[4] Soon thereafter, the Brand Promotion Grant (BPG) unit was created, armed with millions of dollars worth of grants and subsidies to assist companies to brand themselves.

> *"Branding is an important aspect of improving the competitiveness of products and services. It has been my desire and belief to see Malaysian brands achieve distinction on a global level. However, there is so much more tapped potential among so many more local brands. We must find more ways to overcome this situation if we want to succeed regionally and internationally. That is why I am glad that there is a growing awareness and appreciation about the importance of branding."*

> Dato' Seri Abdullah Haji Ahmad Badawi, former prime minister of Malaysia

In Singapore, successive government ministers and senior officials have long heralded the importance of branding by framing it in the context of the "Singapore" brand, and championing the importance of being different. Speaking at the Global Forum in 2004, Senior Minister Mentor Lee Kuan Yew declared that "Singapore's new leaders must protect the nation's 'brand', which stands for transparency and integrity," explaining that the latter provided the basis for the country's differentiation. "We systematically set out to be different. To tell the world that we are different" from the image of Third World countries that Lee said were "corrupt, inefficient and have bad infrastructure."[5]

Three years earlier, in an interview with *Commanding Heights*, Lee's son, Lee Hsien Loong (the then deputy prime minister and present prime minister), had also stressed the importance of transparency and differentiation: "We have to be different. I mean, if we were the same as the rest of Asia, there's no reason why anybody should be in Singapore." And on the subject of brand Singapore: "You can't be slightly transparent. . . . We'd like Singapore to be a symbol of quality; that it's associated with excellence, with perfection, with a constant striving to improve, so that you're never there, but you're always working at it."[6]

It is not surprising, therefore, that the government would place a high importance on branding Singaporean companies and Singaporean products. Beginning much earlier than other Asian countries, in 1983 it launched the Trade Development Board, which eventually went through a rebranding program of its own in 2000. Reconfigured and renamed IE Singapore (International Enterprise Singapore), it was given the mandate to "develop business capabilities" of Singaporean companies, and branding was identified from the beginning as one of the most important of these capabilities. In 2005, under the leadership of CEO Lee Yi Shyan, a very important program—BrandPact—was developed and rolled out. I was privileged to be asked to provide input for this program, and to be invited to deliver a keynote presentation at its launch. Like Malaysia's BPG unit, the objective of the BrandPact program is to help companies formally brand themselves by providing them with advice, services, and generous subsidies and grants.

> "A strong brand is most invaluable, especially in trying times. Yet you cannot build a brand overnight, just before you need it. Therefore, the government has been promoting the use of branding as a strategic business capability. BrandPact, for example, is a joint initiative by IE Singapore and SPRING to help local companies meet their brand development needs. Since the launch of BrandPact in April 2005, 6,702 companies have benefited from various BrandPact initiatives, which included training workshops and use of brand assessment. Companies have in total received $17.7 million worth of co-funding support for brand development projects."

> Lee Yi Shyan, Minister of State for Trade and Industry
> (former CEO of IE Singapore), December 3, 2008

Alas, years later, in spite of the hype, the speeches, and the money invested, branding continues to languish in the business sectors of virtually all Asian countries. In this chapter, we will examine the top five reasons that have contributed—and continue to contribute—to the malaise affecting Asian brands. Specifically, they are:

1. Myopic CEO leadership
2. Corporate culture that is by default, rather than by design
3. Charlatan brand practitioners

4. Government agencies that mean well, but should perform better

5. Advertising agencies with little to no branding competencies.

MYOPIC CEO LEADERSHIP

Over the past eight years, I have interviewed more than a hundred CEOs and other C-level executives from multinational companies, regional conglomerates, and SMEs in more than half a dozen Asian countries—from mainland China to Singapore, and from India to Korea. Most of the interviews were structured and were conducted in the context of formal branding projects which our firm had been assigned to undertake. They were generally of one and a half to two hours' duration and covered general themes as well as specific questions consistent with the needs of a comprehensive brand audit (see Chapter 6).[7] Beyond questions that related to the specific performance or culture of their companies, we also included several generic questions that probed executive—especially CEO—beliefs about and attitudes to management, leadership, values, and concepts such as "company mission." The impressions gained from these interviews, coupled with those I had collected from a hundred more informal sessions with other CEOs over the years, have—along with secondary research—contributed to the observations made in this section.[8]

The evidence shows beyond any doubt that the most obstructive hurdles preventing mediocre and good Asian companies from breaking through a decades-long glass ceiling and achieving brand greatness are CEO mentality and ignorance about the branding process—in that order. **Mentality**: The CEO is driven almost exclusively by a desire to (only) make money—and rarely by passion. He will often over-promise and under-deliver. He will take short-cuts and consider himself clever for doing so. He rarely looks beyond today and lacks a vision for tomorrow. **Ignorance**: He misunderstands branding and sees it as the company name and logo, and its promotion as taking place almost exclusively through the media. Its conceptual, business, and strategic dimensions are totally lost on him, and his impatience causes him to dismiss or undermine the process before it even gets underway. As a result, Asian consumers fail to love, lust after, or be inspired by most Asian brands.

In much of Asia (mainland China, Hong Kong, Taiwan, Singapore, and Korea), traditional management philosophy rooted in Confucian-based values has created an environment where many CEOs operate, and see themselves, as patriarchal figures: individuals who are at once irreproachable, as well as unapproachable. The resulting management style resembles a "by decree" approach, rather than one that is inclusive. Tom Doctoroff, JWT North Asia CEO, has commented: "Chinese companies are sales-driven and managed by emperor-kings who rule in a defensive, even self-protective manner. . . . Quite often, the instructions are promulgated in an ambiguous manner, resulting in an undercurrent of anxiety on lower levels, not an all-for-one future focus."[9] Interestingly, many CEOs from non-Confucian-influenced countries such as Indonesia, Malaysia, and even Thailand also exhibit these styles of leadership and management.

"To make money," is the most common—almost universal— reply given by CEOs to the question: "What is the mission of your company?" This single-minded, primary, and often exclusive goal of most Asian CEOs is commonly inculcated in the minds of their senior managers, from where it is filtered down to the lower ranks of employees. *To make money*—period. While there is nothing inherently wrong with this (after all, it is the goal of business to be profitable), most of these decision makers, hailing from the smallest SMEs to the largest Asian conglomerates, persistently pursue this goal in a manner that is self-defeating. First, they fail to recognize that making money for its own sake is a flawed strategy; that making money is, rather, the result of a coherent strategy. Secondly, in their haste to deliver on the goal, they misunderstand the business and brand strategy development process (one that has evolved dramatically because of the dynamic environmental changes of the past two decades) and try to fast-track it or gloss over it. Instead, they adopt a command-and-control business management style that fails to recruit and encourage all members of the company to work together to deliver a product or a service that can effectively compete with compelling Western brands. They fail not only to harness the energy and intellectual contributions of all the constituents they have on hand (not to mention their untapped intrinsic enthusiasm, whose loss or absence is impossible to measure), but also to create a culture that works to ensure that the customer promise is delivered on a consistent basis.

The practice of managing by decree, and the reluctance to share and include most, if not all, members of the company in policy and direction, results in a brand identity (company or product) that is defined by a narrow group of individuals with narrower perspectives and biases of their own. The end-result is almost guaranteed to fail.

Two factors commonly contribute to this mentality. The first is an anachronistic obsession by CEOs and their top executives with keeping everything "secret." They believe that sharing plans with employees and external stakeholders (such as shareholders) makes the company vulnerable to competitors. Consequently, it is most often only the inner circle that is familiar with the company's direction and objectives. In many cases, however, not even the inner circle is apprised of these objectives or asked to contribute to their formulation. In these companies, the CEO reigns absolute and unchallenged. He (and it is most often a "he") alone decides everything. The other factor is related to "face." Many CEOs feel compromised or diminished in some manner or measure if they solicit opinions (or, worse, advice) from lower-level employees.

The result is that Asian companies tend to rely overly much on a handful of individuals (and sometimes on the CEO alone) to steer and move the organization forward. In addition to placing unnecessary and onerous pressure on relatively few individuals, these companies are rarely as competitive and as successful as they could otherwise be, because they suffer from an absence of fresh and creative thinking—and the ideas this generates—from the general population of the company. Ultimately, this can lead to a chronic absence of innovation. (For a more comprehensive discussion on innovation in Asia, see Chapter 5.)

> *"Asians are very empirical. If they put money into*
> *branding, they ask where the result is on sales.*
> *It's a very hard thing to quantify."*
>
> Tony Fernandes, CEO, AirAsia[10]

The CEO's tunnel-vision obsession with making money for its own sake highlights a widespread misunderstanding of the purpose—and value—of the corporate mission (at least, in its Western business definition): that it is an opportunity for the company to connect all employees behind a galvanizing overarching goal that provides reliable and sustainable forward momentum (which, in turn, ultimately delivers profit).

While this misunderstanding about the role and value of the corporate mission might be excused—even expected—from less experienced and less sophisticated managers of smaller companies, it is surprisingly prevalent among CEOs and senior-level managers of larger companies who have benefited from intensive field experience as well as formal education from leading business schools in Asia, the US, and Europe. (For a more comprehensive discussion on corporate mission statements, see Chapter 4.)

Another debilitating CEO characteristic that contributes to the development of relatively weak Asian brands is the inability or reluctance to view the brand as a tangible asset. It is not necessarily an oversimplification to say that many decision makers in this part of the world continue to consider only those things they can see and touch as valuable. Consequently, the branding process isn't given due consideration, and certainly not the appropriate funding it requires.

> . . . managers at all levels consider all decisions based on a criterion that prioritizes "price."

This skewed view of branding leads to yet another CEO characteristic that not only profoundly affects branding but also has a major impact on business generally: the price question. Cultural conditioning and values have made the open pursuit of money and wealth a desirable virtue. The business corollary is the ingrained belief that everything can and should be secured at the cheapest possible price point. This attitude has translated into an expectation that managers at all levels consider all decisions based on a criterion that prioritizes "price." This practice is particularly true of government tenders and how they are awarded—regardless of how often government officials refute this. Price always primarily influences the decisions made. The reason is obvious, but no less damaging: Middle and lower managers feel that their best hopes for recognition and reward are linked to their acquisition of products and services at the lowest possible price. They are rarely interested in, or influenced by, the possible consequences at a later date.

Not only are CEOs no different; they are, as alluded to above, the principal instigators of this mentality. When presented with formal branding project proposals (where no two are ever comparable because the "briefing" process is almost always inconsistent—see Chapter 6), too many CEOs demand to know "how much is it going to cost me?" before understanding or even listening to what the branding process entails. Furthermore—regardless of what that cost is—they then automatically demand that it be delivered at a fraction of the cost.

While cost control is an important component of effective management, this practice hardly qualifies. And as far as a branding project is concerned, it can often have serious consequences. It is like a patient haggling over the price of treatment with a professional medical specialist for a serious condition he likely doesn't fully understand, and opting to go to a practitioner who offers a cut-price service. This scenario should be as improbable in the business context as it is in the medical field, but it is not.

CEOS DON'T KNOW WHAT THEY DON'T KNOW

*"Many of these people never understood what they didn't know
and were either too wary, or too cocksure, to seek advice from
others more experienced in the ways of the world."*

Michael Moritz, *Return to the Little Kingdom*

Having said all of this, it is important and fair also to say that these
same CEOs suffer from an affliction that is difficult to "cure": They
basically don't know what they don't know—at least as far as branding is concerned. This is a critical and crucial diagnosis, and one of
the many reasons for the absence of great Asian brands. MATRADE
officials in Kuala Lumpur are very familiar with the consequences of
the problem. They describe it in simpler language: ignorance of branding. When you don't know what you don't know, you are not aware of
what you are missing out on—and sometimes ignorance isn't bliss. It
can be painful and expensive. Related or not, they pose a real problem
to BPG officials at MATRADE. Mandated and authorized to provide
surprisingly generous subsidies and outright grants to Malaysian companies, millions of taxpayer dollars meant for brand building end up
being given away to companies and their CEOs, who instead spend it
on advertising. "Free money," one cynical senior MATRADE official
ruefully observed.

Figure 2.2 sets out 10 illustrations of the "CEO problem." The
last point in the figure is particularly problematic. When you don't
know what you don't know, you automatically assume that you know
enough to make some basic decisions: such as judging a branding "proposal," for instance, on the basis of what you like or what you find
easy to do. Or choosing a brand practitioner because he or she tells you
what you want to hear. And, of course, doing it as cheaply as possible. Beyond a substandard process, the irony is that all branding projects have a threshold level in terms of minimum scope (and, therefore,
cost). Thus, excluding an element that is outside the absolute minimum
needed doesn't just deliver a less effective solution; it effectively destroys
the integrity of the solution altogether. In other words, if that threshold
has been determined by a reputable consultant to be at a certain level,
spending less than that level requires ends up being less productive than
not going through the process in the first place. In reality, what is happening is that the relatively blind are being led by the unscrupulous in a
process that delivers a flawed outcome. So, far from "saving" money, as
many CEOs congratulate themselves on doing, they end up effectively

Figure 2.2 Ten illustrations of the "CEO problem"

Because CEOs and other C-level executives lack an understanding and appreciation for branding:

1. They fail to understand the *difference* between product and brand—this is often reflected through communications strategies (advertising) that focus on either product features or price.

2. They fail to understand the *expansive role* the brand plays within their companies. They see brand and branding as isolated functions, instead of as an interconnected process that touches every functional department in the company.

3. They fail to understand the *profound impact* the brand makes on every functional department of the company.

4. They fail to understand how customers, as well as employees, *relate or could relate* to the brand, and in the process routinely fail to benefit from their critical engagement.

5. They fail to understand the role *employees* play in creating and delivering the brand promise.

6. They fail to understand *key brand strategy issues* such as profiling and targeting specific audiences and customer communities (as opposed to aiming for the whole customer universe).

7. They fail to understand the crucial role of *brand architecture*. (An example of this is the popular insistence that a single company name be slapped across all businesses, regardless of whether or not they are related.)

8. They fail to understand the role and importance of "vision": *knowing where exactly* the company needs to be within a specific time frame and creating the *road map* to get there.

9. They are unwilling to commit personal time to *champion* the process.

10. They insist on *quick-fix solutions* and gravitate to providers who promise what they want to hear (as opposed to what they *need* to hear) and price the effort at a *price point they are willing to pay* (instead of the minimum that is required).

throwing money out the window. The lesson here is this: If you, as the CEO, are unwilling—for whatever reason—to do and spend the minimum it takes (and you do need to be knowledgeable enough to know where that minimum is), do nothing.

To be fair, this mentality, while flawed, does not reflect inappropriate business practices per se. It makes sense—on the surface—to make decisions based on the knowledge you have, rather than the absence of knowledge of which you are unaware. Instead, it rather underscores just how alarmingly ill-informed many senior and key decision makers are about something that represents not only the foundational pillar of the organization, but also the central driver of its success. Branding influences the very destiny of the company, and should be tackled from that perspective. It rarely is.

> If the CEO does not *get it,* or does not get behind it, the overall result of any branding initiative will almost always be compromised

Regardless of the reasons or circumstances, this is the bottom line: If the CEO does not get it, or does not get behind it, the overall result of any branding initiative will almost always be compromised. And it is not an exaggeration or a generalization to say that this is exactly what is happening right now across most companies in Asia.

CORPORATE CULTURE IS BY DEFAULT, RATHER THAN BY DESIGN

Whether understood or misunderstood, and whether created by design or through circumstances, culture exists in all organizations. Where it is "positive," it can be harnessed and leveraged to influence people to do extraordinary things. Where it is "negative," it tends to have the reverse effect. While every company has, to a certain extent, a unique culture, certain characteristics are commonly found in Asian companies.

Most Asian companies began, and many still operate, as family-owned businesses. Business decisions are typically made by one key individual, and accountability to a third or external party is generally not the norm. Even in publicly listed companies, the usual practice in Asia is for the CEO to retain control and relinquish only a small percentage of ownership to outside parties.

The CEO is the supreme leader. He (as mentioned earlier, the chief executive is almost always a male) generally believes he knows best, and he expects others to agree with him. He believes that success in business is about keeping secrets, so that only the "inner circle" has any idea about what is going on, and that employees should do as they are told and not be permitted to make mistakes (which has the effect of discouraging risk taking and initiative in the first place).

I don't wish to suggest that these practices and values are a product of an inherently harsh, unfair, or exploitative management mentality. There is no evidence that employees in Asian SMEs and multinational corporations (MNCs) are deliberately "mistreated" for the sake of profit—at least, no more than are employees in other markets, including those in the West. What I am referring to here is more intangible in nature: employees who are denied the opportunity to fully embrace and enjoy the work they do because their employers are either simply unaware that this is important and valuable, or just don't know how to make it happen.

The life-blood of great brands is creativity and innovation that originates from *within* the organization, and its source is corporate culture.

As a result, the culture that characterizes most present-day Asian companies suppresses creativity and innovation. Employees are not encouraged to express themselves; as a consequence, they tend to progress slowly, and to learn or contribute little—and the cycle becomes vicious. This situation is completely at odds with what is possible, and very desirable, in modern-day corporate cultures. The life-blood of great brands is creativity and innovation that originates from within the organization, and its source is corporate culture.

Richard Branson took the corporate world by surprise when he declared that the consumer is not number 1—something that had been considered a basic, inviolate business tenet by generations of business executives. In an address to the British Institute of Directors in 1993, Branson said: "We give top priority to the interests of our staff, second priority to those of our customers, third to our shareholders." Surprise or not, there was nothing particularly radical about this declaration. Branson was simply articulating what Asian CEOs would do well to take to heart: that there is no point in spending money to find out what customers want if one's employees have little desire or encouragement to follow through and make it happen. Branson understands that companies are effectively held hostage by their employees. It doesn't matter whether the company delivers a service or manufactures a product. Customer experience and product quality are delivered by employees. The absence of the right culture prevents this from happening and retards the development of great Asian brands.

CHARLATAN BRAND PRACTITIONERS

Some brand practitioners disseminate substandard advice either deliberately or inadvertently, because they too don't know what they don't know. In a business environment replete with alpha-type CEOs who know exactly what they want, and believe they know what they need, there is no shortage of "consultants" who are willing to give them what they want and tell them what they want to hear. The "branding category" is not like the medical sector, where practitioners need to be properly trained and accredited before they are allowed to practice. In the branding field, there are virtually no regulations and anybody can call himself or herself a "brand consultant." The ramifications of this are broad and profound. As alluded to earlier, branding is a little like a zero-sum game. The wrong "solution" will *not* result in a benign outcome. Effective branding goes beyond the formulation of a positioning statement for the company. (This topic will be covered in more detail in Chapter 3.) Positioning, which includes the promise the company makes to its constituents, amounts to 50 percent of the task. Effective and consistent delivery of that message represents the other 50 percent. As delivery is dependent on a group effort, the entire process relies on an internal systemic structure that effectively involves every functional department in the company. Very few CEOs are interested in hearing this. Very few practitioners are willing to say this.

There are two ways in which the company can self-inflict significant damage: (1) when the message is "right," but employees are not motivated to deliver it; and (2) when the message is "wrong," but the company has somehow managed to persuade most of its employees to get behind it. Both scenarios amount to qualified statements, because "right" and "wrong" are relative concepts and difficult to define. In the first case, a message that is formulated with only customers in mind might theoretically deliver to their expectations. But if employees have not been involved in the process the delivery will, sooner or later, falter or fall short. When this happens the company will have compromised its credibility, as well as wasted significant communication funds. So, even "right" ends up being wrong. In the second scenario, companies that take short-cuts in formulating their brand positioning and brand promise invariably end up with a message that fails to resonate with customers. Invoking all employee resources to deliver a fundamentally flawed proposition delivers little material return and, as in the first scenario, ends up costing the company a great deal in communication funds.

In the end, both scenarios will deliver equally baleful results: instead of just dismissing the effort, customers invariably form a new negative perception, which means that the company ends up being further behind than the point they started from. Once again, this is a reminder that if, for whatever reason, companies are not fully prepared to do and invest the minimum, they should do nothing. And they should actively seek out branding practitioners who are willing to tell them that.

The brand represents the beginning, the middle, and the end of everything the company is and can become. As such, it is a very powerful catalyst. Used wrongly, the brand can cause significant damage.

The key learning here is that companies that are keen to strengthen their brands, or that are ready to go through a formal branding process, need to do their homework in order to identify the right partner for their needs.

Different strokes for different folks: Beyond "good" and "bad" lie "right" and "wrong," as far as matching different brand practitioners to different client company needs. Think of branding companies occupying a continuum (see Figure 2.3). At one extreme will be the graphic designer companies and production houses (A). Some of these call themselves "brand consultants," but many provide only visual (graphic) solutions such as logos and corporate identity services. Somewhere in the middle of the continuum are advertising agencies (B), most of which call themselves "brand consultants." At the other extreme are the strategy-centric consultancies (D), which provide branding solutions delivered through a comprehensive process that starts with business strategy and ends with operational implementation. And somewhere in-between the advertising agencies and the strategy-centric consultancies are companies whose strengths lie in providing strategic and graphic solutions, with an emphasis on the latter (C).

The question that companies seeking brand advice and assistance should ask themselves is: "Which type of provider is right for my needs?" Clearly, there are no generic branding solutions that fit all companies in

Figure 2.3 Branding companies occupy a continuum

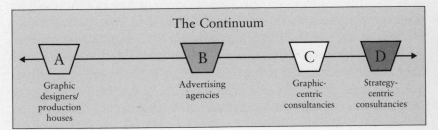

Source: "The Brand Positioning Continuum," BrandAsian, 2008. All rights reserved.

equal measure. Different companies have different issues and problems that need to be addressed, all potentially influencing the scale and scope of any branding process in different ways. But beyond this lies the question of where the (corporate or product) brand finds itself on its "evolutionary curve." Is it a new brand, a well-established brand, or a mature brand? Does it need a makeover or a transplant? Each of the four types of branding providers (and there are more) identified along the continuum in Figure 2.3 is differentiated by its primary competencies and capabilities—what it is good at and what it does best.

Companies seeking a branding partner would be advised to spend some time considering which one best suits their needs and the needs of their brand. For companies that have successfully built a strong brand proposition that resonates with both its customers and its employees, a branding effort might conceivably be limited to a freshening up of its visual identity—for example, modernizing its corporate logo. In this case, a (D)-type strategic consultancy would be less appropriate for their needs than, say, an (A)-type provider. At the other extreme, companies that have—for whatever reason—reached a crisis point and are facing loss of traction with their constituents might want to consider a strategic repositioning. For these companies, considering (A)- and (B)-type providers would likely be a waste of time (and money).

PERFORMANCE OF GOVERNMENT AGENCIES

It is encouraging to see government agencies from two or three Asian countries leaping ahead of the private sector in recognizing the role and importance of strong branding. The more active ones are from Singapore and Malaysia. While these agencies have, by and large, succeeded in delivering valuable services to their client companies, they have also demonstrated bureaucratic and policy-related shortcomings that have visibly compromised their overall declared goals.

In Singapore, significant brand assistance in the form of capabilities support via training and grants has been available for the better part of the past decade from two key government agencies: International Enterprise Singapore (IE Singapore) and SPRING. Both agencies were created with mandates that are broad and go beyond branding. In generalized terms, IE Singapore focuses more on helping and encouraging companies to internationalize themselves, whereas SPRING focuses on the smaller SMES that have a mostly domestic presence. Among the forms of brand-related assistance available is a leading program that was created in 2005 as a joint initiative by both agencies—BrandPact.

> *"BrandPact is a multi-agency initiative to better meet the varied*
> *brand development needs of local enterprises as they grow and*
> *expand within Singapore and into the global marketplace. It is*
> *a holistic initiative that will raise awareness and understanding*
> *of branding, develop brand savvy executives and catalyse the*
> *adoption of branding as a strategy for business competitiveness."*
>
> SPRING Singapore website

Significant effort and funding was allocated to develop and launch this initiative and, as mentioned earlier, I was privileged to have the opportunity to contribute some input. I was also invited to be a keynote speaker at the launch. A portion of my address is reproduced as follows:

> *In any environment, but particularly in a highly evolving and increasingly competitive environment like the one that prevails in Asia, the role and value of branding emerge as critical, central drivers to business success.*
>
> *There is a revolution taking place in Asia today that will profoundly change the lives of hundreds of thousands of Asians and impact the lives of millions more outside of Asia in the decade and more to come.*
>
> *Some already label it the "Chinese Century."*
>
> *There exists a massive opportunity for Asian businesses on a scale that is not only unprecedented, but to many ironically so large that it is almost invisible.*
>
> *Asian brand owners need to wake up! Some will do so faster than others. But soon there will be a wave of indescribable strength sweeping over the region.*
>
> *Great Asian brands will rise. This is an inevitability (for) those who have the mindset that eschews short-term gains in favor of long-term success.*[11]

While expressing my conviction that great Asian brands will emerge and take their place on the global stage, the point I wished to make was that the inability or unwillingness of some CEOs to recognize the oncoming sea change was not only futile, but would likely result in their missing out on great and unprecedented opportunities. For others, the scale of the opportunity effectively rendered invisible something that was in plain sight. A preference for short-term focus over long-term planning continues to be one of the main reasons for CEOs' resistance to change.

It is, of course, unreasonable to expect that either of the two Singaporean government agencies referred to above should contribute to changing this ingrained attitude. The best type of assistance that agencies such as these can and should provide is practical in nature, and both have been making credible and sincere efforts to do just that. Indeed, the strategy these agencies have adopted has been sound enough: a combination of advice, training, and monetary support. But as far as advice and training are concerned, both agencies—at least in the early years—had limited in-house expertise they could draw from, and so they relied on brand practitioners to fill the void. While this makes sense on the surface, the landscape in Asia—and Singapore is no different—was, and continues to be, cluttered with substandard providers and even some outright charlatans. In an environment where CEOs and other decision makers need disruptive, honest, and strategic advice to encourage them to explore new ways of doing business, the absence of branding partners that are willing to give them what they need, as opposed to what they want, compounds the overall problem of misunderstanding and ignorance. Out of this environment emerged a real challenge for companies seeking solid branding advice: "Who should I work with? Who is the right provider for my company?" And "Who can help me find out?"

One central challenge for companies seeking a branding partner lies in separating not just the good from the bad, but the right from the wrong. "Who" in the first two questions referred to branding companies; the third one—"Who can help me find out?"—should, in my view, point in the direction of government agencies, and in the case of Singapore, IE Singapore and SPRING. In the wake of the launch of BrandPact, it emerged that neither agency had made practical allowance for this important need. On the contrary, in their rigorous efforts to demonstrate impartiality to all companies providing brand advice (a list posted on the IE Singapore website at one point numbered close to 100 companies), they implemented a policy of providing no advice. This inadvertently created a real problem.

Over the years, I have consistently voiced the view that this procedure is problematic. It is a view that has failed to find much support among my colleagues, perhaps out of fear of the consequences of such public criticism. However, over the years, many middle managers from both IE Singapore and SPRING have, off the record, not only expressed agreement but also frustration about their inability to change the process from within.

In May 2007, IE Singapore hosted a major business event at which I was invited to deliver a paper on branding. During the event, I struck up a conversation with the agency's deputy CEO, Ted Tan. He had been kind enough to compliment me on the content of my paper, and I took the opportunity once again to express my concerns over the progress of brand development in Singapore and the role that organizations like IE Singapore could play.

In a follow-up note to Mr. Tan, dated May 14, I wrote:

> *The role that IE plays is not only essential but, in my view, central to the achievement of national competitive advantage. Do I believe that the branding program at IE is perfect? No. And I have said so on several occasions. I believe that IE can do much more for its clients. There is a lot of room for improvements and, like all leader organizations, I have always believed IE to be open to learning more about how to do it better. To this end I will continue to express my views when called upon. As always, I would be most pleased to share some of my thoughts with you at any time perhaps over coffee. Just let me know.*

He replied:

> *I appreciate(d) your frank opinion and comments when we spoke, which I read with pleasure when it was reflected in your article on "Brand Singapore" in* The Business Times *the next day. . . . As we continue to help Singapore companies become bigger Asian brands and to compete more effectively internationally, your comments and suggestions would be very valuable to us. I will contact you to arrange for a discussion over coffee some time this week if you are available. Thanks for your continuing support to IE.*

I met Mr. Tan and one of his senior colleagues over coffee on May 15. At that meeting, I again expressed my concerns and then handed him a document I had prepared the day before that provided a formal point of view. An extract of that document is provided below:

> *The #1 issue that conspires to adversely affect the efforts by companies in Singapore to brand or re-brand themselves is a lack of understanding as well as appreciation of what branding is and does at the CEO level. It does not matter how much effort is taking place at other levels. If the CEO does not get it, or does not get behind it, the overall result is almost always compromised. This problem must be directly tackled. If it is not addressed, all (IE) efforts will continue to deliver sub-optimal results. In many cases, the result (may be) even grimmer—wasted effort, time and money. For organizations like IE Singapore, its well-intentioned efforts,*

not to mention significant financial investments, can and should be better disseminated.

The role of IE Singapore as it relates to branding: Today IE plays a central and crucial catalytic role for most if not all companies considering or engaged in branding or re-branding projects. In our view, as essential as this role is, certain circumstances contribute to the emergence of counter-productive influences.

As mentioned above, most companies approach the subject of branding with a less than clear understanding of what is involved. Most rely on IE for counsel and advice. Arguably, for help in better understanding what their needs might really be; what a project should arguably include and cover; determining realistically (relative to the unique issues of their companies) how long it should last and how much it should cost; what kind of providers are appropriate and inappropriate for their needs (never mind separating those that might be "good" from those that are manifestly "bad").

There are profound implications and consequences if the lack of understanding among client companies triggers action in the "wrong" direction. It is like a domino effect. It not only delivers sub-par results, it risks perpetuating the suspicion that branding is a waste of time and money (a vicious cycle).

The present IE policy of non-preference or non-specific brand provider recommendation is fine and fair in principle but it does little to direct companies to appropriate partners. "Appropriate" is important because apart from not all brand consultancies being created equal, the straightforward reality is that some specialize in specific areas. At the risk of over-simplifying the point, the landscape can be plotted across a bi-polar matrix:[12]

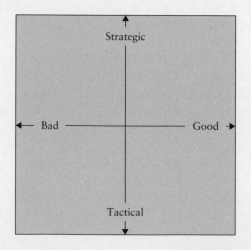

I concluded the letter with some suggestions that IE Singapore might consider. There was no further response from Mr. Tan or IE Singapore. Indeed, months later, when I wrote to Mr. Tan to invite him to a meeting so that I could share with him the development of a new initiative, he excused himself and directed me instead to meet with Mr. Tan Kok Hoe, who had been recently appointed to the role of head of capabilities.

During the course of that meeting, I was struck by something Mr. Tan Kok Hoe said that was unrelated to the initiative I was there to discuss. I am paraphrasing: "IE Singapore is no longer focusing on providing companies with brand-building advice. We believe that phase is over. We are now focusing on more practical operational issues." Given the more accurate dismal condition of Asian branding (as well as branding practices among Singaporean companies), I was stunned by this statement, and by its implications for Singaporean companies.

Some five years have passed since the launch of BrandPact, and yet brand building in Singapore is as moribund as ever. Both IE Singapore and SPRING have a done a great deal of good in promoting branding in Singapore. But that effort has been compromised by the inability of both agencies to recognize and address some of the core causes of poor branding among Singaporean companies, as well as to assist them in addressing an elementary but critical need: choosing which branding providers might be appropriate and relevant to their needs. As a result, much effort and money have been wasted.

ADVERTISING AGENCIES' LACK OF BRANDING COMPETENCIES

The advertising industry has been in a state of perpetual turmoil for decades, addressing one problem after another with varying degrees of success. The problems have ranged from resistance to change (particularly in the face of media fragmentation) and to more transparent fee and billing mechanisms, to poor recruitment practices and inconsistent efforts in cultivating human capital, among many other things. These problems have contributed to a significant across-the-board devaluation of the industry's effectiveness, as well as its reputation. In some quarters an increasingly vocal debate is being conducted about the very legitimacy and sustainability of the advertising agency model in its present iteration.[13]

In parallel to these developments and challenges, agencies around the world have dramatically thinned their ranks. As many as 80,000 jobs in the US alone disappeared between 2004 and 2008. And those who left were not just junior and non-performing executives; the best and the brightest left in droves for more encouraging fields. This has resulted in ever-heavier workloads being placed on less experienced and less capable individuals.

> *"Some of the first to go were senior agency people. Professionals that were probably fairly expensive but past their peak in productivity. Historically, these folks did much of the mentoring of younger agency staffers. They had the experience, the wisdom, and most importantly, the time to help young talent develop. The good ones believed in giving back to the next generation of agency professionals the skill gifts that they had received in their youth. While their mentoring contribution was not easily quantifiable, it was of incredible value. There is hardly an accomplished agency professional who cannot point with appreciation and warmth to a senior mentor (or two) that years ago helped make his or her ultimate success possible."*

> Mike Carlton, *Who's Going to Do the Work?*[14]

Exacerbating these problems is the inability or unwillingness of global advertising agencies to invest in educating and training the (diminishing) platoons of executives marching in and out of their offices around the world. This has been particularly damaging to the industry's real and perceived capacity to be effective. With the exception of small numbers of fortunate individuals (mostly always based in head offices in New York or London) who have benefited from structured training and exposure to genuine mentors, the sustainable discipline needed to run and implement training programs rarely exists in other network offices where priorities are different and resources are fewer.

Worse than not providing effective training is the half-hearted, inconsistent training of young people who are keen to explore a future in the business. This leads to impaired and incomplete learning, so that young executives develop misconceptions and misunderstandings, which, over time, often become ingrained beliefs that are very difficult to change and generally are damaging to the business of clients—particularly brand building. Around the world, we now have multiple generations of confused and ill-prepared advertising executives who are ill-equipped to deal with today's increasingly complex business challenges and increasingly demanding and more sophisticated clients. Compounding this problem has been the practice of agencies settling for lower-caliber individuals, as the best and brightest are recognizing the limitations and risks of a career in advertising and choosing alternatives in areas that provide visible career planning, development, and higher remuneration, such as finance, banking, consultancy, client-side marketing, and the like.

> *For years, agencies have been their own worst enemy,*
> *devaluing their services through competitive pricing. There*
> *is a knock-on effect—the tendency to hire cheaper people*
> *and have less quality control."*

Mark Ingrouille, CEO, McCann Erickson Singapore[15]

Hardest-hit are account executives—at all levels. They join agencies with great enthusiasm, but with little substantive understanding of business in general and the advertising business in particular. Instead of solid on-the-job training, they are thrown in the deep end with little or no assistance. Most of the time they exist in a perpetual state of confusion and anxiety. As a defense mechanism of sorts, they learn to pretend to know when they don't know; in time, some develop bluster and bravado instead of expertise and wisdom. Paradoxically, many are promoted too quickly in a culture that both celebrates self-congratulation and uses titles to reassure clients that "senior" people are handling their business. At the junior levels, this environment damages the individual. At the senior levels (and there are vast numbers of senior and executive vice presidents in agencies around the world, but especially in Asia, who just don't have a clue), the damage is done to the agency—and by extension, the client.

Today, the advertising industry has a poor image, perhaps comparable to that of the used-car industry. This is ironic and troubling for a business that is partly about image. Market research conducted in Malaysia in 2008 revealed that "a majority 55% of marketers are neither satisfied with nor loyal to their current advertising agency."[16]

> *"They (ad agencies) have a high staff turnover and they*
> *don't live the brand. My creative director knows me inside*
> *out, she knows the brand, lives with our staff. Most creative*
> *directors come here for a few hours—they don't see the*
> *pain we have gone through."*

Tony Fernandes, CEO, AirAsia[17]

A Damaging Side-Effect

The industry's inability to build a solid human knowledge base has, in turn, created many consequences across a range of issues. Of central

concern to branding has been the knock-on effect which poorly educated account executives contribute to the dissemination and understanding of branding and brand strategy (within both their own industry
and the client community), and their inability to differentiate these from
advertising and advertising strategy.

> . . . even today, a fair proportion of executives at agencies believe branding
> and advertising are one and the same thing.

"Brand image," "brand positioning," "brand promise," "brand strategy," "advertising strategy," "slogans," and "taglines" are concepts that
are routinely lumped together and referenced by advertising executives
in the course of internal discussions and external client presentations.
They are used interchangeably because most account executives believe
them to be identical concepts. This is not surprising where, even today, a
fair proportion of executives at agencies believe branding and advertising are one and the same thing. And when advertising executives believe
this, clients end up believing it. I was appalled to read the take on branding of one agency senior executive—a regional "network boss" of one of
the world's largest ad agencies: "A lot of agencies are now adding brand
consultancy to their current offering. I am not sure how this is any different from strategic planning."[18] It should be of absolutely no surprise
that this senior management mindset trickles down to the lower levels.
    Advertising agencies compound the branding crisis that exists in
Asia by formulating communications strategies and creating advertising that are unsupported by formal "brand blueprints." The brand
blueprint (which is discussed in detail in Chapter 3) is a mission-critical
document that provides the essence of a brand upon which everything
is built—from decisions that involve company operational issues, to
(and especially) advertising. Instead, most of the time advertising is created in a vacuum. Even when consumer insights are used, they tend to
be uncorrelated to the brand's essence (which is not surprising, when
no brand blueprint is in evidence). In some cases, a "brand blueprint"
crafted by the agency will be used. But these hastily created documents
usually provide neither relevant direction nor a robust frame of reference. Part of the reason this happens is because existing agency business models are not delivering sufficient margins that warrant the kind
of time and effort that is required to generate properly what needs to be

generated. Agencies are usually forced into crafting brand blueprints by clients wanting to get better value for their fees. Of course, usually the opposite happens.

CONCLUSION

Asian brands face a double challenge: both from within and from without. Within the company, the CEO is unwittingly creating formidable barriers and obstacles that effectively all but smother the brand. This is the root cause of the current crisis in Asian branding. But most CEOs don't even recognize that a problem exists, so they take no effective action to correct it.

When a serious problem exists, it is often only a neutral and objective third party that has the ability to make the individual concerned recognize the fact. Government agencies that encourage and support brand building (such as Singapore's SPRING and Malaysia's MATRADE) are perfectly placed to do exactly that. They have not only the resources, but also, in most countries, the necessary credibility. Unfortunately, they are not doing enough and a major opportunity is being wasted. They need to do more. Most agencies could enhance their roles by adopting two initiatives: (a) get tough; and (b) get smart. "Getting tough" simply means evaluating more carefully who they dole out money to and under what conditions. Too much "free money" is being given away in markets such as Malaysia where it is being used for everything *except* branding. And in markets like Singapore, branding "proposals" that form the basis for approving grants are not being scrutinized closely enough. The result is that poorly thought-out proposals are getting funding when they shouldn't. Getting smart will neutralize many of these problems. Good intentions aside, the reality is that many of the officers responsible for assessing companies' needs and approving grants are not qualified to do so. They are often junior-level individuals who are learning on the job (from only slightly more experienced colleagues). They are, nonetheless, making judgments regarding advice and (taxpayers') money. Government agencies in most markets have at their disposal plenty of reputable and qualified brand consultants whose expertise and experience can and should be harnessed. This is a low-hanging fruit solution, but many more should be adopted. The relevant government ministers and the chiefs of these agencies need seriously to review and restructure their operations, given the importance of what is at stake.

Rounding off the external challenges to Asian brands are charlatan brand consultants and the role that advertising agencies play. The former can be dealt with to some degree by government agencies that are better placed to spot less-than-qualified providers and have (or will have) the mechanisms in place to warn clients away from unsuitable providers. At the same time, better-trained government agency officers will also be better placed to steer companies with specific needs to relevant providers with specialized expertise or services that address those needs. And "impartiality" need not suffer.

Lastly, advertising agencies are reluctant actors in this drama. While they contribute to the problem, much of that comes from unreasonable client demands that ironically—and client CEOs should pay attention to this—result in poorer output. Agencies are usually not going to walk away from accounts, even if they come bundled with demands that extra services—such as brand development—be included "free of charge." Given that very little is really free, something always has to give. And in most cases that "something" is going to be "quality" brand building—the same quality that many Asian CEOs are presently incapable of recognizing.

Asian brands are struggling in a brutal environment.

NOTES

1. *The Straits Times*, Singapore, March 12, 2003.
2. "Media Top 1000 Asia-Pacific Brands," *Media*, 2010 (Haymarket Media Limited, Hong Kong).
3. Jim Collins, *Good to Great* (New York: HarperCollins, 2001), pp. 1, 11.
4. MATRADE website: www.matrade.gov.my.
5. Senior Minister Mentor Lee Kuan Yew, speaking at the Global Forum, August 16, 2004, UPI.com.
6. Minister of Finance and Deputy Prime Minister Lee Hsien Loong, *Commanding Heights*, May 5, 2001.
7. For a more detailed explanation of what defines a brand audit in the context of a branding project, see Chapter 6.
8. Structured interviews were mostly videotaped with the permission of interviewees. A typical questionnaire would include some 40 questions, 75 percent of which would refer directly to the interviewee's company, with the remaining 25 percent being generic questions on management style and business philosophy.
9. Tom Doctoroff quote extracted from "Recession Bodes Well for China's Global March," *Media*, March 26, 2009, p. 25 (Haymarket Media Limited, Hong Kong).

10. Tony Fernandes, "CEO AirAsia, Fernandes Declares 'War' as Airlines Feel Chill," *Media*, March 12, 2009, p. 17 (Haymarket Media Limited, Hong Kong).
11. Joseph Baladi, keynote speech, "How Singapore Companies Can Build Stronger Brands," Launch of BrandPact & Inaugural Brand Exploratory Workshop, April 7, 2005, IE Singapore and SPRING.
12. Joseph Baladi, "Branding and Singaporean Companies," presented to IE Singapore, May 15, 2007.
13. Brian Fling, "The Agency Model is Dead," www.blueflavor.com, August 1, 2006.
14. Mike Carlton, *Who's Going to Do the Work?* (Carlton Associates Inc. 2009, www.CarltonAssociatesInc.com).
15. "Marketers Place a Premium on Value for Money," *Media*, March 12, 2009, p. 25 (Haymarket Media Limited, Hong Kong).
16. "Marketers' Feel that Advertising Agencies Need to Focus on Account Orientation," *ADOI Magazine*, May 29, 2009.
17. Fernandes, "CEO AirAsia, Fernandes Declares 'War' as Airlines Feel Chill," *op. cit.*
18. Tracey Furniss, "Can Ad Shops Become Consultants?" *Media*, April 9, 2009 (Haymarket Media Limited, Hong Kong).

3

REDEFINING BRAND, BRANDING, AND ADVERTISING

BRAND AND BRANDING: THINKING DIFFERENTLY

"What is a brand?" and "What is branding?" are arguably two of the most often asked questions when it comes to the business landscape in Asia. The irony is that key decision makers are still no closer to understanding the role, value, and application of brands and branding, not to mention what differentiates one from the other. Part of the reason for this is that branding is "invisible," and Asian CEOs tend to value more the tangible: what they can see and touch. And yet, companies must focus on brands and branding if they hope to be successful. This fact is neither complicated nor hidden. It is in plain sight, and managers need to make an effort to see it. To use a metaphor: Branding is to a company what foundations are to a building. Both are, in a manner of speaking, invisible. One supports an edifice, the other an organization. Both have a critical role. Foundations give a building integrity and strength, in much the same way a brand does for a company. Simply put, without foundations, a building will fall; and without a strong brand, a company will fail. Yet, while Asian CEOs have no difficulty in understanding the purpose of a building's foundations, as invisible as they are, they struggle to recognize how brands and branding play the same role in their companies.

Most Asian CEOs look at branding as either an optional extra or a luxury expense. This illustrates a significant lack of understanding by this singularly important group, with dire consequences.

Beyond the misunderstandings, "brand" and "branding" also suffer from an extreme case of serious underestimation. Most Asian CEOs look at branding as either an optional extra or a luxury expense. This illustrates a significant lack of understanding by this singularly important group, with dire consequences. Asian CEOs, in particular, have an obligation to revisit the concept. The effort would prove to be illuminating: It would provide major revelations that would trigger a series of actions and initiatives that would literally change the destinies of their companies.

> Brands amount to some of the most important things in life.

I am going to preface my own definitions of brand and branding with a statement that is intended to be provocative: **Brands amount to some of the most important things in life.**

I often make this comment at the conferences I am invited to speak at in Asia and elsewhere. It never fails to surprise. I always add: "'Sure, brands are important,' I can hear some of you thinking. 'But among the most important things in life? Come on, get real! What about love, relationships, values. . .?'"

I assure the audience that I am very serious indeed. I genuinely do believe that brands represent some of the most important things in life. And I will say here the same thing I say during my conferences: It is my aim to have readers of this book more or less agree with this statement by the time they finish reading it.

At its very simplest, brand = positioning and branding = process. Positioning is what the brand stands for in the minds of customers (and other stakeholders). It also directly influences what the brand promises. Branding is the process that creates, builds, and sustains the brand (see Figure 4.1 in Chapter 4, "The Business and Branding Flowchart"). What is important to grasp at this stage, however, is that: (a) the process begins inside the company; (b) it reflects the values and contributions of the majority of internal stakeholders, which, in turn, impacts them, their roles, and the operations of their functional departments; (c) this impact is neither linear nor siloed, but dynamic and multidirectional; and (d) unless all individuals and functional departments willingly work in an orchestrated manner, the brand positioning and promise are weakened. Why? Because everything within the organization is connected.

Thinking Differently

One of the best ways to understand seemingly confusing or complex concepts is to reconsider them from a different perspective. Often, the more unconventional that perspective is, the more surprising the revelation. Central to recognizing why brands are so important in life is being willing to look beyond traditional definitions of "brand."

> Brands are *not* limited to goods and services. Brands are *not* the exclusive domain of business and commerce.

Brands are *not* limited to goods and services. Brands are *not* the exclusive domain of business and commerce. That they are not, will surprise many Asian CEOs, who may even scoff at the notion. Nevertheless, brands should not be limited to these narrow parameters. And it is precisely because we traditionally equate brands almost exclusively with business that most of us fail to see how they manifest themselves as other things that influence and affect our daily lives. And anything that affects our everyday life is powerful and deserves closer scrutiny.

Unfortunately, the word "brand" is weighed down by a debilitating amount of baggage that mostly serves to confuse its real meaning. Dictionary.com defines brand as: kind, grade, or make. According to *The New Penguin Dictionary,* a brand is "a characteristic or distinctive kind: his own lively brand of humour." What both these definitions infer is a broad application for the word. It is useful to divorce the word from the business context and reconsider it as simply a "label." As a label, it has equal applicability to areas other than business. And if you can understand how "brands" work in other, non-business contexts, it becomes possible suddenly to begin to see their infinite potential.

Brands Define Who People Are

While the role and importance of branding are often underestimated, other conventional perceptions contribute to needless over-complications. Visit a bookstore and pull out 10 leading business titles that include explanations of branding, and chances are that you will read 10 different definitions. Some may cover only one dimension of the several that collectively contribute to an accurate expression of the concept. They will all likely provide explanations that are best described as tangible and practical—the conventional "What is branding?" approach. Here are five examples of these:

1. "A brand is a trusted promise of quality, service and value, established over time and proven by the test of repeated use and satisfaction." John Mariotti, *Smart Things to Know about Brands and Branding*

2. "At its simplest, a brand is a recognizable and trustworthy badge of origin and also a promise of performance." Paul Feldwick, *Advertising Planner*

3. "A brand is a store-house of trust that matters more and more as choices multiply. People want to simplify their lives." Niall Fitzgerald, chairman of Unilever

4. "(A brand is) a singular idea or concept that you own inside the mind of the prospect." Al Ries, *The 22 Immutable Laws of Branding*

5. "A brand is a brand is a brand." *Gertrude Stein*

Brands help people define themselves.

There is a better way to define "brand." Instead of looking at ways to explain what it is, it is infinitely more useful to look at it from the point of view of what it does. What do brands do? Answer: **Brands help people define themselves.** I have underscored the statement because it is one of the major themes of this book.

Consider the characteristics of an effective brand:

- It offers a proposition (positioning and customer promise).
- It has values.
- It has attributes.
- It has associations.
- It has personality traits.
- It conjures up an image in the minds of people.

The characteristics listed above contribute to a brand's blueprint. Their value depends entirely on whether they are relevant in the first place and whether they are applied consistently. Expressed differently: Brands = Promise & Delivery.

Any "thing" that reflects or delivers these types of characteristics in a credible and sustainable way ultimately attracts specific groups of people to it. The stronger its characteristics are, the more likely it is to stand for something and the stronger the attraction is likely to be. The more compelling the attraction is, the more we adopt it and the more it tends to define us. All of these things qualify as brands.

Brands Help People Define Themselves: Elvis the Brand

Elvis Presley has often been described as "The Artist of the [20th] Century." The singing sensation and mega-celebrity became a symbol not just for his generation, but for every one that followed. The music was the trigger, but Elvis Presley's importance derived from the values and lifestyle he embodied—the image he created (both real and mythical). He was a rebel who shocked much of conservative Middle America with his music and provocative on-stage performances; yet, through his public displays of affection for his mother and his willingness to serve his country by accepting the draft, he portrayed a clean-cut image that electrified women and inspired men the world over. Even during the latter part of his career, when he publicly began to lose control over his life, he remained an untouchable icon. He would forever remain "The King." Millions of people lived vicariously through Elvis. The Elvis Presley brand was an important part of their lives, influencing how they saw themselves: "I am 23 now and I've been listening to his music for exactly 13 and a half years now. He changed my life, my way of thinking and everything I was, am, or ever will be. I've cried, smiled, made love and started singing in public because of Elvis."[1]

Whether it was manifested in aspiring to sing like him, dress like him, or live like him, many people began to define themselves based on some aspect of the Elvis Presley brand: "In 1977 there were 170 Elvis impersonators. By 2002 there were 85,000. At that rate of growth, by 2019 a third of the world's population will be Elvis impersonators. Impersonators include black Elvises, disabled Elvises, Jewish Elvises, Greek Elvises and child Elvises. A Mexican one is called El Vez. Elvis Herselvis is a lesbian one."[2]

(Continued)

Elvis Presley has everything to do with branding. In 2002, a remixed track of the 1968 song "A Little More Action" was released to accompany a Nike World Cup TV commercial and instantly became a runaway global hit. Social media networks buzzed with excitement and glee:[3]

- "If someone had told me, that there was to be a remixed version of an Elvis Presley song released, and it would be a smash around the world, I would have told them to keep taking the pills. It aint gonna happen! BUT thank heaven it did." June 25, 2002
- "This may be the biggest pop music event of the year. I can't stop playing the thing." July 28, 2002
- "WHO ELSE BUT ELVIS PRESLEY COULD HAVE A NO. #1 HIT AFTER HE'S BEEN GONE FOR 25 YEARS!! ALL OVER THE ENTIRE WORLD IT WAS A BIG #1 HIT SONG!!" February 24, 2004
- "This is the kind of music that gets in your head and you can't get it out." August 6, 2005
- "Elvis is still the best singer to walk the planet. He's got the groove, the style, and he does it with heart and grace . . . all these years later. We need music like this today to feel good about." March 14, 2003
- "Elvis may have left the building, but his song, '(A Little More Action and) A Little Less Conversation' has entered the charts at #1 in England." June 25, 2002

In 2007 the Elvis brand was estimated to be worth over US$600 million[4] and the man has been dead for over 33 years! Such is the power of this brand. What makes the Elvis brand "great" is its power to excite, inspire, uplift, and even empower people.

Religions, Ideologies, Terrorism, Countries, and People

It may surprise many to hear that religions are powerful brands. Consider the Catholic Church: Its reason for being stems from a central premise—its proposition (and, critically, the promise that comes within it). It has values and attributes. It exhibits specific personality traits. Ultimately, it earns associations that others give it. As a result, it has "customers"—people who choose to adopt that brand. And like any other brand whose proposition does not appeal, there are scores of others who choose not to be customers. Make no mistake: religions are, in every way, legitimate brands.

Every single day, millions of people around the world "use" the Catholicism brand. What determines whether people "buy" into this brand is what it stands for—its promise—and what it does to deliver that promise. So, every day, by calling themselves Catholics or Christians and behaving as such, millions of people define themselves. And the same applies for millions of Muslims, Hindus, Jews, and so on.

Similarly, **ideologies** make equally powerful brands. Ideologies, like religions, possess all the basic characteristics that define brands. If you believe in capitalism, you will behave in a certain way. If you believe in communism, you will behave in a certain way. By believing deeply in something, we behave in a manner that is consistent with its tenets. We define ourselves through our beliefs and actions—actions that create a bond between us and that "brand."

A more troubling extension of the ideological brand is being manifested through the rise of **global terrorism**: ". . .Al-Qaida has become a global brand driven by the power of the World Wide Web. . . ."[5] Al-Qaida (like the more conventional ideologies) provides a specific proposition that appeals to some people and not to others. That makes it a brand for those with whom the proposition resonates (as much as for those for whom it does not). The former become "customers." They *remain* customers (brand-loyal) depending on whether they perceive the brand as delivering on its promise. As loyal customers, they then behave in a certain manner: They define themselves, and are defined by others, by their behavior relative to this brand.

Source: Olivier Roy, "Al-Qaida Brand Name Ready for Franchise," *Le Monde Diplomatique,* September 2004, http://mondediplo.com/2004/09/02alqaida.

Countries are brands. Consider brand USA. I grew up in a generation that venerated America. America—notwithstanding the anomalies of Watergate and Vietnam—stood for freedom of expression, and inspiration as much as aspiration (for everything from the middle-class lifestyles of suburbia, to striking it rich as an entrepreneur). It was about liberty of the body and spirit, experimentation (in thought and behavior), and fabulous, enviable achievement. Everybody loved America. It was a hell of a brand. And for those who "bought" that brand, their feelings and opinions influenced the decisions they made and the lifestyles they chose. Whether they were Americans living in Alabama, or Britons living in Brixton, they lived by the ideas and ideals they admired; they dressed in the fashions that Hollywood movies dazzled them with; they enjoyed burgers because . . . well, because everyone enjoys burgers. The point is that brand USA influenced hundreds of millions of people, and in the process, it helped them define themselves. And its ability to retain this franchise today depends entirely on the relative appeal of its promise and its consistent delivery—something being strongly tested by a new generation living in an entirely new world.

Madonna fans transcend age and gender

Source: CORBIS.

People are brands. Consider celebrities, singers, movie stars, politicians, captains of industry . . . terrorists. Madonna is a brand. So was JFK (and he continues to be one), and so is Jack Welch. These people are associated with specific values and other associations that they themselves cultivate and/or that are attributed to them by others. They "stand" for an idea, a sound, a value, a style, or a belief that resonates with specific groups of people: their "customers." They are symbols that embody specific things—along with the authority, fame, admiration, or notoriety that comes with those things. People brands infiltrate their customers' lives in sufficient measure to influence their behavior in some manner. A Madonna fan usually does not limit herself or himself only to listening to and buying her music. Often it goes far beyond this. A hard-core Madonna fan will relate to Madonna's personality, empathize with her experiences, find common ground with her values, and ultimately allow her into his or her world. The manifestations of this will emerge as both tangible and intangible expressions—and almost always through behavior. People define themselves through the vehicles that resonate with them.

But it is not only celebrities that are brands. "Ordinary" people represent strong individual brands—not in a metaphorical sense, but in a real and, for the purposes of this book, very instructive way.

BRANDING MADE EASY: THE PEOPLE ANALOGY

By understanding how people emerge as individual brands in their own right, it is possible to understand brands in a commercial context. We can cut through the clutter of definitions by using a model we call the People Analogy. This useful tool provides more than an approximation of meaning: It provides an almost mirror-like, accurate reflection. By revisiting a process we can all relate to—human growth and development—it is possible to couple the individual phases of human development to those of brand development and growth.

Over time, we all develop into individual, stand-alone brands. Not "some" or "many" of us—every one of us is a walking, living, *bona fide* brand. We may not all be "good" brands, but brands we remain nonetheless. This notion may offend some people, but the concept of brands and branding as it applies to our everyday lives, as well as to business, should be devoid of sentiment. As a "label," it just is. It is a descriptor. How it is applied, however—in business or elsewhere—may be deserving of criticism or praise.

Our own human development process (*The Human Blueprint*) provides us with a model that allows us to understand the development of commercial brands. The development of brands parallels our development as human beings in many fundamental ways. Consider the process that contributes to the evolution of our human values and belief systems; the way we create and sustain relationships; the very fabric of those relationships; what happens when we sometimes damage those relationships; and the role of "second chances" in life. All have parallels with aspects of the development of commercial brands.

The People Analogy model identifies seven effective chronological and progressive phases that also reflect the development phases of commercial brands. Figure 3.1 provides a snapshot summary:

Phase 1: Time

Phase 2: Differentiation

Phase 3: Make it right the first time

Phase 4: Target segmentation

Phase 5: Avoid change/embrace innovation

Phase 6: Don't exaggerate, lie, cheat, or misrepresent

Phase 7: Find ways to be bigger than yourself

Phase 1: Time

The early years of life—our childhood and adolescence—are influenced and largely controlled by our parents and other authority figures. It is during these formative years that we are exposed to internal and external variables that will influence the people we become later in life. And "what" we become—the end-product, so to speak—is equivalent to the brand "me" proposition. In other words, I am brand "Joe." And like all brands, I am made up of a set of certain core characteristics that define who I am to myself as well as to others: I have a brand proposition that explains what I believe in; what I stand for. I value specific things that define me in specific ways. I have my own unique personality and a host of definable attributes. My collective characteristics don't emerge overnight. They take time to form and to reveal themselves to me. In time, I adopt some and reject others. It is a journey.

As I become more and more comfortable with these characteristics, I begin to express more confidently to people around me what I think and what I believe in. This "message" will appeal to some, but not to others. The former become my friends (the equivalent of "customers"). My ability to maintain my friends' interest lies entirely in my capability and willingness to match my words with my deeds. But this takes time. I will need multiple opportunities to demonstrate in deed what I say I mean in words. Friends, for their part, will require multiple demonstrations of my sincerity before they will believe what I say. This also takes time. This process of matching deeds to words is the social equivalent of the commercial promise and delivery brand equation.

Commercial parallel #1: "Friends" are to people what customers are to companies and brands.

Commercial parallel #2: Many (not merely some) Asian CEOs are under the mistaken impression that strong brands can be created overnight. But as the People Analogy illustrates, a position, a point of view, a proposition requires not only time to explore, develop, and finally emerge, but also to *stick*. Once formulated, a company's position will take even more time to settle in the minds of its intended customers. Why? Because the company will have to demonstrate and prove two things over and over again: (a) "who" it is, and (b) that it is serious and committed to being who it claims to be. This will require time.

The branding process—whether formal or informal—starts from within. . . . Companies must not abdicate their responsibility for crafting their own brand positionings. This cannot be outsourced. The very idea of doing so is absurd.

Commercial parallel #3: Like people, commercial brands need to undergo a process that deliberately explores possibilities that lead to a position. In the case of companies, this process may take the form of a formal, structured branding project. The branding process—whether formal or informal—starts from within. There is a widespread misconception that branding is built externally—typically by vehicles such as advertising, promotions, and public relations. In fact, it is employees who build (and deliver) the brand, not account executives from ad agencies, who often neither have a real understanding of the company's culture nor share in the CEO's vision for its future. (For more about the role of advertising agencies, see Chapter 2.) The brand "essence" evolves from within the organization. It is the "self" of the organization that can only be created by it, not by a separate entity that may or may not be on the same wavelength as the company, but could never

Figure 3.1 The People Analogy

The People Analogy: Understanding brands through the understanding of people				
	VARIABLE	PEOPLE	COMMERCIAL BRANDS	KEY PARALLELS
Phase 1	TIME 1. To develop 2. To demonstrate	**The Human Blueprint** 1. People need time (typically during early adulthood) to explore and eventually decide on: • The values they believe in • The personality they will exude • The attributes that will identify them • The strengths they will build 2. For the above to be "believed" by others, people need time to demonstrate them; opportunities to show that they are who they claim to be.	**The Brand Blueprint** 1. Commercial corporate and product brands also need time either to evolve or to formally explore their identity. They cannot be dictated by the chief executive or a management committee. • What will the brand value? • Personality: aggressive/easy-going; conservative/liberal, fun/serious, etc? • What strengths (core benefits) will the brand become known for? 2. Simply because a company settles on a blueprint and expresses it through advertising does not mean that customers are ready to believe it. *Actual delivery* over an extended period of time is critical to earning confidence and trust.	1. Both processes start from *within*. 2. All brands (both "people" as well as commercial brands) *take time to build*.
Phase 2	DIFFEREN-TIATION	Many would argue that to succeed in life we need to make an effort to stand out. To become an individual in a literal sense—different from others. We do this by building our Human Blueprint (Phase 1) and by paying attention to those drivers that highlight our more emotional side—those that make us more compelling to other human beings.	The single most valuable dimension that will drive a brand to success is differentiation. "Me-too" propositions get the scant attention and respect they deserve. Differentiation must on the one hand appeal emotionally to customers and, on the other hand, always provide functional benefits (practical benefits) that are considered a given.	Focus on the emotional, but never lose sight of the practical.
Phase 3	MAKE IT RIGHT THE FIRST TIME	We only have one opportunity to make a good first impression. If that first opportunity is wasted, it is always a struggle to make up for it.	Brands are judged immediately and without compassion when they first emerge onto the market. An irrelevant or undifferentiated message—or worse, no message at all—relegates the brand to a position that is often impossible to overcome in the future.	It is critical that a brand's very first exposure to customers communicates a message that is relevant and compelling to them.
Phase 4	TARGET SEGMENTA-TION	Once our character is defined, we are likely to appeal to some people who become our friends, but not to all people. If we try to pretend to be someone we are not (to please others), we are soon found out and often we risk alienating our original friends, who begin to think twice about us.	Very few brands can successfully engage all people. Truly successful brands **choose**. The conscious choice of a specific identity (via the Brand Proposition/Phase 1 above) dictates that it cannot and will not be equally appealing to all customers. It can't. It is, by definition, specific. The focus must, instead, be on one or two key target segments.	1. Friends are to people what customers are to companies and brands. 2. If we are to be true to ourselves, we need to recognize that we will never be able to appeal to *all* people. Similarly, it is a mistake for brands to try to appeal to *all* customers. Doing this inevitably compromises them and they end up appealing (in a strong way) to no one.

	VARIABLE	PEOPLE	COMMERCIAL BRANDS	KEY PARALLELS
Phase 5	AVOID CHANGE/ EMBRACE INNOVATION	**1. Change:** (A) Once we reach a certain age—when we "mature"—the values and belief systems we adopt form the basis of our character DNA that we more or less retain and strengthen all through our lives. We rarely fundamentally change this foundation. This frame of reference defines who we are (to ourselves and to others). (B) Further, the fact that we interact with groups of people every day parents, colleagues, friends, children,etc—does not give us reason to communicate different identities to each. We remain the same person. We simply tailor-make our messages differently to cater to different people. **2. Innovation:** As we strengthen and reinforce our core identities during our lifetimes, we must also pay attention to the changing landscape. The world moves forward, delivering change. As individuals, we must maintain currency and relevance-particularly with new and emerging generations of people as well as technology and how it impacts on work, home, and relationships. This means we need to continuously innovate or run the risk of being left behind. But we must do this without compromising our core beliefs and values.	**1. Change:** The strength of a brand lies in its clarity of message, purpose, and values. These cannot change over time to suit ever-emerging opportunities or changing fads. Doing this would confuse customers at best, and alienate them at worst. Further, brands should not have different identities to suit the perceived different needs of different markets. A brand may only have one identity, but it may be expressed differently in different markets as needs and circumstances dictate. **2. Innovation:** Whilst a brand never changes, the absence of innovation in an environment where markets and customers develop and evolve is a death sentence. A brand may be true to itself by continuously reflecting and living its values. But if it fails to recognize the ever-changing nature of markets and customers, it risks becoming boring, old fashioned, or worse, irrelevant.	1. Brand identities, once established, should not change over time. On the contrary, the very point of view they take and the values they embody must be reinforced. Consistent action over time creates solidity, trust, confidence, and ultimately, belief. 2. Different markets should not provide an argument for the expression of different brand identities. A brand can only own one identity. It may, however, choose to express that identity differently in different markets. 3. But, to maintain relevance, brands must incorporate or reflect the latest thinking and remain at the leading edge of relevance to customers. To do this, they must innovate.
Phase 6	DON'T EXAGGERATE, LIE, CHEAT, OR MISREPRESENT	1. Individuals who over-reach beyond their known capabilities are often embarrassed, sometimes compromised. Their image in the eyes of others suffers. 2. Individuals who spend a lifetime earning trust and confidence run the risk of losing it all if they misrepresent or deceive or disappoint—even once. When this happens, people feel betrayed. Often the relationship is lost forever.	A commercial brand takes years to build confidence with customers. If it fails to deliver or fails to live up to its proposition or values or, worse, deceives its customers—even once—loyal customers will feel betrayed. And in that moment they will desert in droves a brand that might have taken years to build. And if that were not enough, they will also tell their friends of their disappointment via the internet!	1. Be careful what you promise. Why? Because you will need to deliver it all the time—every time. 2. In an era of hyper-competition where customers not only have infinite choice but are informed and sophisticated, any deception, or worse, any hint that the brand disrespects the customer, will be dealt with ruthlessly and swiftly.
Phase 7	FIND WAYS TO BE BIGGER THAN YOURSELF	Self-centered individuals rarely enjoy enduring warm and rewarding relationships with others. The capacity to see the world outside of one's personal needs and to contribute positively to it makes us not only more worthwhile human beings but also more appealing to others.	In an era of global challenges (many created by business), the practices of companies are increasingly coming under scrutiny—not only from regulatory bodies but from customers themselves. Not only is corporate social responsibility increasingly mandatory, but so are the values that brands themselves are seen to "live." The closer the correlation between individual values and brand values, the more likely it is that a brand will be chosen and adopted.	Corporate social responsibility is as relevant to companies as personal responsibility is to individuals. The former impacts the relationships customers have with brands, the latter the relationships people have with one another.

Source: The People Analogy, "Understanding Brands through the Understanding of People," BrandAsian.

understand it as it understands itself. Companies must not abdicate their responsibility for crafting their own brand positionings. This cannot be outsourced. The very idea of doing so is absurd.

Phase 2: Differentiation

As individuals, we spend our lives trying to stand out—to be different. Being different is the core essence of being an individual. And this is a universal need that transcends cultures, and even Asian cultures where responsibility for the collective is also deeply ingrained.

What makes us different from the people around us is partly the end-result of our human development process (described in phase 1), which turns us into the individuals we become. In becoming different, we also discover that what we know impacts people differently than how we behave and interact with them. Raw knowledge provides us with the ability to build expertise, but it is the chemistry we have with others that allows us to build relationships. It is not that the former is less important; on the contrary, it is very much a mandatory component. However, it is also mostly considered a "hygiene factor"; in other words, it is a "given" which people would expect you to have in order for them to consider talking to and getting to know you. It is what one adds on top of that—the emotional dimension—that generally leads to successful relationships. It is the quality of one's emotions that makes us special and human to others.

Commercial parallel #1: Products that solely offer features and functional benefits often discover that customers don't find this is enough. To stand out, to attract the attention of customers, products need to demonstrate and offer a difference that is compelling.

Commercial parallel #2: In today's hyper-competitive environment, it is increasingly difficult to effectively differentiate products and services on the basis of attributes and features alone. In today's sophisticated marketplace, best-in-class attributes and features are simply expected; these emerge as basic category price-to-play. Relying solely on these only results in "me-too" products. Effective differentiation therefore lies beyond (not instead of) functional benefits in the area of emotions.

Phase 3: Make It Right the First Time

This is a pretty straightforward, easy-to-understand phase. We usually have only one opportunity to make a good first impression. Being the not-so-rational creatures that we are, we are often quick to judge people on first meeting them—whether rightly or wrongly. That being the case, it is in our interests always to be ourselves and not try to project an image that we think suits the circumstances. Being ourselves may not provide the impression some people can or want to relate to, but it does ensure that we deliver an accurate and consistent expression of our real selves. This reinforces the appeal we have with existing friends who do "patronise" us. Being true to ourselves will always serve us well in the long term.

Commercial parallel #1: In the incredibly competitive environment in which brands do battle today, it is difficult enough to attract any customer attention. But when brands do so, they had better communicate the *right* message the first time. If they don't, they will rarely get a second chance.

Commercial parallel #2: For the message to be right the first time, it needs to reflect the brand's true identity and values, even if this risks alienating some customers.

Phase 4: Target Segmentation

The more different and unique we become, the more interesting and appealing we end up being to certain people. These people become our friends. I say "certain people," because we learn very quickly how futile it is to aim to be appealing to or popular with everyone we meet. What makes us unique correspondingly attracts only specific types of people to us, and not others (by definition). Any persistent effort to try to please everyone generally backfires and we end up pleasing no one, including those who might otherwise have responded to our true selves.

Commercial parallel #1: "Friends" are to people what customers are to companies and brands.

Commercial parallel #2: Strong and successful brands need to communicate a specific brand identity. The operative term here is specific. A brand cannot, by definition, appeal to all people. Its very design is intended to appeal only to specific people. The strength of any message lies in its clarity and purpose. Both must be focused. Decision makers need to choose who their intended customers are, and then focus on them to the exclusion of others.

Phase 5: Avoid Change/Embrace Innovation

This sounds like a paradox, but it isn't. "Change" is generally a good thing. The change I am referring to here is of a different type.

Once we finally settle on the basics of our core identity, especially our values, we find that these never really change. In fact, the passing of time serves to strengthen them. We are able to understand ourselves better, and we feel more confident about the decisions we make because we make them within the context of the rock-solid frame of reference that we have built. Further, we find that our ability to be consistent contributes to the trust our friends continue to have in us. They find us dependable and true to our word.

Constant change—character flip-flops—would undo a lot of this. At best, it would confuse our friends or elicit their sympathy. (They may think that we either "have not found our way" or "have lost it.") At worst, it might convince them that we are not people to be trusted.

At the same time, most of us recognize the complementary relationship between solid core beliefs and the need to accommodate—and in some cases, embrace—the constant change that affects our lives. The world today is very different, in an infinite number of ways, from that of just 10 years ago. As individuals, we need to adopt a dual strategy in order to survive: hold on to our core values (the immutable things that make us who we are), while at the same time innovating as the world changes so that we remain current and relevant.

> "Our corporate philosophy . . . has not changed (in 32 years)
> since the first store was opened. This has remained the same.
> Although we have, of course, had to change in the way we
> respond to (external changes) over the years."
>
> Tadashi Yanai, CEO and Chairman, Fast
> Retailing Co. Ltd. (UNIQLO)[6]

Commercial parallel #1: It is a tough challenge to create a brand identity that is effective and relevant, and that will pass the test of time. Time, as mentioned earlier, is a fundamental element of the brand development and building process. It provides the means for brand identity to "stick." It stands to reason that one would aim to strengthen it with consistent reinforcement, rather than weaken it with inconsistent delivery or constant change. Once crafted, brand positionings should be changed only under very extreme and specific circumstances; otherwise, credibility and customer relationships may be adversely affected.

Commercial parallel #2: Brands must not adopt or express different core identities in different markets. Although "change" brought about by globalization and technology is making the world smaller and more accessible to customers, both physically and virtually, the risk of message dissonance is correspondingly higher in today's connected world. Dissonance, as alluded to earlier, creates confusion and results in outright brand erosion. What may differ in different markets is the specific promise the brand makes locally, and how that promise is delivered (execution). (See "Brand Proposition" later in this chapter.)

Commercial parallel #3: Yet, the world *is* always changing. Change is the one constant we can be sure of. To keep up—to maintain currency and relevance—brands need to be innovative, but never at the expense of their core identities.

Phase 6: Don't Exaggerate, Lie, Cheat, or Misrepresent

It can take years, sometimes decades, to build personal relationships— those we have with our families, our friends, and our work colleagues. Those relationships are characterized by trust, which is built up over time. But just one indiscretion, one lapse of judgment, or one conscious misdemeanor can destroy that trust—often instantly and for good. With family members we sometimes get a second chance; with others, we may not enjoy that luxury.

Commercial parallel: Once a brand's positioning has been formulated, its strength and credibility are entirely dependent on consistent, reliable delivery of the brand promise. Why some companies continue to believe that they can get away with over-promising and under-delivering is a mystery. Even more absurd is the practice by some of lying outright to customers. This approach is particularly mystifying in times of aggressive competition on the one hand, and highly sophisticated, educated, and informed customers on the other.

Phase 7: Find Ways to Be Bigger Than Yourself

This last phase, while critically important, may be as elusive to many people in life as it is to many companies and their decision makers in the business context. "Life" conditions us first to look out for ourselves and our immediate loved ones. We are primed for survival in a world that is becoming ever more complex, competitive, and even dangerous. Nevertheless, many among us make an effort to do more: to recognize that the welfare of the collective is important for the survival of the individual. This translates into sensitivity toward others, especially those less fortunate than ourselves, as well as toward the living world around us—our climate and our environment. For some people, the goal of helping others or the environment becomes an end in itself; it provides a purpose in life.

Two decades or more ago, when the world was more parochial and far less "connected" than it is today, "doing more" might have been interpreted as giving money or doing charity work according to one's capability. In this way, many people were able to do something, but without really getting involved. Today, while charity still has its place, people are getting more involved. The issues of global poverty, political corruption, human trafficking (especially of children and women), and global warming are being incessantly communicated through 24-hour global news channels and internet social networks. The result is that people are getting involved because they feel they have to. Many people feel they are part of the problem and therefore should also be part of the solution. Involvement contributes to the character we create for ourselves, strengthens the values we hold as important, and reinforces the reasons why others may feel attracted to us.

Commercial parallel #1: Company donations to charities and special causes, as well as corporate sponsorships—as welcome as they are, don't amount to modern-day corporate social responsibility (CSR) efforts. Very much like people, responsible companies are waking up to the reality that, by virtue of whatever product they produce or service they provide, they are leaving behind a carbon footprint. Sooner or later, they will either have to account for this themselves or be made to account for it by their customers.

Commercial parallel #2: Beyond making profits for themselves and their shareholders, some companies are also realizing that recognizing their responsibility translates into goodwill for increasing numbers of customers. The more that companies are seen to "live" certain values, the more empathy—and loyal customers—they generate.

Summary

The idea behind the People Analogy is to demonstrate how people and commercial brands develop in parallel ways. These parallels are intriguing and revealing. The goal is to provide business decision makers with a familiar "tool" (themselves) that helps them understand the concept of brand and branding in a more personal, clear, and revealing way (see Figure 3.2). Benchmarking the brand-creation and brand-building process to the development of personal core beliefs is a useful way for decision makers to rid themselves of sound bites, convoluted definitions,

Figure 3.2 Brands are like people

Just like **people**,
brands take time to develop their individual identities

Just like **people**,
brands have attributes that are simply expected (price to play)

Just like **people**,
brands have values that take time to be believed

Just like **people**,
brands need to prove themselves over and again when they break trust

Just like **people**,
brands have but one chance to make a first impression.

and misconceptions that are obscuring their comprehension of a subject that they simply cannot afford to misunderstand.

Does toothpaste define me?

While some might concede that religions and ideologies, and perhaps even some celebrities, might contribute to people's self-definition, they may have reservations about the ability of less-exalted products, such as the car they drive or the toothpaste they use, to define them.

The fact is, *all* our preferred brands define us in some measure: The choice of authors I read, the car I drive, the clothes I wear, the music I listen to, the bank I use, and the dog food I buy all say something very specific about me and help define me: whether I read Steinbeck or Grisham; drive a Toyota or a Mercedes Benz; wear GAP or Prada; listen to Bach or rock out to Bon Jovi; bank with Citibank or DBS; or buy Caesar-brand dog food or a supermarket own brand. These are choices that I deliberately make; and if they become regular choices, they become part of my life, which means part of me. These brands help define who I am to myself while also sending a very strong signal to others.

> *"I am irresistible, I say, as I put on my designer fragrance. I am a merchant banker, I say, as I climb out of my BMW. I am a juvenile lout, I say, as I down a glass of extra-strong beer. I am handsome, I say, as I don my Levi's jeans."*

John Kay, Economist

To many people, a BMW is much more than a car—even a prestige car. To some, it might be "the ultimate driving experience." To others, it makes a more general statement either about themselves—"I am a BMW kind of guy (or girl)"—or about someone else: "There goes a BMW kind of guy (or girl)." Embedded in the statement is what we assume to be true of such a person: they are likely to be a young, upwardly mobile professional—probably an investment banker, a lawyer, or similar; they are likely to buy Armani clothing; they probably prefer to wear black. Of course, the brand is bought by a far larger range of people than this generalization would suggest. However, the broader reality doesn't invalidate the popular perception that surrounds the brand, because even those who fall outside of the generalization buy into it. The generalization itself is aspirational. While it defines some, others aspire to be defined by it—even if vicariously.

This applies in different measures to other car brands as well. There are Toyota owners, just as there are Toyota-type people; and there are Volvo owners, just as there are Volvo-type people. The brand characteristics *always* transfer across to the owners in some measure and say something about them (whether or not they are aware of it): "I am a practical person" (any Honda model); or "I like small cars" (SMART car); or "I am environmentally conscious" (Toyota Prius); or "I like cute cars" (VW Bug); or "I worry about the safety of my children" (Volvo). The choices we make reflect who we are and who we wish to be, and thus help define us.

Consider the toothpaste you use. If you consistently buy, say, Colgate toothpaste, you are making a statement to and about yourself. To others, you may be indicating you are "a Colgate kind of girl." Because you may have grown up using Colgate, the brand is about authenticity and heritage. Making the choice to continue to use this particular brand helps remind you of who you are.

During a seminar that I delivered to UOB senior bankers in Singapore, I asked them if they could recall using more than one toothpaste brand when they were growing up. Most people said that they had used just one brand, and had grown emotionally attached to it. Now, as adults, they continued to use the same brand and were unlikely to switch to another.

In a brand audit focus group that I conducted in 2002, one respondent commented: "I grew up with Colgate. . . . It reminds me of my mother nagging me to brush my teeth . . . of being a teenager and that special minty taste just before a Saturday night out. . . . It reflects so many memories and is so much a part of my life. . . ." The prospect

There are legions of people all over the world who believe that the iPod in particular, and Apple, in general, say a great deal about the kind of person they are

Source: Newsweek, July 20, 2004.

of that brand suddenly disappearing from this person's life (and others like her) would likely result in a sense of loss. We have the capability of forming strong bonds with brands that enter our orbits and stay there. Those bonds inevitably contribute in some shape or form to the mosaic we become, whether we are conscious of this or not.

Brands are thus very powerful. Whether they are religions, ideologies, people we are inspired by, or the cars we drive or the toothpaste we use, they find a way into our lives and, in the process, help define us. The value of a brand should be obvious to the marketer. In some ways, brands are some of the most important things in life. Yet, Asian companies and their CEOs are failing to harness this enormous power and to create great, iconic Asian brands.

THE BRAND BLUEPRINT

Simply defined, the brand blueprint provides a strategic manual that influences virtually all of a company's operations—not just the brand. It is the company's Holy Book, in a sense; the pillar that holds up the company edifice. It not only provides a blueprint for proactive action, but also serves to clarify the company's strategic direction and redirect its efforts. Whenever someone in a department is in doubt or confused over an issue that is strategic in nature, or in those more serious situations when the company is experiencing a crisis, the brand blueprint provides a frame of reference that can be used to help resolve the issue. And because it is a document that is circulated and distributed company-wide, it provides the means for making decisions in a manner that is consistent with company strategy. As such, it is a key strategic document.

Seven Key Elements of the Brand Blueprint

The brand blueprint includes seven critical elements, as set out in Figure 3.3.

Core brand values

A company's core brand values are those things it really believes in—whether they are moral code values or practical values—and which, in one

Figure 3.3 Key elements of the brand blueprint

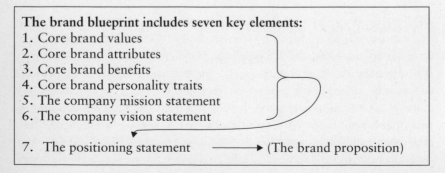

The brand blueprint includes seven key elements:
1. Core brand values
2. Core brand attributes
3. Core brand benefits
4. Core brand personality traits
5. The company mission statement
6. The company vision statement

7. The positioning statement ⟶ (The brand proposition)

way or another, motivate employees to behave in a certain manner. Brand values—because of their emotional dimensions—also contribute directly to the brand's appeal to customers. Typically, a company will have no more than four "core" values. This subject is analyzed in Chapters 4 and 5.

Core brand attributes

Attributes are to a company or product what garments are to people. They are key characteristics that help "clothe" the company, and may be tangible or intangible. Typically, a company will have no more than four "core" attributes.

Core brand benefits

Many Asian companies communicate a laundry list of "benefits," many of which are not seen by customers as being very compelling or even relevant. "Core" brand benefits are those that customers find compelling, and which make the brand unique and desirable. Core benefits are drivers of brand differentiation. Typically, a company will have no more than four "core" benefits. These are discussed in more detail in Chapter 5.

Core brand personality traits

Brand personality is the assigning of human characteristics and traits to a brand. These traits permeate the entire organization and are ultimately reflected in the behavior of staff and the identity of the brand. Brand personality is, along with the brand's values and the company's mission statement, probably the strongest contributor to a brand's emotional dimension. Typically, a company will have no more than four "core" personality traits. This subject is discussed in more detail in Chapter 5.

The company mission statement

In its simplest form, the mission statement spells out the reason why the organization exists—that is, its purpose. That purpose may not necessarily be business-centric. It is mostly internally directed, and contributes to the creation of the organization's corporate culture. Its principal benefit lies in helping to motivate employees, and making them feel more fulfilled by what they do. This subject is discussed in more detail in Chapters 4 and 5.

The company vision statement

A vision has an aspirational end-point that reflects where the CEO would like his or her company to be within a predetermined period of time. A vision sets the direction and the framework for defining and accomplishing goals. The vision statement is rooted in reality, but is focused on the future. This subject is discussed in more detail in Chapter 4.

The positioning statement

The brand positioning statement refers to how the brand is mentally perceived by the customer. It should reflect a selection (if not all) of the characteristics of the first six brand blueprint elements mentioned above, in order to provide an overall perception of the brand's image: what it stands for. This central image is theoretically permanent or fixed, in as much as it defines the brand. It is independent of the "customer promise," which is another essential, complementary component of the positioning statement, but is dynamic. This subject is discussed in more detail under the heading "The Brand Proposition," below.

The brand blueprint works off the premise that management and operational policies and decisions take their cue from the brand, making the company effectively brand-centric. This is an important premise because, while the term "brand-centric" has some currency, most companies in Asia have not adopted it as an operational philosophy. A brand-centric approach explicitly delivers primacy to the brand. Marketing, sales, and indeed virtually all the other functional departments within the company, take their cue from the brand.

> Companies that are brand-centric understand that their brands act as connective threads that hold together the fabric of the company. Companies that are brand-centric depend entirely on their brand blueprint.

Companies that have adopted a brand-centric mentality and operational structure recognize that everything—from marketing and communications of the brand, to human resources, to sourcing and assembly line operations (and more)—is, in some measure, influenced, if not dictated, by the brand blueprint. The core brand personality traits influence the tone of the advertising; the core brand values influence the kind of people the company hires; the core brand benefits determine what kind of materials are purchased and used to make the brand, and so forth. Ultimately, a brand-centric company typically creates a self-sustaining culture that allows the emergence of positive dynamics. Where everything is connected, one positive element linked to another leads to virtuous circles. Companies that are brand-centric understand that their brands act as connective threads that hold together the fabric of the company. Companies that are brand-centric depend entirely on their brand blueprint. For more on brand-centric companies and employee engagement, see Chapter 5.

Developing the Brand Blueprint

For brands to be powerful, they need to be "real." Reality and truth can only come from within the company. They cannot be manufactured by an advertising agency and then be translated into an expression—even if the expression is "creative" or compelling. Without truth, the message is not sustainable. Truth underpins the company's brand blueprint.

Uncovering the truth provides opportunities for internal company reflection, discussion, debate, and—finally—consensus. This requires a process. The problem with "truth" is that it seldom stands in stark contrast to the "untrue" or the "false." Companies generally discover that multiple truths emerge. The challenge for CEOs, company managers, and their employees lies in choosing the real truth—as opposed to the *easy* one—that defines their company not only in the present, but also in the near and long-term future.

Most companies that make the strategic decision to brand or rebrand (position or reposition) engage in one of several alternative brand development processes. The most common approach is discussed in more detail in Chapter 6. Whatever process type a company adopts, as long as the methodology is reliable, the end deliverable will be the same: the brand blueprint.

The brand development process will take the company through several phases. It is during these phases that the seven key critical elements—along with several others—will emerge to shape the brand blueprint.

Individually and collectively, the seven elements of the brand blueprint provide the company with purpose, differentiation, identity, and a destination. Once crafted, they provide the company not only with its structural foundation for support, but also the engine to power it forward.

The brand blueprint is the single most effective document in delivering a company's real strategic advantage in an ever-changing, dynamic environment. It allows companies not only to forward plan in a proactive manner, but also to deal with and overcome threats and challenges systematically. The absence of a brand blueprint, on the other hand, produces the exact opposite outcome: poor planning and a reactive management mentality.

There is an overwhelming resistance among Asian CEOs to undertaking formal brand development exercises. Not completely understanding the value and purpose of the outcome naturally prejudices the initiative being considered and adopted in the first place. But even more significant than this is resistance that stems from an almost universal belief that branding is mostly an external effort that should be delivered by advertising, promotions, and public relations companies. One of the key goals of this book is to overcome this persistent and damaging misconception.

For all that the brand blueprint offers a company, it remains not much more than a piece of paper. Without activation, it is of little value to the company. Activation is also known as internal alignment—the process that that "brings alive" the seven elements of the brand blueprint. Chapter 7 provides an in-depth explanation of internal alignment and identifies the kinds of benefits a company can expect from the process. Ironically, those few companies that actually take the important step of engaging in a formal brand development process more often than not fail to conduct an internal alignment. Internal change is required in order to bring the brand blueprint alive within the organization. In Asia, this is anathema to many decision makers, who find change uncomfortable and threatening. These individuals are responsible for hindering the growth of their companies and, in many cases, depriving them of greatness.

THE BRAND PROPOSITION

The brand proposition is the expression of the brand blueprint. It is to a company what the heart is to the human body: it is connected to all the other functional department organs and pumps the equivalent of blood and energy into the company's brand. And the brand, in turn, influences everything and everyone in the company. If that influence is positive, the very final manifestation—delivery of the brand promise to the customer—will also be positive. If the influence is negative, it will infect everything in the organization on its way to the customer, and the customer experience is almost guaranteed to be negative. So, the company doesn't have the luxury of getting the brand proposition wrong.

Predictably, though, many companies do still get it wrong. This basic concept is commonly misunderstood by the two most important business audiences: the company CEO (and, by extension, those who report to him) and the managers of the advertising agencies with whom they work with. The casualties are the brand and the customer.

What is basic should be clear to everyone, especially advertising agencies—but often it is not. As the managing director of FutureBrand Australia pointed out in an article that debated the strategic credentials of some providers, there is a big difference between brand strategy, communications strategy, and media strategy.[7] Equally, there is a big difference between brand positioning, brand strategy, brand promise, and the brand proposition. That this should be self-evident infers that people— especially senior agency heads—understand the roles they each have. The overwhelming evidence, however, is that they don't. As a result, they develop a mentality and philosophy that is then passed on to the lower ranks, who, in turn, confuse the company's clients and ultimately create havoc among Asian brands: what the CEO of the Singapore office of a global network refers to as the "dumbing down of our industry."[8]

Some basics: brand positioning precedes brand strategy—see Figure 3.4. Sole responsibility for the former lies with the brand owners, not the advertising agency. The latter is also a brand owner responsibility, but it can be influenced by agency input. It is also important to note that the brand positioning provides a *fixed* position, meaning that it does not change over time. The brand strategy, on the other hand, is dynamic and can change with evolving circumstances. Both provide the basis for the brand promise, which is—to some degree—also *dynamic*. **All three constitute the brand proposition.** Only when these three are formulated (and aligned internally in the organization) can the communications strategy and creative development take place (see the business and branding flowchart in Figure 4.1, in Chapter 4) and have a chance of succeeding.

Brand Positioning

The brand positioning is the single central catalyst that will drive the future destiny of the company. The company *must* get this right if it hopes to survive—much less grow and expand. Expressed as a statement, it amounts to the central idea the brand stands for in the minds

Figure 3.4 The brand proposition is the sum total of the brand positioning, brand strategy, and brand promise, and influences the creative work

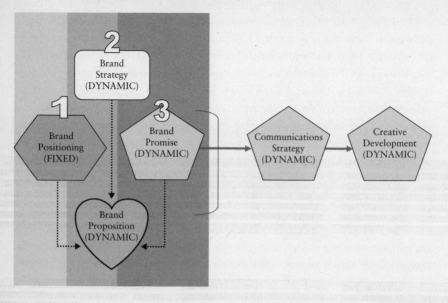

of all constituents—especially customers and employees. It should sum up many of the core characteristics that define the company—those that are found in the brand blueprint. The brand positioning is not a concept that changes or is adapted to the peculiarities of different groups of people in different geographies, or to changing circumstances. It is a central and immutable core idea that represents the brand to everyone, everywhere. It is the foundation of the edifice upon which the company is built. It doesn't change over time. On the contrary, the passing of time strengthens and reinforces that central idea. The aim is to ultimately own the idea.

As a fundamental and essential construct that drives the brand and therefore the company, its creation needs to be carefully considered and orchestrated. As mentioned earlier, the responsibility for this lies entirely with the CEO. It cannot be delegated.

Brand positioning statements are generally crafted soon after a new company is set up. Brand repositioning processes, on the other hand, are adopted by existing businesses which are experiencing severe adverse circumstances that threaten their ability to compete effectively.

Chapter 6 discusses the methodology companies must adopt in order to position or reposition themselves. It is important that the CEO understands and participates in the multi-step linear process, and engages with it fully, to ensure that the end-result is a statement that is both strategically relevant to the company's needs and sustainable. The process, while typically moderated by third-party brand consultants, is an internal one. The final positioning statement is crafted through discussions, exercises, and consensus by selected employee groups—normally, through a series of workshops.

Figure 3.5 provides an example of a CEO-led and employee-crafted positioning statement for the Singapore-based Eu Yan Sang Company. Eu Yan Sang is a leading Asia-wide manufacturer and retailer of traditional Chinese medicines (TCM). Over the years, it has expanded its business to include medical clinics and wellness centres. In the early 2000s the company felt increasingly challenged by rapid category transformation that was being fueled by changing consumer habits and usage patterns. The changes that were taking place were so dramatic, the entire category risked becoming irrelevant. In 2005, Eu Yan Sang took the initiative and decided to reposition itself in the marketplace in order to better appeal to younger target audiences with more sophisticated expectations, as well as remain relevant with its existing customer franchise. The positioning statement shown in Figure 3.5 was the product of a comprehensive multi-market branding project that solicited input from not only different customer groups, but also more than 100 company

Figure 3.5 The Eu Yan Sang positioning statement

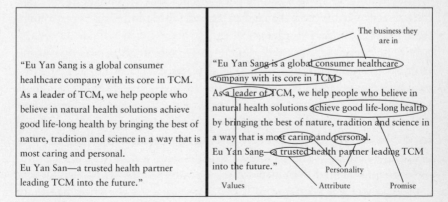

Source: The "Eu Yan Sang Brand Positioning Statement," extracted from its branding project's brand blueprint, 2002. Reprinted with permission.

employees—from the CEO to R&D technicians, administrators, and retail salespeople. The statement provides an excellent example of the kind of key components that are needed to create a clear, differentiated, and compelling position in the minds of targeted audiences. The left-hand side of the diagram provides the statement, while the right-hand side identifies the key components that make the statement work. All components originate from the Eu Yan Sang brand blueprint. The willingness of Eu Yan Sang employees to embrace its new brand positioning and deliver it consistently to customers contributed to the company's ability to reverse its fortunes and emerge as the region's number one TCM player. In the process, Eu Yan Sang also single-handedly redefined the category.

Brand Strategy

In this book, I have simplified the concept of brand strategy to include just the eight key cues that activate the brand. (Brand strategy is discussed in more detail in Chapter 5.) In basic terms, brand strategy is the strategy a company must adopt to best deliver on the brand positioning it has created for itself. The brand positioning says something very specific about the company, because part of the goal is differentiation. This dictates that specific target audiences will need to be focused on. This, in turn, means that specific measures and initiatives will need to be taken and activated internally with employees. This means that specific innovations will need to be pursued and a specific type of brand architecture adopted. And overall, a specific type of corporate social responsibility program may need to be implemented. The key word, of course, is specific. Brand strategy is about making choices that deliver specifically to the brand positioning. Once that strategy is identified, it is possible to formulate the brand promise.

In an effort to stem what is likely to be some confusion, it is useful to look at **brand promise** as having two iterations: strategic and tactical. Within the framework of the brand proposition, the promise is largely strategic. In this context, the customer promise is influenced by the brand strategy choices the company makes, and is very closely tied to the brand positioning. In this sense, the brand promise helps to define the company. The second—tactical—iteration of the brand promise is communicated through advertising to reflect insights and circumstances in local markets. It is framed within the creative idea—all of which will always be consistent and connected to the brand positioning and strategic brand promise.

It is the collective forces of the three elements that combine to create a **holistic brand** proposition. The brand proposition not only gives light and direction to the communications strategy, but in the brand-centric company it also influences virtually all the decisions made within the organization.

THE RELATIONSHIP BETWEEN BRANDING AND ADVERTISING

Chapter 2 identified how advertising agencies have contributed to the arrested development of strong and great Asian brands. In this section, we will explore the relationship that should exist between the two disciplines.

Most advertising executives wrongly equate advertising with branding. Further, the absence of robust brand development processes on the client side ends up all but effectively eliminating the role of the brand blueprint from the communications strategies coming out of agencies. This issue results in a great deal of misdirected creative work, and is at the source of much of the criticism leveled at agencies.

Figure 3.6 provides a basic and simplified illustration of the relationship that connects branding to advertising. As the diagram shows, the two disciplines constitute two separate functions that complement one another. This alignment effectively creates a two-phased process.

The first phase—the brand development phase—is a formal and structured process that begins within the organization. This fact may surprise some corporate decision makers, especially young advertising account executives who have been conditioned to believe that company identity and promise begin and end with a television commercial. Any identity (meaning "essence," be it of a brand or a person) comes from within. It is astonishing, therefore, how the advertising industry has for decades convinced both the business community and itself that it alone creates the magic that persuades people to buy. This self-perception has all but buried awareness and comprehension of, and credit being given to, a less glamorous but invaluable pillar of the overall mix—the brand blueprint. A reasonable analogy might be the storyline in a movie that has attracted attention for its compelling actors and special effects; sometimes the story—which has made it all possible—gets lost.

The end deliverable of the brand development process is the brand blueprint. As identified earlier, the blueprint provides stakeholders both from within and outside the company—especially customers—with the key pieces of the puzzle that will, in time, emerge as the identity of the company. It also provides advertising people with the building blocks that are critical in developing the communication strategy and, ultimately, the creative work itself.

Phase 1 of the brand blueprint enables phase 2. As Figure 3.6 shows, the main output of the advertising communications strategy is the brand promise the company makes to the customer. Ultimately, the brand promise is translated into a creative execution. Of all the elements that contribute to the development of the brand promise, three are key: (1) consumer insights—an understanding of the local drivers that

Figure 3.6 The branding—advertising construct

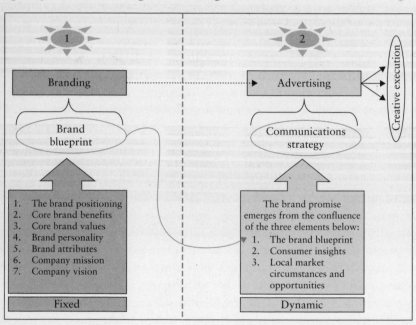

It is very important to note the two boxes at the base of the illustration: "Fixed" and "Dynamic." While the communications strategy will, by necessity, change over time (from season to season or year to year), the brand blueprint does not change. Understanding why this is so goes a great distance in removing the obstacles that prevent both clients and advertising executives from creating and building truly great brands.

Source: The Branding–Advertising Construct, BrandAsian—Brand Education Seminar series, 2008. All rights reserved.

trigger behavior in each of the markets in which the brand is marketed; (2) local market circumstances and opportunities—an appreciation for individual or indigenous market characteristics or developing opportunities; and finally—but critically—(3) the brand blueprint, which injects the brand's essence into the mix.

The vast majority of advertising in Asia (and a not insignificant amount of advertising in the rest of the world) is created in the near absence of phase 1. This consequently robs the communications strategy function (phase 2) of one of its three critical ingredients: the brand blueprint. The end-result is as damaging as it is difficult to detect initially: off-brand messaging.

Off-brand messaging is another example of people not knowing what they don't know. Very often, clients may not be aware that a campaign created by their agency—while perhaps being funny, witty, provocative, or touching—fails the most critical test: relevance.

Relevance is key. Consider the total universe of possible creative executional alternatives as being a circle comprised of as many possibilities as there are degrees. In other words, there are 360 different messages to choose from. Any one of these messages is capable of being communicated in a powerfully creative manner. Which one is "right"? It is at this critical point that many clients make a fateful error that triggers a series of adverse outcomes. The correct answer to the question is impossible to discern without some frame of reference. It is impossible to tell which direction will be the most effective one unless the agency has created, or has been provided with, a "strategic zone" from which to work. We call this the positioning or strategic tranche (see Figure 3.7). The illustration shows the black arrows as alternative creative campaigns/executions. And while some may be attractive, even compelling, it is useful to remember that they are all different. So, again, which one is "right"? In fact, all are "wrong," because they are all off-brand.

The triangle tranche, on the other hand, represents the area of strategic relevance created by the brand blueprint. As is clearly visible, this tranche is sufficiently wide to accommodate a broad scope of creativity. The difference is that any direction within this area (illustrated by the dotted arrows) will be relevant to the needs and issues of the company (on-brand). It is between these dotted arrows that the real choice of creative ideas and campaigns for the client lies.

Many clients are simply unaware that the tranche even exists. Worse still, many advertising account executives don't know of its importance. At the more professional agencies, reputable creative directors will welcome any construct that takes the guesswork out of the process.

Figure 3.7 The strategic tranche created by the brand blueprint

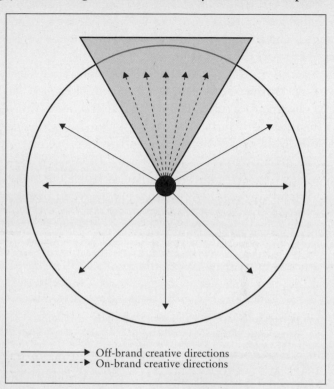

→ Off-brand creative directions
--------▶ On-brand creative directions

It makes their lives easier and the final work more powerful in a sustainable way, instead of being temporarily titillating but ultimately failing.

To be fair, most agencies have neither the business models nor the competencies to develop robust brand blueprints. The protracted and painful fee restructuring negotiations of the past decade have severely and adversely affected the profit margins of most agencies, essentially forcing them to do two things: further reduce their operating expenses (including further devaluation of their human capital); and create new value-added services that might be chargeable. In Asia, the work of developing robust brand positionings for clients that need them has *not* been one of these services. For a variety of reasons, clients expect this to be a free benefit thrown in, and many agencies have perpetuated this misguided sense of self-entitlement by agreeing to provide this. As

A series of Pepsi ads that don't reflect the brand's core values and personality

"I think it's pretty disturbing...."

"I think it's disgusting.... it lowers my respect for Pepsi."

"I think they should pull the ads and apologize."

"This is no way to promote a product. I think it's really sick."

"It doesn't even seem like a very smart marketing move ... and seeing that ad certainly doesn't make me think 'Pepsi'."

"Very insensitive. Doesn't do much for Pepsi's brand image, if you ask me."

"Pepsi is obviously trying to stir up some kind of controversy.... What kind of an idiot would think that suicide would be a good marketing idea?"

"How could this ever persuade someone to actually buy Pepsi?"

"Such a stupid concept by the ad agency and I am surprised Pepsi actually accepted it."

"I have NO IDEA how a supposedly world-class agency ...? could have come up with such an insensitive ad campaign ... nor can I comprehend how a brand like Pepsi could approve this kind of garbage."

What were they thinking?
The image of an animated, forlorn calorie committing suicide in a number of explicitly disturbing ways, including by gunshot, hanging, self-immolation and wrist slitting, raises questions about the campaign's taste and sensitivity on the one hand, and its alignment with Pepsi's core brand values and brand personality on the other. This is a good example of an advertising effort being conceived outside of the brand blueprint strategic tranche. It may be provocative (surely the intent of the creatives), but the effort is irrelevant in as much as it fails to reflect or strengthen the brand's long-standing positioning. The immediate reaction on the message boards was to be expected and mostly indicated that the campaign had caused damage to the brand.

Sources: BNET: www.bnet.com/blog/advertising-business/bbdo-airs-8220suicide-8221-ads-for-pepsi-max/164; Trenhunter: www.trendhunter.com/trends/controversial-soft-drink-ads-pepsi-max-lonely-calorie-campaign; Yumsugar: www.yumsugar.com/Pepsi-Targets-Controversy-Suicidal-Calorie-Campaign-2563895?page=0%2C1#comments.

a consequence, the quality, strength, and sustainability of Asian brands, and the creative work that supports them, have been damaged.

> . . . there is an awful amount of off-brand advertising polluting the landscape in Asia.

Despite all of the self-congratulation that goes on in the industry (there is a slew of awards events), there is an awful amount of off-brand advertising polluting the landscape in Asia. Bad advertising has thus contributed to deferring the development of great Asian brands.

If most advertising agencies are not equipped to deliver robust brand blueprints, whose responsibility is it to ensure that the blueprint is formulated in the first place? It is the responsibility of the client, of course. But most Asian CEOs either consciously abdicate this responsibility or are unaware of it in the first place.

This needs to change.

Logos and Slogans

It is useful and appropriate to make brief mention here of the role of logos and slogans, given that they dominate the visual landscape of brands, as well as the perceptual thinking of many Asian CEOs as to what amounts to "branding." Mid-level and senior decision makers in the region almost always equate logos and slogans with branding. In other words, they consider the mere existence of a trademark and a quirky slogan as amounting to effective branding.

Given that this perception is ingrained and entrenched, and amounts to a fundamental obstacle to building great Asian brands, it is important to state unequivocally that (like advertising) *neither a logo nor a slogan amounts to branding*. But like advertising, both play critical roles that complement the branding function. For this reason, it is important to understand the role of each.

Logos play important roles within the communications construct of all brands. Because of their prominence, they are usually the first visual expressions of a brand to which customers are exposed. In that brief opportunity to engage with the customer, the logo must immediately and effectively impart the essence of the brand's identity. The essence of any brand's identity is to be found in the brand blueprint. Very much like advertising that is created outside of the strategic tranche (Figure 3.7), a logo created in the absence of a brand blueprint will likely not reflect the brand's positioning and will amount to not much more than a pretty picture (at best). It will be irrelevant and ineffective. The logo is a vehicle that triggers a shorthand visual snapshot of the brand's positioning. Those that are created in a vacuum miss out on a vital opportunity to capitalize on the most ubiquitous symbol a company has to reinforce those characteristics that makes it unique and compelling.

Unlike logos, which usually either don't change or only evolve very slowly, slogans tend to have use-by dates that roughly correspond to the life-spans of the advertising campaigns they support. In that sense, slogans are very much (*dynamic*) tactical tools that more accurately reflect communication strategies (or creative executions). Consider some of the 172-odd slogans Coca-Cola has used over the past 121 years: the simple call to action of 1886: "Drink Coca-Cola"; 1905's somewhat wordy and bizarre "The favorite drink for ladies when thirsty, weary, and despondent"; 1917's boastful Three million a day; 1925's more triumphant Six million a day; 1942's *really* wordy "Wherever you are, whatever you do, wherever you may be, when you think refreshment, think ice-cold Coca-Cola"; 1970's memorable "It's the real thing"; 1982's enduring signature "Coke is it"; and today's somewhat cryptic "The Coke Side of Life" (2007).[9] Each was as effective as the campaign it was created to reinforce. And each was replaced with new and evolving (dynamic) advertising campaigns.

While slogans tend, for the most part, to be tactical support tools, they can also be deployed as strategic expressions of brands. In other words, slogans can reflect the fixed side of Figure 3.6. But it is important for brand owners and advertising executives to understand that this amounts to a choice that needs to be made consciously—not haphazardly—and for the right reasons. "Volvo. for life" is a good example of a strategic slogan that aims to activate and reinforce a profound core brand benefit, rather than reflect the brand's advertising campaign *de jour*. A strategic slogan has a much longer shelf life than a tactical slogan and needs to be used in a careful and considered context. Typically, such slogans emerge during a brand-repositioning phase or at a time when the company needs to reinforce its core brand blueprint characteristics.

Whether used tactically or strategically, slogans and logos are meaningless words and images if they fail to reflect the brand's strategic positioning or other elements of the brand blueprint. Like advertising campaigns, slogans and logos that are created without relevance do little more than take up space.

NOTES

1. Customer Review, "A Little Less Conversation," May 6, 2004, Amazon.com, www.amazon.com/Little-Less-Conversation-Elvis-Presley/product-reviews/B000068QZW/ref=cm_cr_dp_all_helpful?ie=UTF8&coliid=&showViewpoints=1&colid=&sortBy=bySubmissionDateDescending.
2. "The Wonder of You—75 Fascinating Facts about The King," *The Sun*, February 7, 2010, www.thesun.co.uk/sol/homepage/features/2799410/75-facts-about-Elvis-Presley-for-his-75th.html.
3. Customer Review, "A Little Less Conversation," *op. cit.*
4. Neelam Verjee, "Business Big Shot: Elvis Presley," *TIMESONLINE*, June 2, 2007, http://business.timesonline.co.uk/tol/business/industry_sectors/media/article1873110.ece.
5. John Lettice, "Internet Has 'Given Al Qaeda Wings' Claims BBC Potboiler, Shock Discovery—Terrorists Use Computers Too," *Music and Media*, July 27, 2005, www.theregister.co.uk/2005/07/27/bbc_al_qaeda_internet.
6. *Today*, April 18–19, 2009.
7. Tim Riches, managing director, FutureBrand Australia, "Design Companies Look for Life Beyond the Logo," *Media Magazine*, June 4, 2009, www.media.asia/searcharticle/2009_06/Live-Issue-Design-companies-look-for-life-beyond-the-logo/35868.
8. "Marketers Place a Premium on Value for Money," *Media*, March 12, 2009, p. 25 (Haymarket Media Limited, Hong Kong).
9. "Coca-Cola Advertising Slogans by Year," www.2collectcola.com.

4

PRE-BRANDING

*"Kung fu lives in everything we do, Dre Parker. It lives in how
we put on our jacket; how we take off the jacket. It lives in how
we treat people. Everything is kung fu."*

Mr. Han (Jackie Chan) to Dre Parker (Jaden Smith),
The Karate Kid (2010)

The branding process requires, and is dependent on, a pre-branding phase that puts in place foundations that support the brand positioning and brand strategy. In this chapter, we will examine the role and purpose of two of these critically important foundations: (a) business goals and business strategy; and (b) corporate guiding principles.

We will also examine the Business and Branding Flowchart[1] (see Figure 4.1). The flowchart provides a snapshot view of an interconnected process that begins with the formulation of business goals and strategy and concludes with delivery of the brand message to the customer. The interrelationships between the different phases provide an early illustrative view of the interconnectedness and interdependence of business strategy and brand positioning in particular, along with everything else. Everything is connected.

> Branding . . . provides direction to the marketing function—not the other way round.

88

Figure 4.1 The Business and Branding Flowchart

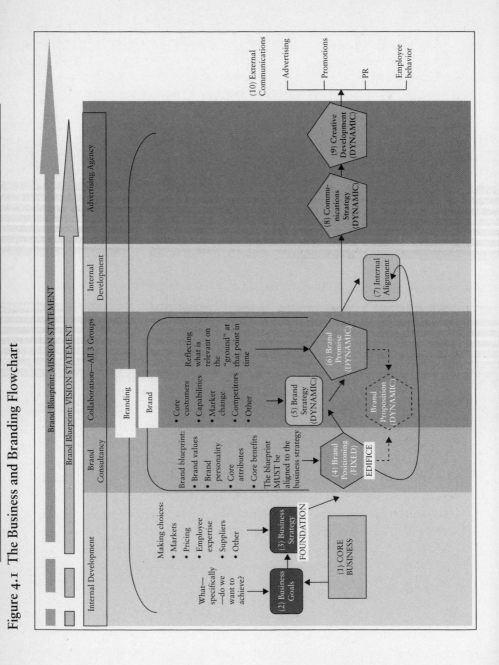

OVERVIEW OF THE BUSINESS AND BRANDING FLOWCHART

There are different ways of looking at the 10 phases of the Business and Branding Flowchart. One way is to start near the top and recognize the parameters that cover brand and those that cover branding. The latter clearly shows a breadth that encompasses all activities within the organization from beginning to end—that is, from recognition of the core business, to formulation of the business and brand strategy, to the eventual expression and delivery of the brand message to the customer. *All of this is branding.* Thus, branding can be said to be the process that extends across all functions and functional departments of the organization (see Chapter 3). Further, as might be visually inferred, branding is not a subset of the marketing function as is commonly believed. If branding is reinterpreted as an element shared by all functional departments, then it provides direction to the marketing function—not the other way round. Though not illustrated, the marketing function in the evolved corporation of the 21st century lies between phases 5 and 9 as set out in the figure.

Core business (phase 1) provides the basis for the formulation of both the **business goals** (phase 2)—which includes corporate and/or brand vision—and the **business strategy** (phase 3), which will deliver these goals. As the top row of the figure indicates, this amounts to an internal process and responsibility. These three elements need to be discussed and debated by senior management and ultimately be ruled on by the CEO. They should not be ignored or done on the fly. The process must be structured and disciplined. Too often in Asia, it is not.

Once defined, goals and business strategy provide context and direction for the vital brand development process, which is made up of three interconnected phases: **brand positioning, brand strategy**, and **brand promise** (phases 4, 5, and 6).

Many senior managers and their advertising partners in the Asian region either ignore or misunderstand these three phases. This has significant consequences, as they are all strategic in nature and form the foundations of any strong brand. If their role, makeup, and application are systematically sidelined or undermined, this can be expected to have negative implications for the robustness of Asian brands. This is presently happening on a large scale in Asia.

Of these three elements, brand positioning—a critically important phase—is most often misunderstood or ignored. It is—essentially—the leading driver of the seven found in the brand blueprint. These drivers are the pillars that support the product or corporate brand. A brand that is built without these pillars—as are many brands in Asia—can and should expect erosion and fault-lines, and the likelihood of eventual collapse.

While the development of the brand blueprint (inclusive of the brand positioning) is a fundamentally internal effort, it is often led by external brand practitioners. Though this is arguably something that competent internal management teams might choose to do themselves, very few managers in Asia have the requisite expertise and experience to deliver an effective outcome. Further, the many ingrained biases and prejudices that would almost certainly emerge would also conspire to adversely affect the outcome. Phases 5 and 6, on the other hand, are best carried out through the collaboration of the three key partners: the company, the brand consultancy, and the advertising agency.

All three phases collectively deliver the more consumer-directed brand proposition. These phases are discussed in more detail in Chapter 3.

Internal alignment (phase 7) is the vitally important (and common-sense step) of aligning the company to the new brand proposition before going to market. This phase will be comprehensively covered in Chapter 7. As indicated in Figure 4.1, this is a mostly internally led process that can be assisted by external consultants.

The last three advertising agency-led phases—**communications strategy, creative development,** and **external communications** (phases 8, 9, and 10)—deliver the message that the consumer will experience. That message will need to be relevant as well as compelling. Too often the latter obscures the importance of the former. The only way to avert this is to ensure that all the preceding phases of the flowchart are addressed. In Asia, very often they are not.

Providing an overall overarching direction, as well as being influenced in some manner by some of the flowchart phases, is the formulation of the **mission** and **vision** statements. The former states the purpose of the company, the latter its long-term visionary goal.

BUSINESS GOALS AND BUSINESS STRATEGY

> Too many companies across Asia are flying blind.

Too many companies across Asia are flying blind. They are headed by CEOs and management teams that either don't know where they are going, or fail to reach their goals because of a lack of focus.

They also suffer from questionable motivation. Ask 100 senior Asian C-level executives what they believe should be the purpose or key business goal of their company, and 99 of them will tell you: "To make money." As mentioned in Chapter 2 and explained in more detail later in this chapter, this is often identified as an "end," instead of as the means to a different end. This view is myopic and ultimately damages the organization in a way that becomes apparent only when much of the damage is already done and it is too late to do much about it.

Following our interviews and group discussions with CEOs, managers, and factory-level workers from companies across key Asian markets, one central and troubling revelation stood out: the virtual universal absence of business strategy from corporate toolboxes.[2] The absence of formal business goals, or the inability of managers to stay focused on declared goals, also emerged as a negative characteristic of many companies. Simply stated, the absence of a destination, or, conversely, the existence of an environment where that destination keeps changing, precludes not just the formulation of a way to get there (business strategy) but also the notion that any special way is needed in the first place. Both are bad news for companies.

"The point is this: how can you hope to mobilize a large team of employees to pull together, accept new and different job assignments, work in an uncertain environment and work hard despite the uncertainty of their future, if the leader of the company can't or won't articulate the shape of the other side of the valley? Clarity of direction, which includes describing what we will not be going after, is exceedingly important at the late stage of a strategic transformation."

Andy Grove, "Only the Paranoid Survive"[3]

Businesses in Asia often demonstrate a mentality that is best described as opportunistic. Where the main goal is defined as making as much money as possible (as opposed to achieving something definable that results in making money), the company's "strategy" effectively becomes tactical: Every opportunity is seized, with little thought given to the possible consequences. Making money in the short term clouds the strategic imperative of knowing what to aim for in the long term (in a sustainable way) and committing to its delivery. One of the side effects of this is a general lack of focus that impacts the company in an insidious way, with devastating results.

When companies meander along with no clear destination and no visible goals, everyone from management down to lower-level hires becomes demoralized. When that happens, nothing works the way it should. Discussing the remaking of the State Bank of India, its chairman Om Prakash Bhatt, said: ". . . the bank's employees were not energized anymore. They had lost their pride and sense of belonging. From the very top down through the branches, everybody was pulling in different directions. The people weren't performing poorly as individuals; they just weren't aligned along a common set of objectives—no goals, no vision, no commitment. I didn't like what I saw."[4]

Bhatt is somewhat of an exception. For many Asian CEOs, making money in the short term trumps risks posed to the core business or core brands in the long term—those risks that are too far off on the horizon to worry about, or that may not even have been recognized. In the case of acquisitions, for example, many companies are bought for the wrong reasons and without sufficient thought being given to issues such as alignment with the core business and whether the company has the relevant competencies, expertise, and experience in the category to which the new acquisition belongs. Focus is almost always on the short term. This explains why Asia continues to have a disproportionately higher number of conglomerates than other regions in the world, particularly the United States, where the trend for the past decade or more has been the reverse—divestiture or rationalization of assets to focus on the core business.

In an environment characterized by the absence of either clear business goals or the discipline to stay focused on those goals that have been identified, it is perhaps not surprising that ignorance about what business strategy actually is or covers prevails across the board—from C-level management down to middle management. In most cases, the core concepts taught in business schools are either completely unknown or are not practiced. To overcome this, larger corporations routinely import this knowledge by appointing high-profile global management consultancies to assess their strategic needs and effectively do their thinking for them. That in itself is not necessarily a bad thing. After all, the purpose of external consultants is to provide specialized expertise and perspective in areas where corporate management has recognized it lacks depth. The problem lies not in the practice, but rather in the absence of implementation after the assessments and recommendations have been made. Too often, little or nothing happens.

"If we focus on price, we don't have a future."

Chen Hong, VP Overseas Markets, SVA Group (Chinese television)

As a result, far too many Asian companies adopt a default business strategy that invariably revolves around end-price to customer—but not in the manner that would be advocated by Michael Porter's cost leadership approach, where price parity with competitors is achieved but at a lower manufacturing cost point.[5] Most of the time, product price and manufacturing costs are determined independently of one another. This leads either to a drop in quality, or to an operating mentality that fails to consider quality as an important constant in the first place. Result: The brand image for such products ("cheap" and continuously "on sale") is poor and brand loyalty is generally limited.

And the situation is even worse with smaller companies. There, business strategy is absent altogether, either by choice or because the decision makers don't know what they don't know.

The business of brand and branding is not well served by this situation. Apart from constituting the elementary pillars that support sound and effective management, business strategy also provides the foundation for brand positioning and brand strategy. (Both concepts are discussed in more detail in Chapter 5.)

As the Business and Branding Flowchart shown in Figure 4.1 illustrates, brand development is a largely linear process, with business strategy playing a vital and integral role. Business strategy covers a wide area of operations, ranging from the macro to the micro.

Business Strategy: The Macro Dimension

"Macro" represents those relatively key fixed characteristics of the business that make the business what it is. For example, Malaysia's AirAsia promises customers the lowest fares in Asia. Their slogan—Now Everyone Can Fly—makes the explicit suggestion that flying is affordable for everyone. Many people would reasonably describe the core business of AirAsia as being low-cost air travel; that it is positioned, among other things, as a budget airline. The airline will likely have in place key characteristics such as a structure, processes, systems, training, and others, all of which will be geared to routinely delivering low-cost travel to passengers on an ongoing basis. In other words, AirAsia is configured to deliver this specific service. Its ability to make money (operationally via economies of scale and perceptionally through the delivery of consistent promises) will also be dependent on its focus on low-cost travel (core business/business goal). Bigger, more established airlines would find it difficult to match AirAsia's services and prices because they, too, are configured in a specific but different way.

AirAsia's brand positioning

Source: AirAsia. Reproduced with permission.

Configurations add up to the big choices companies make in setting up their basic infrastructures. In the case of AirAsia, we can use the Business and Branding Flowchart to assume, reasonably accurately, what macro choices (business strategy) it adopted before and after the company became operational. AirAsia's core business (budget air travel) provides it with big-picture business goals (to get as many people as possible to fly by providing the lowest possible prices). These goals, in turn, create business strategy choices that focus on: low prices, no frills flights, alternative or lower-tier airports or terminals, less experienced ground and cabin crews, low operating cost air ticket purchase points and outlets, and a myriad of other allied elements consistent with a budget operation. These choices inevitably find expression within the company's key customer offering that provides the platform for the creation of the broader brand positioning.

> It is therefore almost impossible to expect a relevant brand positioning to emerge unless the company has first clearly defined its business goal(s) and business strategy decisions.

It is therefore almost impossible to expect a relevant brand positioning to emerge unless the company has first clearly defined its business goal(s) and business strategy decisions.

As important as a company figuring out what it needs to do, is figuring out what it should *not* do. While facilitating business directions, the big choices also create obstacles to experimental forays outside the tight perimeters of the core business—obstacles companies should carefully consider before choosing to ignore them. AirAsia's core business theoretically dictates a relatively narrow business strategy and competitively pits it against other budget airlines. Any effort to compete directly against "first-tier" (full-service) airlines would likely result in significant challenges that its infrastructure might find difficult to address. Thus, the airline's launch in 2007 of a new company, AirAsia X, offering budget services to London and other long-haul destinations raises questions about whether the move is strategically sound or is an example of a company taking its eye off the ball of its core business. To date, all efforts to operate long-haul budget airlines have failed—most notably, Freddie Laker's Skytrain and later the US-operated Peoplexpress. The challenge that these airlines faced some decades ago is the same that AirAsia faces today—logistics.[6] Anything longer than the four-hour radius that has allowed AirAsia to operate successfully as a regional airline tests its infrastructure and stretches its resources. The question is not whether AirAsia X can do it; it is more a question of: Can it do it sustainably? But from a business point of view, an entirely different question has to be asked: Will the attention, effort, and resources diverted to AirAsia X threaten the success of AirAsia? At least one of its direct competitors seems to think so. Indeed, the managing director of Singapore-based Tiger Airways used the word "distracted" to explain why her airline would not be following AirAsia and adding long-haul services. The airline would "not compromise (the) business model" that had made it so successful, she said.[7]

The same thing that has made AirAsia successful—its budget airline business strategy—also acts as an effective barrier to entry for more established, first-tier airlines. Malaysian Airlines, for example, would likely find it difficult to compete directly with AirAsia (if it chose to) because its own business strategy is geared and configured to a different type of business—one that operates at a higher level of service as well as a higher cost. This would theoretically suggest to the management of that airline that any shift into that space (at least, one using its master brand) might be inadvisable. Conversely, the same thing would apply if AirAsia was to consider competing in the more "conventional" airline space in which Malaysian Airlines—and airlines like it—operates.

Senior Asian decision makers usually instinctively "get" the macro side of business strategy. It is common sense to put in place and pursue initiatives that permit the company to deliver on its declared reason for being. But, as mentioned earlier, the problem lies in the attention span of these same individuals: getting them to stay focused on what they are doing (and to get better at it), rather than being distracted by pursuing business opportunities that are often unrelated to their core businesses and outside their core competencies.

Business Strategy: The Micro Dimension

While most managers may do a reasonably decent job of delivering the macro dimension (as long as they focus on their core business), they often fail miserably at the micro side of business strategy. The micro side represents the specific choices related to every conceivable operational driver that is linked to creating and maintaining competitive advantage. These drivers represent developed and structured concepts that need to be understood and then applied. In other words, they go beyond the instinctive, gut-centric decision making that characterizes the command and control styles of Asian CEOs.

This is the nitty-gritty of strategic development that impacts everything: from investment and resource allocation strategy to customer segmentation strategy, to competitor strategy, to innovation and growth strategy, to organizational strategy, to brand strategy—and everything else that eventually leads to implementation (which is then followed by performance measurement strategy). All of these strategies contain multiple sub-elements that need to be understood and considered in concert with other elements within the organization. This requires relatively sophisticated human resources and an organizational culture that allows for effective implementation of all strategies.

Companies aiming to grow and deliver based on a broader vision cannot afford *not* to get their business strategy right.

It is in the area of micro strategy development that Asian companies—both large and small—would do well to seek outside professional guidance from qualified consultants. Companies aiming to grow and deliver based on a broader vision cannot afford *not* to get their business strategy right.

THE ROLE OF CORPORATE GUIDING PRINCIPLES

While the CEO must be prepared to lead, he must also put in place the circumstances that will persuade his troops to follow him. One of the most valuable tools available to Asian CEOs is one that is also routinely misused or not used at all: corporate guiding principles, also known as core ideology.

Corporate guiding principles are akin to a three-legged stool: **vision**, **mission**, and **values**. Although mostly created and crafted in phase 2 (business goals) of the Business and Brand Flowchart, these three drivers are so important that they are included in the brand blueprint. They contribute in a very large measure to the creation of corporate **culture**. Corporate culture influences employee behavior and enables the company to deliver its promises to customers. But this doesn't just happen on its own.

While some might find reassuring the widespread existence of declared guiding principles in many Asian companies, in the majority of cases they are not real and thus provide little meaning or relevance to employees and little in the way of tangible value to the organization. And it is difficult to work out which is more profoundly problematic—the fact that employees are bereft of motivational principles, or that

CEOs are oblivious to the role these principles play in influencing and encouraging behavior in the first place.

In Asia, the existence of guiding principles provides not much more than a superficial veneer that contributes nothing practical to the enterprise. In some companies, the principles are framed and hung in boardrooms and meeting rooms, only to be ignored. In others, they may be referred to occasionally, but in the overwhelming majority of cases, guiding principles play no effective role. These companies are failing to realize that a competitive advantage that is relatively easy and free to harness—the instinctive human need to do something important—is being left on the sidelines for lack of understanding and appreciation. This management lapse is both bizarre and absurd.

Part of the problem is that guiding principles are considered by most managers and their CEOs as "nice to have." Nothing could be further from the truth. Guiding principles, if properly formulated and consistently implemented, emerge as one of the key enablers of brand promise delivery to customers.

Vision

> *"The most direct way to predict the future*
> *is to create it yourself."*
>
> "Vision," Fast Company

For a company to succeed, its leader must figure out where it needs to go. Then he must tell his employees about it. As simple as that sounds, this rarely takes place in Asia and its absence creates a wasted opportunity. As mentioned earlier, many Asian CEOs are driven by an opportunistic mentality that places primacy on short-term gains. Most of the time this precludes any long-term vision, which, in turn, adversely impacts strategic planning.

Part of the problem is that vision (like mission and values) is often misunderstood. For starters, most CEOs will freely admit that they cannot differentiate between vision and mission. To them, the statements are more or less interchangeable. (This doesn't prevent them, nevertheless, from crafting separate—often meaningless—statements for each.) In other cases, the "vision statement" is a box the company feels it needs formally to tick, before forgetting or ignoring it from that point onward. Too often, that ticked box consists of statements that either barely reveal a hint of a future opportunity or ignore it entirely. Instead, most provide a laundry list of tactical goals or self-serving plaudits that

Figure 4.2 A company's vision statement: Employees' feedback

"No articulated vision. Depends on how often you talk to the CEO." (Singapore)
"No corporate vision ... only departmental targets." (Singapore)
"Don't know, but if one exists, only management knows about it." (Hong Kong)
"No vision beyond growth." (Malaysia)
"No vision." (Hong Kong)
"Not sure. I don't know." (Malaysia)
"No real vision: nobody knows or understands." (Thailand)
"More brands ... more stores." (Hong Kong)
"I believe that they have, but personally I am not aware." (Malaysia)
"Nobody has told us anything." (Thailand)
"No vision—we work day-to-day." (Singapore)
"We are curious." (Thailand)

Source: Carlyle Brand Consultants, findings from multiple brand audits (2000–2005).

undermines the purpose and intent of the statement. Although Figure 4.2 illustrates feedback from employees at all levels in just one leading Asian multinational retailer, the feedback is remarkably consistent across employees in dozens of other companies who were similarly surveyed and asked to describe their company's vision.[8]

More damaging, however, is the reality that Asian CEOs don't really consider the concept all that important, anyway. Because guiding principles amount to a foundational pillar that a strong brand is built upon, the widespread absence of understanding and application of vision by CEOs emerges as a profound and fundamental cause of weak Asian brands. Once again, CEOs not knowing what they don't know is handicapping Asian companies and preventing them from realizing their true potential.

"Vision" defined

A vision has two important components: It is (a) an aspirational end-point that reflects where the CEO would like his company to be within (b) a predetermined period of time. So, it is about deciding on a destination for the company and setting a deadline for getting there. Very helpfully, a vision also provides a frame of reference for defining and accomplishing goals. Expressed differently, a vision provides a road map for how to get things done.

"Vision" may also be defined simply as the ability to see beyond one's nose. If you are the CEO, vision is about seeing a greater truth, which most others around you are either incapable of seeing or unwilling to see, and persuading them to trust you; to follow you; to believe

Figure 4.3 Jollibee's vision statement

We are the best tasting QSR...
The most endearing brand...
that has ever been...
We will lead in product taste at all times...
We will provide FSC excellence
in every encounter...
Happiness in every moment...
By year 2020, with over 4,000 stores worldwide,
Jollibee is truly a GLOBAL BRAND (and the Filipino will be
admired worldwide).

Source: www.jollibee.com.ph

that the great goal you can see is achievable and beneficial. The alternative—the absence of vision—Franklin Roosevelt pointed out, is grim: ". . . when there is no vision the people perish. . . ." The corollary equally applies within the business context. The absence of vision handicaps the company by limiting the contributions of its employees, who otherwise—everything else being equal—are willing and generally eager to contribute effort that helps the company realize its vision. This, in turn, handicaps the capacity of the company to be competitive. But because this potential is invisible until it is actually realized, it continues to be avoided, either actively or passively, by CEOs in Asia.

It sounds deceptively straightforward and completely logical to say that a company—like people—needs to know where it is going (particularly if it wishes to get there). As obvious as this is, Asian CEOs continue to demonstrate an unwillingness to see and plan for what lies over the horizon. There exists an infectious mentality that prompts most CEOs to focus on making money here and now and as quickly as possible.

While this mentality is prompted and exemplified by the CEO and management, it trickles down to all levels of the organization and becomes embedded in the corporate culture. Its side effects can be devastating. One particularly debilitating consequence is the absence of internal innovative and creative thinking—an imperative driver for sustainable competitive advantage, growth, and development.

Proactive, visionary thinking delivers a goal. Samsung's declared goal—to own the digital technology market—is a good example (see the accompanying box). A company's broader—strategic—goal, when declared to all internal stakeholders, allows them to participate. Moreover, it allows them to consider their own roles and responsibilities—regardless of level or seniority—and provides them with the opportunity to shape their approach to their jobs in a manner that is consistent with the realization of that goal. In other words, a declared goal allows everyone to contribute in a direct and relevant way. Apart from creating a collective unified energy that helps drive the company forward (in the right direction), it helps employees feel good about themselves.

Nevertheless, many CEOs continue to give lip service to, or totally ignore, vision. Of the dozens of chief executives of SMEs and larger companies whom I have personally interviewed in markets such as Singapore, Malaysia, India, and Thailand, the vast majority have expressed a preference for exploiting immediate and near-term opportunities, explaining that "worrying" about the distant future would

---

A Vision-Driven Company: How Samsung Became the Strong Brand it is Today

It is difficult for many people to believe that Samsung was not always the giant powerhouse that it is today. The popular impression is that, like Sony, Samsung has been around forever and has always been successful. In reality, the company's success can be measured in less than two decades during which it went from literally a near zero start to the position it holds today—a company whose brand is worth US$17,518 million according to the *Business Week/Interbrand* 2009 annual "Top 100 Best Global Brands" survey, where it came in at number 19—well ahead of Sony at number 29. Most would attribute this meteoric rise primarily to the vision it pursued.[9]

Between the early 1980s and the early 1990s, Samsung was just a conglomerate OEM—like so many other Asian companies. It struggled with perceptions that ranged from low quality to invisibility. In 1993, its chairman and CEO, Kun-Hee Lee, declared Samsung's ambition to be a global brand synonymous with world-class products, employees, and processes. He said: ". . . if we keep selling low-end products it will damage our corporate image. . . ." Moreover, what he was also signaling was recognition that low-end products meant low and declining margins with a doubtful future. He saw the future and he was determined to exploit it, while others either ignored it or were blind to it.

Doing it the right way: Simply seeing the future is clearly not enough. The CEO needs to have the will to act and the clarity of mind to do so in a rational and courageous manner. Kun-Hee Lee's

(Continued)

declaration was followed by swift internal restructuring to flatten the organization to achieve nimbleness, a management reorientation that became globally focused, and a real commitment to true innovation. Staff was given autonomy and empowerment, leading to shorter lead times in decision making.

Strategically: Samsung's commitment to build its brand began with a visible investment in R&D in the early 1990s that continued throughout the decade, culminating in a total expenditure of US$2.4 billion in 2002. Its policy then was to invest 6–8 percent of its annual revenue in product and technology development. In 2010, Samsung announced that it would increase R&D expenditure to a record US$6.5 billion "despite questions about the global economic outlook."[10] In 2000, Samsung took an extraordinary decision that stunned many industry observers: It withdrew all its branded products from Wal-Mart stores. The reasoning was straightforward: Samsung was aiming to become the provider of premium-quality digital products that would consistently provide innovative benefits to customers. Never mind that Wal-Mart contributed a major portion of its revenues at the time. The point was: Wal-Mart (at that time) was wrong for the brand.

consume too much attention and resources. And yet the evidence of what a vision-driven company is potentially capable of achieving is incontrovertible and, in many cases, inspirational.

The power of dreams: Human rights, Arnold Schwarzenegger, and Microsoft

History is filled with examples of visionary leaders who chose to walk down roads less traveled in a deliberate and determined effort to realize what they felt was essential to achieve or accomplish, despite the associated difficulties and challenges. The Civil Rights Movement in the United States owes its entire existence to the vision of one man, Martin Luther King, Jr. He "saw" what other African Americans at the time considered an impossible dream and what many white Americans rejected as an impossible reality. Anwar Sadat and Menachem Begin were willing to put aside centuries-old enmities that had come to define their countries, their peoples, and their region, and reach out to one another in the hope of achieving peace.

> (Lee Kuan Yew) had a vision of Singapore *then* that is only visible to most people *today*. Without this vision, and the will to realize it, Singapore would not be the "First-World Asian Tiger" that it is today. Singapore is what it is almost entirely because of the vision and tenacity of one man.

The single most dramatic illustration of visionary will creating an extraordinary end-result that Asian CEOs—and particularly those from Singapore—would do well to recognize and appreciate is that of Lee Kuan Yew. Putting aside the debate about whether or not Singapore is a true democracy, the indisputable fact is that, in 1965, Singapore was an underdeveloped colonial backwater. Tiny in size compared to its neighbors, it possessed no natural resources and no regional benefactor willing to subsidize its road to development. Few people within and outside Singapore gave it much chance of becoming anything more than a failed state. However, Lee Kuan Yew had a vision for Singapore. He "saw" a different future: one so fantastically different from the reality the island state was then experiencing that, had he fully articulated it, he would have likely met with incredulity, if not derision. He had a vision of Singapore *then* that is only visible to most people *today*. Without this vision, and the will to realize it, Singapore would not be the "First-World Asian Tiger" that it is today. Singapore is what it is almost entirely because of the vision and tenacity of one man.

Examples of how impactful a vision can be are not found only in historical or political spheres. The visions of ordinary people can have extraordinary results. In 1962, at the age of 15, Arnold Schwarzenegger dreamed of winning the "Mr. Universe" title. Despite his modest origins and limited opportunities, Schwarzenegger dreamed big. He saw a future that others in his world were incapable of seeing and, intent on achieving his goal, he lived his life in a disciplined manner. He was not tempted by opportunities that occasionally came his way. He focused on what he considered the "prize," putting all his mental and physical energies into winning it. At age 22, he won the "Mr. Universe" title. He then went on to win the "Mr. Olympia" contest a total of 22 times.

Recognizing the power and utility of having a single-minded vision and allowing himself to be directed by it, he made it a life-long habit. In the 1970s he was determined to reinvent himself as a Hollywood "star." Once again, he focused on that vision and directed all his energies into realizing it. Over the next two decades, he would become one of the world's biggest action movie stars. Not surprisingly, Schwarzenegger set his sights even higher once that goal had been realized. In an interview with *Fortune* magazine in August 2004, in which he discussed his ambitions for political office, he explained his philosophy on life and the approach he favored: "I can see my goals very clearly." Power, he explained, required a clear vision and a steadfast commitment to delivering that vision. "Arnold could see himself running (for office) and winning. He could see himself as governor."[11]

It doesn't take too much imagination to see what Schwarzenegger's next vision might be. He "sees" himself as the first non-American by birth to run for the presidency. That the US Constitution currently prohibits this is only a minor hurdle to a man who believes that greatness can be realized first through the willful act of "seeing" it and then pursuing it.

The Schwarzenegger example illustrates one of the key differences that separate vision from mission: vision is a goal that is defined by, among other things, delivery within a specific time frame. All vision-related goals and objectives need to be rooted within the framework of a deadline. Once the deadline is reached (and the vision is achieved), the company moves on to its next goal-driven vision—very much in the same way that Arnold Schwarzenegger moved systematically from one visionary goal to the next. Mission, as will be explained later in this chapter, is a goal that, among other things, is not chained to any time frame.

To illustrate the point, consider the two Microsoft vision statements that have emerged over the past 32 years, and the impact that the realization of those statements has had on the company, its community of global customers, and ordinary people around the world. In around 1978, Paul Allen and Bill Gates articulated an audacious vision they had for their company: "A computer on every desk and in every home. . . . It is a dream we believe is within our reach, and within our capabilities."[12] On the surface, some might interpret this cynically as a grand goal to make a lot of money. While this is indeed exactly what happened, making money as an end in and of itself was not what Allen and Gates likely had in mind. Their vision was about transforming both the work and home environments on a grand scale by introducing computers into them at a time (the 1970s) when the technology was the preserve of universities and very large corporations. Exactly how that transformation was to manifest itself was something that they were probably uncertain of—but likely excited by—at the time. That it was going to be big was clear. Exactly how big was revealed within one generation, when a global paradigm shift saw the world make the transition from typewriters to laptops.

The realization of that vision has impacted the lives and destinies of millions of people around the world, and continues to do so. As with all strong vision statements, this one also had a shelf-line due date. A new vision for the company was crafted and publicly released in March 2008: "Create experiences that combine the magic of software with the power of Internet services across a world of devices."[13] This vision statement reflects the company's intention to leverage its significant resources to harness the growing global shift toward the empowerment of individuals through the myriad of (mostly personal) devices that will continue to make their way on to markets for the foreseeable future. While perhaps not as pithy, simple, and dramatically compelling as its first vision statement, this latest expression identifies a clear future opportunity and declares the company's intention to exploit it in a focused and single-minded way.

Microsoft's two vision statements have provided a context for its business strategy. Both have shaped its corporate brand positioning as well as its brand strategy. All four elements have been the engine that has delivered the extraordinary success the company has enjoyed over the past four decades. The two vision statements have provided direction for management, as well as its employees worldwide. They have encouraged consensus and a like-minded attitude and effort toward delivering a common goal.

> *"Even more to the point, Facebook founder Mark Zuckerberg possessed a clear vision of empire: one in which the developers who built applications on top of the platform that his company owned and controlled would always be subservient to the platform itself."*
>
> Michael Wolff, co-author, "The Web Is Dead. Long Live the Internet," *Wired*, August 17, 2010

Too many Asian companies—both large and small—are driven by relatively underpowered engines. Instead of the entire workforce pooling their efforts and ideas to develop a clear and agreed goal that galvanizes everyone to move forward solidly and confidently, the effort mostly comes from the C-level group: the CEO, the chief financial officer (CFO), and the chief operating operator (COO). These "three musketeers" take it upon themselves to shoulder the burden of driving a company forward on their own and relying on all other staff only for operational support. Why? "Because," as one CEO explained to me, "we have too many secrets and not everyone can be trusted or is competent." This extraordinary statement says volumes about the management philosophy of Asian companies. That it is expressed as a strategy for performance, rather than being recognized as a symptom of poor management, highlights the root cause of the problem. This absence of big-picture thinking leads many business leaders to adopt management styles that stifle growth.

> From the point of view of competitive advantage, it is what lies in the future that has the potential to deliver sustainability. Focusing only on the present condemns the company to playing a tactical, rather than a strategic, game.

Given the dynamic, fast-paced nature of modern business, it is all too easy for company leaders to focus on the company's immediate day-to-day needs and opportunities and to defer or ignore altogether the possibilities that lie beyond the visible horizon. But that is a mistake. From the point of view of competitive advantage, it is what lies in the future that has the potential to deliver sustainability. Focusing only on the present condemns the company to playing a tactical, rather than a strategic, game. This results in a reactive, rather than a proactive, operating mentality that reduces options. When options are reduced, differentiation suffers; products, pricing, and other strategies look like everyone else's; and the company becomes chronically vulnerable.

The role, purpose, and value that an articulated vision delivers to a company doesn't amount to rocket science. But as simple as the concept is to understand, it is adopted by relatively few Asian CEOs. Though that is clearly not a good thing, the flip-side of this is very good news for a new generation of CEOs who may prove to be the exception to the rule. Putting aside the very real competitive challenges posed by top-tier Western brands that have articulated long-term destinations, vision-poor Asian companies provide a "blue ocean"[14] environment (less competitive than the shark-infested "red ocean") for these individuals if they are willing to manage their businesses with an eye to broader horizons. This is an important opportunity, but one whose window won't remain open indefinitely. (In redefining themselves, some brands can also redefine their categories or find themselves in completely new categories where competition is effectively nonexistent. A good example is Cirque de Soleil. In defining its unique offering, it stepped out of the "circus" category into a new category it created, where for a while it enjoyed no competitive threat. This is "blue ocean." "Red ocean" refers to a conventional business environment cluttered with competition ("red ocean" = sharks).

The "exceptions" in Asia

Vision provides a destination that is capable not only of changing the rules of the game, but also, in many cases, changing the game itself. When a company succeeds in redefining its category, or creating a completely new category, it creates an almost insurmountable competitive advantage. Two good examples of visionary Asian leaders who have seen beyond the merely visible realities that characterized their businesses and capitalized on the "blue ocean" opportunities to dominate their respective categories are Richard Eu, CEO of Eu Yan Sang, the Asia-wide manufacturer and retailer of traditional Chinese medicines (TCM), and Ho Kwon Ping, CEO and founder of Banyan Tree Hotels & Resorts.

Richard Eu, recognized by many as a long-time maverick who is open to experimentation and innovation, faced a difficult market landscape in the mid- to late-1990s when TCM lost relevance with younger consumers, who opted for Western medications and treatments that better suited their modern and hectic lives. As the leading regional TCM brand, Eu Yan Sang was also taking the brunt of the downturn. Eu's solution was to reposition the brand to make it more relevant to all consumers, but especially the younger target audiences. His goal was to make the brand more contemporary, not only by making it more approachable (via—among other things—new products and packaging, and delivery systems that redefined the centuries-old category), but also by implementing an exciting vision that tapped into the expectations of all Asians experiencing the rush of the new century. He aimed to make Eu Yan Sang a leading vehicle that would bridge the gap between Eastern and Western medicine and provide services that harnessed the best of both. The vision statement that was articulated, shared internally, and actively implemented was: "We want to be a global consumer healthcare company with a focus in Traditional Chinese Medicine and Integrative Healthcare."[15] The company's vision is directly responsible for the introduction of a series of innovative new services and products that have not only revitalized the company and reinstated its number one position region-wide, but also successfully redefined the category itself, injecting new life and vitality into what many observers had years earlier described as a sunset industry.

Ho Kwon Ping is an entrepreneur who has demonstrated not only vision but also the courage to question conventional wisdom. He is a leader who demonstrates the discipline of pursuing a goal to its complete delivery once it has been set. He rejects the lure of short-cuts and recognizes that the "invisible" steps in building a brand are the most crucial ones. He understands the power of a strong brand and, through his own efforts and those of the people around him, he has built a formidable and uniquely Asian brand.

The hospitality industry is a highly competitive category where brands are constantly attempting to find ways and means to please guests and persuade them to return. As a service industry, customer experience clearly emerges as a critical driver of customer choice. At the high end of the category, Asian hotel brands have failed to break out of the established paradigm that typically defines "five-star" hotels. To most well-heeled customers, they are all elegant, they are all plush—and they all look the same. More critically, the experience seems to be the same. When one brand is not available, many customers simply look at other like brands interchangeably. This conclusion is from the brand audit report of a major hotel brand's repositioning project: "Most hotel brands are poorly differentiated from their competitors. While each may have clearly articulated positionings, these positionings are essentially similar to one another."[16] This common-knowledge insight has not prevented many Asian-based hotel groups from pursuing more or less identical strategies.

The notable exception has been Banyan Tree. Ho Kwon Ping's vision was to create a new brand experience that would "inspire all stakeholders."[17] He wanted to break away from the tried and safe formula most other Asian hotel brands had gravitated toward and provide guests with a unique experience that combined intimacy and romance and an Asian brand personality that also reflected each location's indigenous Asian surroundings. His vision also allowed him to go a step further, demonstrating a keen sense and awareness of important environmental concerns that was well ahead of his time. Banyan Tree pioneered the policy of building eco-friendly resorts in a manner that is socially responsible and sustainable.

Summary

In the business context, a vision has an aspirational end-point reflecting where the CEO would like his company to be within a predetermined period of time. A vision asks the questions: "Where are we going strategically? How will we know when we get there?" A vision sets the direction and the framework for defining and accomplishing goals.

Figuring out what lies ahead and where the key leverageable opportunities might come from are the first challenges. Next, is figuring out how to get there and having the discipline and will to stay the course.

Envisioning the future is not only essential for the modern-day corporation faced with an environment that is changing faster than ever; it also offers a unique competitive advantage opportunity where present market circumstances (relative to the state of Asian company competition) can best be described as relatively "blue ocean." And it is this last point that provides a dramatic and exciting insight for Asian CEOs aiming to join the club of "exceptions": When corporations such as Microsoft and Samsung are cited as vision-led or vision-driven companies, many managers might comment cynically that those companies are rare exceptions and bear little resemblance to the real world or to their own companies and circumstances. The brutal truth is that both these companies, like many others, had humble and modest beginnings. They have become great because their leaders willfully chose to look beyond their own noses. This choice is available to all Asian business leaders who are determined to build not merely good, but great, Asian brands.

Mission

> *"The most effective way to forge a winning team*
> *is to call on the players' needs to connect with*
> *something larger than themselves."*
>
> Phil Jackson, former coach to the Chicago Bulls[18]

The second essential component of a company's guiding principles is its mission, or purpose. Perhaps even more so than a vision statement, a mission statement provides the means to harness human energy within the organization that cannot be harnessed through monetary rewards or incentives, or fear or threats. Like "vision," "mission" is a concept that is often misunderstood in Asia; as a consequence, it fails to deliver the extraordinary benefits it has the capacity to provide. Like vision statements, mission statements offer a major strategic driver for Asian companies determined to build great brands.

"Mission" defined

In its simplest form, the mission of an organization amounts to its purpose, or the reason for its existence. As suggested in the previous section, unlike a vision statement, which is characterized by a deadline, a mission statement is timeless. In other words, a mission, in a sense, is never quite realized—very much like "being happy" is a timeless pursuit, and not a goal that, when reached, is replaced by another. A mission is more like a guiding star: forever pursued, but never reached.

A strong mission statement is also *enduring*—it passes the test of time and is as relevant after 50 years as on the day it was written. A strong mission statement is also *inspiring*. It motivates most, if not all, the organization's employees. Lastly, a strong mission statement is *encompassing*—it is embraced by most members of the organization. In a word, a mission has the means to deliver *capability* to the company.

> The mission statement humanizes the company by declaring to the world that it recognizes that "making money" is just one dimension of its purpose (albeit an important one).

The mission statement has very little to do with the company making money or growing market share. And it should not be used for that purpose. Other "tools" exist whose role is to deliver this and other goals. A company mission delivers an altogether different benefit that most Asian CEOs are unaware of: It delivers the business equivalent of the "meaning of life." The mission statement humanizes the company by declaring to the world that it recognizes that "making money" is just one dimension of its purpose (albeit an important one). It declares its recognition that, as an entity, it interacts with people internally (employees) and externally (customers and others), and—importantly—that it creates displacement by manufacturing a product or delivering a service. In other words, the very act of existing triggers and touches many things, for all of which it bears some responsibility. The great benefit that a mission statement provides a company lies in that very realization and admission, which is appreciated first by the people who power it—employees—and then by those who sustain it—customers.

Most Asian managers will be surprised to discover that a motivating and effective mission is concerned with answering the question: **"How will the world become a better place as a consequence of what my**

company or brand does?" This doesn't mean that mission statements are warm and fuzzy goals that bear no relationship to reality or practical needs. Helping the world be a better place is something that every company is able to deliver to some degree. For example, a toy manufacturer can help "make the world a better place" by making safer or more environmentally friendly toys. A sports apparel and equipment company can help "make the world a better place" by developing innovative fabrics and materials that might have other applications in other fields; or by supporting certain values, traditionally associated with sports, that might enhance people's self-esteem or perhaps empower them. It is the "why" and "how" that matters.

> *"Great companies are measured by how they help people, and the most important thing is our people and the people we represent."*
>
> Peter Tortorici, CEO of Group M, WPP[19]

Another likely surprise to most Asian managers is that, while a mission statement should be formulated with the right message (purpose) and for the right reasons (relevance), its consistent application (sincerity) amounts to a formula for brand or corporate greatness.

Why so powerful?

Correctly crafted mission statements can be very powerful. Today, they are increasingly offering companies the ability to create meaningful differentiation and customer loyalty. This is not something most Asian senior executives would normally associate with "mission"—something they consider to be a "soft" value. In reality, mission statements can amount to powerful business drivers and therefore need to be carefully explored and leveraged. The reason for this is as simple as it is powerful. As will be discussed in Chapter 5, strong brands can be divided into two basic components: functional benefits and emotional benefits. Most tier-one quality brands across most categories have one thing in common: strong functional benefits. Competition and relentless innovation over the years have ensured this. In an ironic and perverse sort of way, the journey of leading brands has turned some 360 degrees, where the functional product excellence they have in common now results in near parity. In the minds of consumers, most leading brands in many categories deliver to functional expectations more or less equally. As a result, consumers are increasingly looking to a brand's emotional benefits when making choices and bestowing loyalty. This is not because functional benefits have suddenly become less important. On the contrary, they are more important than ever. So much so that consumers have come to expect them as a basic attribute. As will be discussed more fully in Chapter 5, emotional drivers are the real key to strong brands. Emotional benefits can come from different sources or be reflected in different ways. One of these is through the mission statement. What a company believes its purpose to be has the potential to strongly resonate with and influence customers.

What is more interesting and important—and surprising to many Asian managers—is the connection between emotionally touched customers and the internal attitude and state of mind of company employees. Company mission statements are actually more employee-oriented than customer-directed. They are created for an internal purpose that also results in an external manifestation. While both of these are important, the company's internal role takes precedence.

Why is that? First, employees are also human beings and are subject to the same innate need to accomplish something of value or importance in their lives. This is part of the human condition; it is not something that people leave at home when they go to work—unless their company forces them to do so. Unfortunately, many Asian companies are unwittingly doing just that. The irony is that, by suppressing the natural need employees have to achieve something beyond the mechanical requirements of the jobs they do or the roles they have, these companies are depriving themselves of a vast amount of collective energy that could be directed at moving the company forward via two important manifestations: (a) reliable and ongoing innovation, and (b) positive attitude toward work. The latter is particularly crucial. In a manufacturing environment, this translates to attitudes that impact quality of product, safety of product, cost efficiencies, and other critical operational drivers. In service and retail environments, where customer satisfaction is of paramount importance, this amounts to nothing less than a silver bullet. The single most effective way to ensure a positive customer experience is to have employees who are willing to deliver it.

And yet, very much like their vision statements, the mission statements of most Asian companies are haphazardly crafted—and almost always by the wrong people. As a result, they end up delivering their companies next to zero benefit. Figure 4.4 sets out the responses of randomly selected employees from a cross-section of Asian companies who were asked about their company's mission. Most of the responses reveal that employees are either disinterested in or disillusioned with

Figure 4.4 A company's mission statement: Employees' feedback

"No mission." (Hong Kong/Malaysia)
"To make money for shareholders." (Hong Kong)
"Shared only at the top level." (Malaysia)
"(Company name) does not do anything special for the society." (Singapore)
"There is no emotional attachment or commitment felt by people externally." (Singapore)
"To be top 5 in the world or second to (competitor brand name), this is our goal." (Singapore)
"To hit half a billion (dollars) sales in three years' time." (Singapore)
"To achieve significant market expansion." (Singapore)
"We are all not very clear.... We know the year-end goal, but don't know the big picture, long-term plans, etc." (China)
"The mission is terribly boring." (India)
"The mission does not make us proud to come and work for (company name)." (India)
"Lack of clarity." (India)
"No obvious mission." (Singapore)
"Mission is only about money." (Singapore)
"To become the market leader." (Singapore)

Source: Carlyle Brand Consultants, findings from multiple brand audits (2000–2005).

their company's mission statement. To most, they remain vague concepts (because they are not properly explained by management) and largely irrelevant to their day-to-day jobs.

Companies live or die on the basis of a single equation: promise and delivery. How relevant the former is, and how consistently the latter takes place, determines whether consumers engage and stay engaged. As elementary as this equation should be, in Asia far too many companies over-promise and under-deliver. This is remarkable, given the level of competition and the ever-increasing expectations of customers who instantly penalize offenders. The most critical component that makes the equation work consistently is the human resources of the company and their willingness to "play." Companies such as Apple, Harley-Davidson, Google, and others have built strong corporate cultures that benefit from an employee population that is positively disposed to consistently delivering what they consider to be a collective goal—one they have a stake in, because it resonates deeply and emotionally with them. The purpose (mission) that supports a company's right to exist provides that stake.

"It's not just money that motivates Singaporeans. . . . Employee management (is) a high ranking priority. (They) need to be more engaged on a more emotional level . . . and want to be inspired by leaders who walk the talk."

PricewaterhouseCoopers[20]

Most private individuals are able to recognize the value of purpose within the context of their own lives and those of others. They see the importance of establishing a personal frame of reference that validates the road they have chosen to take in life. Most people see how purpose validates their lives and provides meaning, direction—and, ultimately, value. Yet, in the business context, Asian CEOs either ignore or abandon the concept altogether, or struggle to translate it in a manner that is relevant to and effective for their companies. Their brains switch off— or at the very least, logic and common sense take temporary leave—and they craft sentences that fail to capture the basic intent of the construct and instead contain empty, feel-good words or list impersonal, clinical business objectives that are unlikely to move the very people they should be inspiring: employees (first) and customers (second). The Korean cosmetics *wunder*-brand Missha—credited with single-handedly creating a budget segment from scratch and generating revenues of over US$120 million in its first year of business—experienced an abrupt and painful fall from grace in only its second year of operations when more savvy competitors entered the space with differentiated brands and well-defined mission statements. Commented one analyst: "There (was) no brand mission as a beauty provider to women. The product could be anything, because the business was started to make money rather than deliver beautiful skin or make-up to consumers."[21]

I have conducted hundreds of interviews with executives at all levels from companies doing business in markets across Asia, from which two important themes have emerged: (1) management attitudes to employees; and (2) what CEOs believe to be the true purpose of their businesses.

(1) Management attitudes to employees: Senior executives and CEOs more or less view the employee as—in the words of Pink Floyd—"another brick in the wall." While most companies, particularly large ones, don't mistreat or abuse their employees, they also don't as a rule engage with them—particularly with those at the middle and lower levels—in a collaborative and respectful manner. Instead, there is simply an expectation that employees will do their jobs "because they are paid to do so." As mentioned earlier, contributing to this attitude is the belief that most employees either cannot be trusted with sensitive information or empowerment, or are not sufficiently competent to handle it. As might be expected, these circumstances can lead to a vicious circle in terms of employee satisfaction, innovative contributions, teamwork, quality control, and, ultimately, delivery of the customer promise. While it is this last element that translates into direct revenue, all the elements identified above are connected. The customer promise will always be undermined if the chain is populated by weak links.

(2) **What CEOs believe to be the true purpose of their businesses:** The vast majority of the Asian CEOs I have interviewed or interacted with at conferences, seminars, and workshops have provided exactly the same answer to the question: "What do you think is the purpose of your business?" They answered: "To make money." As mentioned in Chapter 2, there is nothing inherently wrong with a company wanting to make money. Companies are in the business of being profitable. However, the issue of what should be the company's main purpose is more subtle in today's increasingly complex business world.

The pace of technological change and the impact of globalization have literally transformed the planet in the past two decades. Some great strides have been made: millions of people have been delivered from abject poverty; and people around the world are connected to one another in ways that would have been unimaginable just 20 years ago. Within the business context, we now face issues and challenges such as global warming and environmental sustainability, as well as increased employee rights and expectations—matters that were of little or no concern before recent times. Addressing these issues successfully is, admittedly, a challenge. Ignoring them, however—as many CEOs in Asia are doing—is a sure-fire recipe for disaster.

> ... some hard-nosed businessmen may scoff at the notion that it is the business of business to be concerned with "doing good," or to be directly involved with social issues. But they would be wrong.

The visionary—and pragmatic—modern-day company leader recognizes the changing landscape of the world and reconciles this with the basic objective all businesses have, which is to make money. This has resulted in what some might describe as a reversal of strategic priorities: from making money and occasionally doing some good (charities, foundations, endowments, etc.), to making money as a direct result of doing good. At first glance, some hard-nosed businessmen may scoff at the notion that it is the business of business to be concerned with "doing good," or to be directly involved with social issues. But they would be wrong.

The modern corporate mission statement provides a road map for company excellence and—depending on the caliber of leadership—greatness. The absence of an effective corporate mission sentences a company to mediocrity. Consider Figure 4.5, which sets out some very powerful corporate mission statements. None of these statements makes any reference to "making money," or to business-centric objectives or goals. None of them makes patronizing promises that people simply expect anyway. Yet, all these statements have contributed directly to the success of these companies.

Let's consider each one in turn.

Disney: "To make people happy." When most people think of Disney, they instantly think of fantasy and wholesome fun; a place of imagination and wondrous characters and stories that engage children and adults alike. From its animated characters created over 80 years ago to its theme parks and hotels, from its library of movies and cartoon series to its licensed products, the one overarching idea around which everything revolves, that encourages employees to deliver to the expectations of Disney's customers and guests, is fun. It is fitting that the very purpose of the organization—the mission that it is dedicated

Figure 4.5 Examples of powerful mission statements

Disney	To make people happy.
3M	To solve unsolved problems innovatively.
Mary Kay	To give unlimited opportunity to women.
HP	To make technical contributions for the advancement of welfare of humanity.
Wal-Mart	To give ordinary folks the chance to buy the same things as rich people (OR) Saving people money so they can live better.
McKinsey & Company	To help leading corporations and governments be more successful.

to—is something lofty, elevated, and detached from business. "To make people happy" encapsulates a broader contribution to humanity that is positive and nurturing. Beyond the customers, this objective resonates with employees and invites them to be part of something bigger than themselves. Delivering on the Disney purpose isn't hard work for them; it is fun. Indeed, the simplicity of the statement acts as a call to action for them. It provides a directive that is both compelling and clear. It also doesn't have a shelf-life. Making people happy has no end-point. It is timeless. It is the stuff that makes Disney *great*. And yes, as a *result* of that, Disney makes money.

3M: "To solve problems innovatively." Not all mission statements are warm and fuzzy, and nor do they need to be. The main criterion is that they address an issue that is of common interest or concern to a specific group of people, and that, in addressing it, the statement delivers solutions that will benefit and improve those people's lives. "To solve problems innovatively" promises the use of creativity and imagination to help solve problems and meet the needs of ordinary people. Both the goal and the means of realizing it reflect message elements that resonate with employees. By doing things innovatively, 3M employees choose to challenge themselves to find solutions to problems and create new products that are useful in a creative—even disruptive—way. Much of the motivation to deliver on this promise is anchored in a collective belief that the effort will contribute to the public good. The pursuit of this creates a workforce that is committed to a timeless goal. The results are the household brand names we have come to rely on for everyday use, such as Nexcare™, Post-it®, Scotch®, Scotch-Brite®, and Scotchgard™. A further result is that the company has found greatness—and, yes, it makes a lot of money.

Mary Kay: "To give unlimited opportunity to women." Nothing galvanizes people to feel good about themselves, and to work together to deliver a common goal, like the feeling of being empowered—particularly if they are part of a minority group, such as women. Mary Kay's mission plays to this. The promise, "To give unlimited opportunity to women," not only resonates with the company's existing workforce (most of whom are women), but also acts as a powerful and seductive clarion call to others to join. Its not difficult to imagine how well the company's customer promise is delivered by such a committed, proud, and cohesive group of people. Partly as a result of its mission, Mary Kay has grown to be a global enterprise inspiring employees all over the world, and this has translated into a powerful operational expression. Again, this mission does not lend itself to a time frame or deadline. It is also timeless. Does Mary Kay make money?

HP: "To make technical contributions for the advancement of welfare of humanity." HP's mission is interesting in that the company aims to harness its existing resources, collective experience, and expertise to develop technically centric solutions, not to (directly) enhance its bottom line but to benefit "humanity." To what extent HP has been successful remains an open question given the stormy years the company has experienced over the past decade. This highlights the importance of bringing alive the mission internally, in a credible and sustainable way, so that employees will then choose to carry the company forward. Technically, "To make technical contributions for the advancement of welfare of humanity" qualifies as a mission statement. But that is not enough if it rings hollow to its most important constituency—HP's employees.

Wal-Mart: "To give ordinary folks the chance to buy the same things as rich people." Love it or hate it, most people give Wal-Mart its due. As an organization it has, from its inception, been a strong propagator and champion of its corporate culture, which is the legacy of its founder, Sam Walton. Walton believed that a strong and united team dedicated to a common purpose was the key to a successful business. Over the years, Wal-Mart has become famous for everything from its internal training programs to its company cheer. Impacting over two million employees worldwide, Wal-Mart's culture today is deeply ingrained and is uniform across its 7,800 stores spanning more than a dozen countries.[22] The most important pillar supporting the company culture is its mission. Dozens of websites continue to quote the popularly known "To give ordinary folks the chance to buy the same things as rich people," but those exact words are difficult to find on Wal-Mart's own website, where the official mission is stated as: "Saving people money so they can live better." While the two statements are not exactly the same, most would argue that they aim to deliver a similar outcome. The bottom line is that by coupling its business strategy to its focus on delivering the lowest possible prices to customers, and by harnessing its incomparable resources, Wal-Mart has successfully changed the social paradigm of millions of people—first in the United States and then, increasingly, in other countries as its geographical footprint expands. Through the delivery of its mission, Wal-Mart has transformed the lives of its employees, who have been motivated and inspired to be part of this social experiment, as well as the lives of its millions of customers, who have enthusiastically welcomed the opportunity to improve their lives by flocking to its stores. Is this a mission statement that has a shelf life? No, not likely. Has the company fared better by focusing on its mission, rather than on making money? The answer is self-evident.

McKinsey & Company: "To help leading corporations and governments be more successful." The McKinsey & Company mission statement is probably one of the best illustrations of what a compelling purpose is capable of creating. The world didn't need another management consulting firm when McKinsey first set up shop in 1926. But from the very beginning it set the bar for its purpose and goals very high. The pursuit of money for its own sake was of relatively little interest to the company's founders. They were more interested in achieving excellence and greatness, and they set out to create a company that would be known for the superlative quality of its advice, which would be sought not only by companies, but by governments as well. Its mission statement, "To help leading corporations and governments be more successful," helped create not just a very successful company, but probably the benchmark against which most, if not all, management consulting companies compare themselves. McKinsey started by recruiting only the best of the best, but it quickly found that it was being overwhelmed by the best graduates from the best universities, who were inspired by the opportunity—in the words of one McKinsey executive—"to change the world." Does McKinsey make money?

Summary

The mission statement—particularly in the modern-day world, where our concerns and fears exist side-by-side with our ever-higher quality-of-life expectations—has become a key strategic driver for companies looking for sustainable growth. Employee training and incentives play an essential role. True engagement, however, comes from the fulfillment of a basic human need—to do something important; something fulfilling. At a time when Asia is aggressively ascending, it will take genuinely visionary leadership to recognize the importance of engaged employees in the midst of dynamic, even breathtaking but distracting, growth. Secondly, the widespread but narrow, and frankly modest, expectation that business should be geared to "making money" for its own sake is anachronistic and detrimental to that very goal. This makes the single-minded pursuit of money poetically ironic. Broader, more encompassing, and people-directed company purposes are entirely more likely to create more "heroic" companies . . . that end up making more money.

Core Values

*"In the end, it is our ideas and values
that have built this country."*

President Barack Obama, State of the Union
Address, January 28, 2010

While vision provides direction and a destination for the organization, and mission provides its purpose, values spell out the principles that guide its "behavior." Further, of the three guiding principles, "values" has more mainstream currency—both in and outside of Asia—making the concept more accessible and meaningful to people. This still has not prevented the concept from being underutilized and often altogether disregarded—both in and outside of Asia. In the West, however, this is already changing, for a variety of reasons, and it is in the supreme interest of Asian CEOs to hasten their own understanding, adoption, and application of genuine core values.

Corporate values are extremely important. In fact, in a fast-changing world where technology, growth, and development are creating as many negative side-effects as benefits, consumers are increasingly demanding accountability and social responsibility. Real, genuine, and sincere values are contributing to the emotional dimensions of brands. In some cases (for example, The Body Shop—see Figure 4.6), they have emerged as the leading edge of brand differentiation. Core values form an essential component of the overall process that results in the perception and image the customer has of the company or the product brand. In a climate where dynamic social changes are rapidly taking place, the relationship between core values and corporate/brand image is becoming more and more direct.

Corporate core values versus product brand values

Although "core values" are often better understood within the context of corporate brands (such as Virgin), it is important to understand that product brands (such as Coke, Always, or Crest) also need to own and convey their own values. In the case of Virgin, the issue is relatively straightforward and easy to understand. Virgin's brand architecture strategy (see Chapter 5) is largely "master branded." This means that most of the products and businesses it owns and operates share the Virgin name. As a result, the core values of the Virgin corporate brand are automatically transferred to all its products and businesses. Procter &

Figure 4.6 The declared values of The Body Shop compel certain communities of customers to shop there

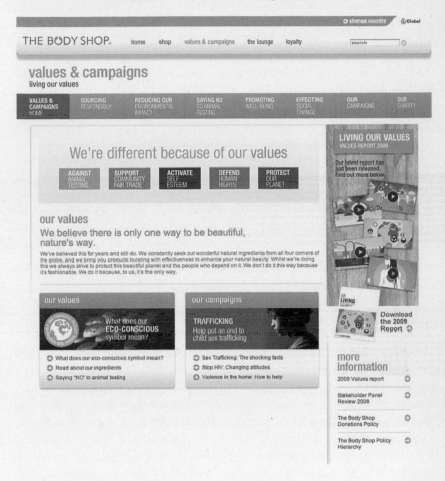

Source: www.thebodyshop.com

Gamble (P&G), on the other hand, chooses an "invisible" brand architecture strategy—also known as "house of brands." While P&G as a company defines itself by a set of company core values (among other things), its hundreds of individual product brands also reflect core values of their own.

"Core values" defined

> *". . . you cannot talk yourself out of things*
> *you've behaved yourself into."*
>
> Paul Polman, CEO, Unilever

The value of values lies in how they encourage—even inspire—people, both consumers and employees, to behave. Within the company, core values, along with *mission*, help shape organizational behavior—"behavior" being the operative term. Increasingly, companies in the West are recognizing that values provide the connection between the promise the company or the product brand makes, and execution—that is, how consistently that promise is actually delivered. Employees are the key drivers in this equation, and values—depending on how genuine and sincere they are, and what they are designed to achieve—provide the motivation. As in the case of mission, employees—like ordinary individuals—are more effective when they are provided with an opportunity to be better people; when they get the chance to contribute in some way to doing good or making the world a better place, in a direct or indirect way. Core values provide a catalyst for this.

While some companies are discovering the potency of this catalyst for the first time, others such as Procter & Gamble are rediscovering their own long-established corporate characters in the belief that the effort will eventually lead to growth, without being growth-centric *per se*. As CEO Bob McDonald put it, P&G is following a "purpose-inspired growth strategy of touching and improving more consumers' lives in more parts of the world . . . more completely."[23] In other words, P&G is looking at the needs people have—not just practical functional needs that the innovative features of P&G products can address, but those needs that help improve people's lives. For P&G in emerging and developing markets, this often means finding new and creative ways to provide new and innovative products that raise the quality of people's lives in an accessible and affordable way.

While corporate values can play a leading role in motivating and even inspiring employees, they are also extremely valuable in persuading customers to consider the company more favorably. One reason for this is that growth and development have contributed in a major way to damaging the world. Company values that result in responsible corporate behavior will increasingly resonate with customers and influence their brand choices. A second reason is that, while product innovation will always be an important driver of brand choice, consumers are increasingly looking at this as a "given." They will simply expect better products as a matter of course from the leading company brands. Satisfied that their functional needs will be addressed more or less equally, their actual choice will navigate to those brands whose values mirror their own.

But there are values, and then there are *values*. The committed modern manager aiming for growth in a responsible manner effectively now has a choice of two categories of values that may power his or her organization.

The moral code type of values

These are the more obvious and usual suspects: honesty, integrity, and morality. Then there are values such as teamwork, excellence, and responsibility, among others in the same vein. Different companies will display different combinations of these generic-type values. They provide the basis for a code of conduct for employees that also translates into reasons for customers to feel good about buying its brands.

Having said that, these obvious values may not necessarily serve all companies equally well. The fine line that separates an essential core value from something that has minimal impact—or even a negative one—on customers is based on how relevant the value is to the business, as well as the prevailing circumstances. For instance, a bank that espouses values such as honesty and integrity might appeal to some customers in an environment that is characterized by questionable moral conduct, such as was the case during the 2008/09 financial crisis. However, other customers might react very differently. To these individuals, those kinds of values amount to a very basic expectation, something they should be able to take for granted: that is, that banks will be honest, and that their employees will demonstrate integrity. Indeed, such customers may well be put off by, and lose confidence in, companies that congratulate themselves on having the sorts of values that they consider a given.

Values which companies are perceived to value

This is why some companies that are universally perceived to have and practice solid moral code-type values (or are, at the very least, trusted) end up focusing on a different set of drivers altogether: practical brand-related values—that is, "things" that companies are perceived *to* value (as opposed to "generic" values). For instance, when asked what is the first thing that comes to mind when they think of 3M, nine people out of ten (particularly in the West) would say "innovation." This suggests that there exists a perception that 3M values innovation. And, indeed, this is true. On its Canadian website, the company describes itself as "A global technology company delivering innovative solutions to life's everyday needs."[24] While I would describe this as a mission statement (though it is not described as that on the site), the statement reflects the value. Its US website, on the other hand, is more specific and identifies innovation as a company value; indeed, it is listed in second place. Yet, even a company as dedicated to delivering to its "mission" as 3M appears to be, doesn't entirely divorce itself from also formally articulating two moral-code values: honesty and integrity.[25]

> When a company successfully establishes an internal mentality, and builds the infrastructure that supports the practice of a value, that value takes on a life of its own and leads to outcomes that are essential to maintaining the company's competitive advantage.

Thus, 3M values innovation. When a company successfully establishes an internal mentality, and builds the infrastructure that supports the practice of a value, that value takes on a life of its own and leads to outcomes that are essential to maintaining the company's competitive advantage. Just as the number of candidate values can literally be infinite, so is the number of competitive advantages each can deliver: new ideas, improvements, higher efficiency, delivery of the customer promises, disruptive and creative thinking—the list is literally endless. Real and relevant core values can be very powerful.

Consider the values at Virgin: fun, entertainment, irreverence, and innovation.[26] Not present are honesty and integrity, which doesn't mean that Virgin doesn't consider these values to be essential. They do. It is simply that they feel they are past the point of reminding people about them (if they ever did), in the sense that these values are solidly embedded within the organization's culture. Having moved beyond them, they are now effectively saying: We value the things we value because they directly result in the experience we want our employees and our customers to have with our brand. Founder Richard Branson describes Virgin values as "the glue that holds (the company) together."[27] And Virgin is a good example of a company that is perceived to live its values successfully. Take fun, entertainment and irreverence as examples. If the company's name was considered rather naughty in 1969, when Richard Branson first dreamt it up, it is today one of the most well known and powerful brand names in the world. To deliver on the connotations of the brand name, Branson has consistently staged a string of publicity stunts for which he has become both famous and notorious. For example, he dressed up in a wedding gown to promote the launch of Virgin Brides, he posed naked in a photo shoot for the launch of Virgin Cola (with only a six pack to preserve his modesty), and he was lowered into New York's Times Square by crane from the top of the Bertelsmann Building wearing only a body stocking and a strategically placed cell-phone. His idea of fun has been internalized and morphed into the company's culture. And Branson's style has extended beyond the simple promotion of his brands. When British Airways made a move in 2008 to partner with American Airlines, which threatened to create a monopoly in the skies above the Atlantic, Branson expressed his dissenting opinion in a uniquely Virgin way: He plastered his fleet of jets with what some described as the world's largest bumper stickers, which said: "No Way BA/AA."

Innovative? Yes, if being disruptive counts. Irreverent? Consistently. Entertaining and fun? Most definitely. Virgin's values and its escapades—particularly those of its chief—have not necessarily made the company a benchmark for excellence or a paragon of virtue. But they send a strong message about what the company genuinely believes in. And to those customer segments it appeals to, it does so strongly and convincingly.

As alluded to at the beginning of this section, the use of values as a strategic driver is only marginally better executed in the West than elsewhere. But this is changing quickly. In light of the massive social, economic, and environmental disruption of the past decade, and as a result of globalization and the ascendancy of countries such as China and India, entirely new consumer groups reflecting diverse cultural characteristics and expectations are emerging. In order to create meaningful dialogues with these groups, Western companies are rapidly reinventing themselves. They are recognizing these developments not as fads, but as permanent indicators of a new and constantly shifting landscape. The more successful companies such as Virgin view corporate values as strategic pillars that evolve as a genuine expression of the company's personality and purpose, not through dispassionate and, in some cases, outsourced processes. Observes Virgin's Branson: "In business schools, brand values are often discussed in terms of marketing, as though they are an end result of a scientific process, rather than embedded in a business's beginnings."[28]

Company values in Asia

In Asia the situation is different, and is characterized by three symptoms: (1) most companies continue to misunderstand the role and power of corporate values; (2) many others simply underutilize them; and (3) to a lesser degree, but nevertheless still visibly and problematically, some companies fail to understand the importance of the "promise and delivery" equation (as well as the implications of failing to deliver it consistently). The CEOs of these companies continue to believe that they can make money by taking short-cuts or short-changing their customers. One exhaustive worldwide brand audit for an Asian-based hospitality brand recorded the perception its employees had of its corporate values. These ranged from "not many values," to "can't think of any," to "values influenced by money," to "greed," to "hard to understand because they are so different."[29]

During the course of another major brand audit we conducted for an Asian luxury brand with operations in four Asian markets, we found company-wide confusion over too wide a spread of perceived values that more closely reflected financial objectives, personal wish lists, and expectations by management of employees, among other things.[30] The COO, for instance, cited "credibility" and "trendsetting" as important values. Another senior executive talked about "passion, professionalism, and expertise." A third cited "confidence" and a "dynamic management team." Yet another believed the company valued "sincerity" and "commitment from its employees" (though the latter value was specifically identified as being absent by another equally senior executive). The CEO himself identified "integrity" and "trust" as important company values. Among lower-level and customer-facing employees, the picture was even more diffused. Perceived values ranged from "trust and reputation," to "services," to "relationships," to "prestige," to "self-image." On a different dimension of the spectrum, words such as "happiness" and friendship" were used. It was a case of everything but the kitchen sink.

This company clearly exhibited an absence of formal institutionalized values. As a result, employees began to assume (or hope for) a long list of disparate and different things. Others were simply not aware that the company had any formal values and were certainly not influenced to behave in any specific way. The result was an internal mess that prevented the company from harnessing what, for the most part, were positive employee attitudes. This was especially true given that the external picture—customers—suggested a perception of an overall (if ill-defined and unfocused) set of good values. The formal customer research that was undertaken at the same time across the same markets revealed that customers viewed this company as valuing "honesty and sincerity" and "personalized service." Whether these three values were "relevant" to the company's strategic goals was something the company management had never explored. As a result, they could never really exploit them, because, prior to the research, they were unaware of them. The managers of this company simply didn't know what they didn't know. This reasonably successful company was successful in spite of itself, which is another way of saying it was not living up to its potential.

> Too many Asian companies across the region are failing to recognize the importance of core values. As a consequence, they are failing to harness the power that core values have to influence two critical stakeholder groups: employees internally and customers externally.

Unfortunately, the above two examples of very high-profile Asian companies that are failing to recognize the importance of core values are not exceptional. Too many companies in the region are failing to harness the power that core values have to influence two critical stakeholder groups: employees internally and customers externally.

In Singapore, customer service standards is a hotly debated public issue. Everyone from customers, to customer lobby groups, to business associations, and especially the government, have weighed in with criticisms, opinions, and recommendations for improving what, most agree, are unacceptably low standard levels for a city-nation that is aiming to be recognized as a leading global destination. According to the Singapore Management University's Customer Satisfaction Index (CSISG), Singapore's score dipped over two consecutive years (2007 and 2008).[31] Yet over this same period, dozens, if not hundreds, of articles appeared in newspapers, countless government ministers addressed conferences and seminars on the subject, and surveys and research were commissioned—all aimed at improving standards. Even national movements such as GEMS (Go the Extra Mile for Service) attracted more than the usual attention. Overall, the effort has been credible and commendable. But as wide-ranging as the discussion has been, it has for the most part failed to recognize the principal driver of human behavior—values. The focus of the thinking—and the solutions—hasn't traveled beyond superficial levels of predictable prescriptions: better business processes, more training, and better technology.[32] Training in the absence of motivation is the equivalent of taking a horse to water but not being able to make it drink. A notable exception is the comment attributed to Ho Kwon Ping, chairman of SMU and CEO of Banyan Tree Hotels. In an SMU article, he was quoted as saying that values play a fundamental role in the service delivery of Banyan Tree Hotels: ". . . that great service, at the end of the day, comes from people who perform consistently, every day with love and quality."[33] Employees who don't want to provide good service simply won't—regardless of whatever training they get, or however much technology improves their working environment. As helpful and useful as these are, they are not sufficient in themselves. Employees need to want to do it. It is about motivation and, ultimately engagement, which rely on core values being in place.

In misunderstanding the potential power that core values are able to harness, company managers in Asia also misunderstand how to go about identifying those values that are most relevant and appropriate for their needs and circumstances. Values, like mission statements, need to be carefully chosen at the very beginning of a company's history. The more frequently they are demonstrated, the more tangible and credible they emerge and the more synonymous with the company they become.

Whether the company is a start-up looking to position itself (through a formal branding exercise) or a veteran operator seeking to reposition itself, it needs to undertake an expansive brand audit. It will need to audit itself, its customers, and its own category. The output of this effort must be carefully synthesized to deliver a clear and honest picture of the relevant facts—a reality check, in effect. A reality check of market circumstances, of customer needs and expectations, but most importantly, of itself. What are its strengths and weaknesses? What do customers and (essentially) employees really think of its products? Its claims? Its image? Its leadership? But the reality in Asia is that most managers are reluctant to engage in this kind of soul-searching research, to the point of resistance. Most think they already know; the rest don't think it is important.

> A company's most important stakeholders will always be its employees. Without engaged employees who are motivated and willing to deliver, there *is* no company—or, at least not one of present or future substance.

If the first step in a company's identifying its core values is looking around—and then at—itself, the second is taking what it has learned to its most important stakeholders: not its customers or shareholders, but its employees. Without engaged employees who are motivated and willing to deliver, there *is* no company—or, at least not one of present or future substance.

Taking what it has learned to employees means opening a real channel of communication and inviting them to engage in discussions and debates about what the corporate values ought to be. And employees are in an ideal position to be partners to management in this process: they are closer to reality—being on the ground, or closer to customers at the delivery end—than managers ever will be, and their insights count.

> Message to the CEO: You cannot build a company in today's environment on your own.

Message to the CEO: You cannot build a company in today's environment on your own. Yet, that is what many CEOs attempt to do. The thinking in Asia is that values, like goals and objectives, are best decided exclusively by management. But without input from customers (from the outside) and employees (from the inside), the result is normally a very predictable laundry list of virtuous characteristics that are likely to be irrelevant to the company's "character" and unhelpful in helping it deliver its vision moving forward. The values that such an approach creates are either not disseminated to employees, or are dismissed by them as irrelevant or impractical. For all intended purposes, these "values" are useless.

Core values versus the laundry list

Visit the websites of any random dozen Asian companies and click on "Values." Nine times out of ten, you will find a laundry list of values that try too hard to portray the company as an embodiment of goodness. And, it seems, the more values one espouses, the better. One leading private hospital in South Asia listed no fewer than eight values and values-related characteristics: successful partnerships; innovation; flexibility; teamwork; excellence; value creation; and, of course, honesty and integrity.

Real values influence what a company does, how its employees behave, and how it is perceived. They are therefore important and valuable. But nothing that is important and valuable is easy to deliver. It is difficult enough for individuals to live up to their own values. Attempting to persuade groups of individuals—numbered in the hundreds, or even thousands—to bring to life and keep alive those values that a company has declared define it, is a far more difficult challenge. It is never a matter of simply espousing them, as should be obvious. Major initiatives—as well as personal commitments to principles and ideas—are needed if even one single value is to come close to being perceived as "real." It is a process requiring a collective effort. Virgin's Branson: "Catherine Salway (group brand director) has put together a structure to ensure that every company in the Virgin Group is aware of our values and also our customers' expectations. . . . We now operate in 29 countries, employ 50,000 people and serve millions of customers every month—we cannot be complacent."[34] To say that it is difficult to bring brand values to life is a serious understatement. The more focus and genuine effort is invested, the better the chance that they will come alive and accurately define the company.

The more values a company commits itself to beyond a certain number of "core" values, the more difficult it will be to keep each of them "real." It is difficult enough to successfully "live" one value, let alone six, eight, or even ten. People not only expect companies to live up to their promised values, but are sophisticated enough to recognize when that isn't likely to be possible. This can happen when they are presented with a long "laundry list" of values. Where there is no credibility, there is no respect.

Although there is no optimum number of values a company should adopt, I would suggest that four is more than enough to keep the company challenged, real, and honest.

And as to the mix of values? There will always be debate on the merits and appropriateness of moral code-type values versus the more practical, open-ended values companies choose to value. While my point of view might disappoint some for being predictable, it doesn't necessarily diminish its desirability: go with a mix. In many cases, customers will need to be reassured that your company is honest and has integrity. But beyond providing reassurance, you will also need practical values that facilitate the creation of products and services that are unique, ahead of their time, or simply inspiring. Make sure that these values are relevant and real.

The truth about corporate values is that they are not valued by most Asian companies.

The opportunity

The truth about corporate values is that they are not valued by most Asian companies. The brutal truth is that they can be so powerful, that the absence of meaningful or real values can rob a company of a potentially completely different—and better—destiny.

The flip-side of that coin provides two very powerful opportunities that, when properly deployed, are potential game changers.

Opportunity #1: Customers becoming increasingly interested in who they are buying products and services from. And they can afford to be selective, because they are spoiled for choice. Available to them is a wide array of quality products, all of which deliver excellent functional benefits, so there is no need to compromise. They are increasingly demanding brands that are responsible or show visible signs of having a conscience. Asian consumers are no different. The first Asian brands that make a meaningful effort to demonstrate strong and compelling values will likely attract the attention of consumers not only in Asia, but the world over. And the sooner Asian companies "get" this the better.

Opportunity #2: The second opportunity lies within a universally shared aphorism: "You are what you are." As individuals, we cannot escape from the cultures that shape us and the personal characters we create growing up in our indigenous environments. This is true also of Asian companies. When we talk about the importance of values, we need to recognize that, in Asia, we must also include "Asian" values. Independent of linguistic diversity and other cultural differences, all Northeast Asian societies (China, Hong Kong, Taiwan, Japan, and Korea) are culturally indebted to Confucianism. Though more diverse, Southeast Asia (Indonesia, Thailand, the Philippines, Malaysia, Singapore, and Vietnam) is strongly characterized by a broad Malay ethnic identity with substantial non-Malay minorities (in regional terms, as in the case of Singapore). However, both groups have interests in common: orderly society, filial piety, social harmony, and respect for authority, among others. These are enduring values that are rarely mentioned on the websites of Asian companies. Instead, many Asian companies appear to believe that success lies in pretending to be Western. However, pretending to be something you are not never works. You are what you are. Rather than ignore or conceal them, Asian companies need to embrace their Asian values. Knowing who you are, and celebrating it, creates authenticity as well as an internal company culture that generates pride and self-esteem. The opportunities inherent in this are further magnified by the increasing interest of the West in all things Asian, including Asian values. Asian provenance is increasingly the new "cool."

Summary

Our everyday practices, not our espoused values, define who we are. In other words, it is not what we say, but what we do, that matters. What we do is generally the product of what we value. This is as true of business as it is of life. And what we value can range from the ingrained but universally revered moral code type of values, to valuing basically anything that leads directly to a desirable outcome. As elementary as this sounds, there is overwhelming evidence that companies across Asia demonstrate a disturbing absence of practiced values while espousing a virtuous corporate character that claims to "care" (about quality; about customers; about service—and anything else considered important to say to a customer). Many of these companies are simply not "walking the talk."

The widespread absence of real and practiced values by many Asian companies provides many other companies in the region with a unique opportunity. Internally, values can energize employees by engaging them at a visceral level. Externally, values deliver what consumers today expect (beyond good-quality products): a caring, conscientious, and responsible approach to business; or products and services that redefine what is "cool," or which solve a problem in an ingenious way, or address a need consumers didn't even know they had.

In addition to tapping into the universal moral code and practical values, Asian companies have the unique advantage of being able to tap into something that is increasingly gaining global currency: the power and appeal of *Asian* values.

CHARTING THE ROAD TO A SUCCESSFUL BUSINESS

"Pre-branding" consists of a set of strategic steps every company must follow if it hopes to create customer preference and, more importantly, customer loyalty.

Running a successful business is a process, not a secret available only to a select few. Asian managers stand to benefit a great deal simply by being aware of the compelling logic. Looking at the process from a "bird's-eye view" (Figure 4.7), one can see how straightforward and logical are the steps involved. The "bird's-eye view" construct is, in fact, another way to view the Business and Branding Flowchart discussed at the start of this chapter. It is best appreciated if viewed from the end, rather than the beginning.

Preference and loyalty

We start at the bottom of the figure with customer preference and loyalty. This is the end-game. This is what your company should be aiming to secure: customer preference for your brand over the alternatives; and, even more importantly, customer satisfaction that keeps them coming back—loyalty. So, this is the goal. How do we make this happen?

Figure 4.7 Running a successful business: A bird's-eye view

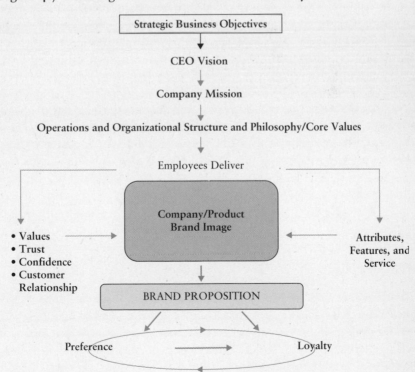

The brand proposition

You don't have to be a branding guru to recognize that people will only try your brand if it offers something that is unique, differentiated, or appealing in some other way. This amounts to the brand proposition: what your product is all about (identity); what it does (function); and what it promises (benefit).

The brand image

You cannot promise something that is unique or different unless it is supported by a positive and credible company or brand image. The image of the brand is, in turn, the product of two elements that complement one another. On the right side of the construct are the "hard" elements: the physical attributes and features of the product or the service—what it literally does for the customer. So, if it is soap, it cleans. If it is a watch, it tells the time. On the left side of the construct are the "soft" elements—those intangible things that support the product attributes and features. They might include what the brand believes in—its values; or the reputation of trust that it has created over time; or the perception of good customer relationships it may have in the minds of some customers. So, in simple terms, the physical product attributes of the brand, combined with the intangible associations customers have of the brand, contribute to the overall image the company enjoys. The image provides credibility to the brand proposition—what is actually promised the customer. Combined, they deliver preference and loyalty.

Many Asian decision makers are sure-footed up to this stage, but not beyond it.

A smart Asian manager will ask the question: What do I need to do to deliver customer preference and loyalty? Just saying, "Buy my brand because it's the best" to a customer is manifestly not enough, but that is exactly what often happens in Asia. What is needed is the understanding and the will to go beyond the "saying."

Employees deliver

This brings us to a central truth that should be self-evident, but often is not. Those who deliver consistent quality at the assembly line, or great service with a genuine smile at the customer point, are the same people who generate the intangibles so valued by customers—such as trust, confidence, and customer relationships. The "doers" are employees. They deliver. No one else does, because no one else can.

So, if we accept that employees are the facilitators of the end-result companies are aiming for, we have to ask ourselves: How do we get them to do this willingly? Incentives (such as bonus payments) and disincentives (such as fear of losing one's job) are not on their own sufficient to engage employees to the extent that they want to deliver. And they need to want to deliver. Great brands are created and maintained by committed stakeholders who love and are proud of what they do.

Operations and organizational structure, and philosophy/core values

What engages employees lies within the management structure and philosophy of the company. How the company is organized (for instance, in a hierarchical or flat structure) has a significant impact on policies such as empowerment. The more (appropriately) empowered an individual is, the more engaged and motivated he or she is likely to be in regards to personal responsibility and collective goals. As for philosophy, company core values are key. If the company truly believes in something inspiring or worthwhile, its employees will rally around it.

Company mission

The pillar that provides the company with its sense of worth and substantiates the core values it lives by is the purpose it has set for itself. And, as mentioned earlier, having as its purpose the making of money will neither motivate a company's facilitators nor—ironically—guarantee financial success. The purpose of the company (its mission) creates an essential frame of reference that provides relevance to its employees and, ultimately, its customers.

CEO vision

For a company's values and mission to be relevant and aligned, the CEO needs to set its direction and declare a destination. What the CEO wants to achieve, and where he or she wants to go, provides context for everyone else in the company to consider and allows them to calibrate their jobs to help get there. The absence of the CEO's vision, therefore, can only result in a rudderless company.

Strategic business objectives

For the right direction and destination to be set, the company needs to be very clear about what business it is in. Diversification, which often translates into distraction, seriously undermines a company's ability to do any single thing well. Confusion over business goals and business strategy either misdirects or totally suppresses the visioning process.

It should be clear by now that the "bird's-eye view" construct is a series of critical, interdependent steps that trigger one another, ultimately impacting the company's ability to do what it wants to do, which is to create customer preference and loyalty for its brands. Fail to include any one of those steps, and the construct will be seriously undermined.

NOTES

1. "Business and Branding Flowchart," BrandAsian, 2010. All rights reserved.
2. Carlyle Brand Consultants/BrandAsian brand audit interviews, 2001–09.
3. Andrew S. Grove, "Only the Paranoid Survive," *Broadway Business*, March 16, 1999.
4. Roger Malone, "Om Prakash Bhatt, Chairman, State Bank of India. Remaking a Government-owned Giant: An Interview with the Chairman of the State Bank of India," *McKinsey Quarterly*, April 2009.
5. Michael Porter, *Competitive Strategy* (New York: The Free Press/Macmillan, 1980).
6. Sarah Arnott, "AirAsia X to Fly No Frills from London to Kuala Lumpur," *The Independent*, March 11, 2009.
7. "Tiger Airways Says 'No' to Long-haul Flights," *Weekend Today*, July 17–18, 2010, p. 24.
8. JosephOnBrands (BrandAsian), repositioning project, Brand Audit Report, 2006.
9. *BusinessWeek/Interbrand*, "100 Best Global Brands," businessweek.com, September 17, 2009.
10. "Samsung Electronics to Ramp up R&D Investment," (AP), *MyPaper*, May 18, 2010, p. 20.
11. Interview with Arnold Schwarzenegger, *Fortune*, August 9, 2004.
12. www.microsoft.com/mscorp/execmail/2002/11-13lookingforward.mspx.
13. Sharon Chan, "Microsoft's New Vision: A Little Wordier than the Old One," *The Seattle Times*, "Business/Technology," September 8, 2008.
14. W. Chan Kim and Renee Mauborgne, *Blue Ocean Strategy* (Cambridge, MA: Harvard Business School Press, 2005).
15. Carlyle Brand Consultants (BrandAsian), "Eu Yan Sang," Brand Blueprint Report, 2003.
16. Carlyle Brand Consultants (BrandAsian), "Millennium & Copthorne," Brand Audit Report, October 2002.
17. Banyan Tree website, "Awards" category, March 19, 2008.

18. Phil Jackson, *Sacred Hoops: Spiritual Lessons of a Hardwood Warrior* (New York: Hyperion, 2006).
19. Andrew Hampp, "New 'We Are the World' Credits: Quincy Jones, Lionel Richie . . . and WPP?," *Advertising Age*, February 12, 2010.
20. PricewaterhouseCoopers, "2005 Asia Human Capital Effectiveness Survey," *The Singapore Business Times*, November 9, 2005.
21. "Why Missha is Falling behind in Korean Cosmetics Race," *Media*, February 11, 2010, p. 13.
22. Wal-Mart, 2009 Global Sustainability Report, www.walmartstores.com.
23. Rosabeth Moss Kanter, "Inside Procter & Gamble's New Values-Based Strategy," *Harvard Business Review Blog* (http://blogs.harvardbusiness.org), January 21, 2010.
24. 3M, "Our Visions, Values & Goals," 3M Canada's Visions, www.3m.com/cms/ca/en/1-30/criRcFK/view.html.
25. 3M, "Our Company. Who We Are," http://solutions.3m.com/wps/portal/3M/en_US/about-3M/information/about/us/.
26. Shaun Smith, "The Customer Experience," London Business Forum, October 24, 2007, www.londonbusinessforum.com/events/customer_experience.
27. Richard Branson, "Secrets Not Taught in Business School," *Today*, May 19, 2010 (distributed by The New York Times Syndicate).
28. Ibid.
29. Carlyle Brand Consultants/BrandAsian, Branding project, 2002.
30. BrandAsian, Branding project, 2006.
31. Mustafa Shafawi, "Singapore 2009 Customer Satisfaction Index up Marginally," January 25, 2010, www.channelnewsasia.com/stories/singaporelocalnews/view/1032865/1/.html.
32. Mustafa Shafawi, "Customer-Centric Policies Pay Off," *Today*, January 25, 2010, p. 10.
33. "When Will Service Standards in Singapore Improve?" September 2, 2009, http://knowledge.smu.edu.sg/article.cfm?articleid=1233.
34. Branson, "Secrets Not Taught in Business School," *op. cit.*

5

BRAND STRATEGY

It is almost axiomatic that if CEOs don't pay sufficient attention to brand positioning, they will pay even less attention to brand strategy. And the evidence in the field bears this out. Whatever brand strategy might be inferred of brands doing business in Asia, most of it is by accident, not by design. Therefore, its impact is usually weak and may even damage the brand itself.

Brand strategy involves important choices that the CEO must make about a range of brand- (and ultimately business-) related issues if he or she is to control and influence events and deliver competitive advantages. The absence of brand strategy, on the other hand, hands control to competitors and results in no competitive advantage.

IF YOU DON'T MAKE A CHOICE, THE CHOICE MAKES YOU

In an environment where business leaders gravitate to wanting it all, "selective choices" as a strategic consideration is largely ignored. "Choice"—in the sense of which opportunities should be exploited, as well as those which should be avoided despite whatever might be gained—is, on the surface, a logical consideration. In reality, this discipline is replaced by an opportunistic mentality, where most of the attention and effort is directed to wherever the making of easy money appears to be most possible. This, at best, results in mediocrity; at worst, it can position the company in a declining trajectory.

Brand strategy includes several essential elements that need to be considered carefully by all CEOs. These elements won't all be relevant to all companies in all industries, but it is the consideration of each in the first place that determines what is—and is not—relevant. Furthermore, in one way or another, everything is connected. If one of these elements is poorly addressed or badly executed, it will inevitably adversely impact all the others in the company's eco-chain.

Among the most important brand strategy drivers that can impact companies in one way or another are the following:

- Differentiation
- Emotional dimension
- Focused target audience
- Ability to innovate and remain relevant
- CEO involvement and leadership
- Employee involvement and commitment
- Intelligent brand architecture
- CSR: the new branding imperative.

Each of these drivers provides several alternatives that CEOs will need to consider before making those choices that are relevant to their businesses. Many of them are interconnected. (For example, differentiation and emotional dimensions both contribute directly to the brand positioning.) There are no right or wrong choices *per se*. What makes one choice "right" for a company depends entirely on its unique circumstances. The choices most suitable to any given company are those that link up to its core business and, most importantly, its business strategy. Effective brand strategy and a compelling brand positioning are directly linked to a clear and articulated business strategy.

DIFFERENTIATION

"Me-tooism," although certainly not invented in Asia, seems to be a practice that Asian CEOs will nonetheless end up perfecting—unless they change.

For what amounts to an elementary driver that influences the choices made by most people, differentiation is notably absent from the strategic considerations of many Asian companies. "Me-tooism," although certainly not invented in Asia, seems to be a practice that Asian CEOs will nonetheless end up perfecting—unless they change.

There is nothing mysterious or complicated about the concept: "differentiation" means delivering real difference. The word "real" doesn't necessarily just mean differences that amount to tangible product features or attributes—in other words, rational (tangible) differentiation. It can also mean (for reasons that will be explained below) emotional (intangible) differentiation. This latter dimension opens up a can of worms for many Asian CEOs, mostly because it is conceptual in nature and generally requires some imagination—and I mean no offense when I say this. Too many hard-nosed businesspeople in the region are focused mostly on what amounts to low-hanging fruit—that is, what is visible or obvious and most readily accessible.

I spent more than 13 months working closely with the CEO and chairman of one of Asia's largest conglomerates. A multibillion-dollar empire, it operates businesses ranging from property development to finance to hotels. The task we had been assigned was to reposition its Asian-based network of hotels as an international network. We undertook a considerable amount of primary research and ran a series of probing workshops in six or so international markets. Our research (as well as common sense) indicated the need to differentiate our client from the other luxury hotel chains. Our research confirmed that, such was the level of commoditization that so many high-end hotel brands had managed to reach, customers were beginning to consider most luxury hotel brands as somewhat interchangeable. In the end, and in spite of our suggesting a number of very different—even inspiring—positioning ideas, the CEO settled for the same international luxury hotel recipe that characterizes most operators. The only difference was that he fabricated an inferior facsimile of the pre-existing, and better-known, global brand names who were there first. He wasn't afraid of the new ideas we provided; he simply lacked imagination.

> *"Unfortunately, most Chinese companies continue to search for the courage to risk being different, and thus prefer to copy or make derivatives of the designs of others. . . ."*
> David Wolf, CEO, The Wolf Group Asia

Though this response is symptomatic of brands in almost all categories in Asia, the hotel category seems to work harder to exemplify this absence of imagination and stubborn persistence in replicating what is believed already works. Consequently—apart from one notable exception—the region's hospitality landscape is awash with Asian hotel brands that look, sound, and even feel the same as the international benchmarks they are effectively trying to copy. The exception is the Banyan Tree Hotel Resort Group. While virtually all other Asian hotel brands are clones of their Western counterparts, Banyan Tree is demonstrating just how powerful differentiation can be. Instead of pretending to be a Western brand, Banyan Tree has embraced its Asian-ness. Its management, headed by Executive Chairman Ho Kwon Ping, has shrewdly and correctly concluded the obvious: (1) Success lies in being yourself. You are what you are what you are. Banyan Tree is Asian; there is no getting around that fact. (2) Why would they even want to get around that fact? Synonymous with Asian values are grace and hospitality—drivers central to the hotel category. To the forward-thinking Ho, it was neither difficult nor complicated to decide on a brand positioning that coupled the idea of the "romance of travel"[1] with the brand values of romance and intimacy and an Asian brand personality. By having the courage to be itself, rather than pretend to be someone else, Banyan Tree broke away from the conventional wis-dom that defined hotel luxury. The hotel resort chain has—from its very inception—successfully defined itself with a clear and compelling, dif-ferentiated brand proposition. In a relatively short period of time, it has emerged as one of the most successful hotel brands in the world.

Differentiation is a crucial part of the effort of any brand to draw attention and interest to itself and is a principal conduit for sustainable success. Young & Rubicam's Brand Asset Valuator® has calculated that brands that demonstrate effective differentiation enjoy up to 50 percent higher operating margins over companies whose products or services demonstrate either little or no differentiation. The numbers were even more dramatic with operating earnings (270 percent) and market cap growth (250 percent).[2]

While the concept of "different = appealing" is neither complex nor complicated to understand, differentiation nevertheless continues to be markedly absent from products and services in many categories in Asia. The usual excuses range from "too difficult" to "we sell commodities" to—as the hotel category illustrates—"why not stick with what works?" The absence of perspective contributes significantly to the existence and perpetuation of the first two reasons. As for the third reason, copying someone else's product, service, or idea manifestly doesn't work—at least, not in a sustainable way. So, Asian companies looking to build long-term futures need seriously to reassess this "strategy."

Differentiation may not be an easy or straightforward process, but it is doable. The inability of some companies to create differentiation for their products or services is often not so much the result of a lack of effort, but a lack of imagination.

Perspective

Perspective—the ability and willingness to look at something from a completely different angle—often provides something where previously nothing was perceived to exist. As Harvard Business School's Professor Theodore Levitt once famously declared: "You can differentiate anything."[3]

Companies that sell commodities are most guilty of believing that a commodity is, well, a commodity, and as such, can only be marketed on the basis of price and quality (often in that order). CEOs of these companies have little time or patience for branding, as their starting point is that differentiation is almost impossible and therefore is not worth spending time, effort, and money on pursuing.

The irony is that business-to-business companies marketing commodities are perhaps most in need of, and may benefit the most from, differentiated brand positionings and brand strategies. It is, after all, manifestly easier (relatively speaking) to differentiate a consumer product that offers multiple permutations of everything from its functional applications to the packaging it comes in, than it is to differentiate one brand of, say, sugar, wheat, or beans from another. Clearly, greater efforts at differentiation must be made with what are perceived to be commodities if a sustainable business is to be built.

Consider water, for instance. My generation grew up taking water for granted. In Australia, it was (and remains) safe to drink water from taps. It is (and remains), relatively speaking, free. And when I was a boy, drinking water was as exciting as watching grass grow. As kids, we wanted Coke®, or at least something that tasted sweet and was fun to drink. Water was boring. The very idea of anyone trying to convince us to pay for something that was dull, and was available for free, would have been considered absurd at the time.

Apparently, that idea wasn't so absurd to the folks at Evian. Although bottled water had been around in one form or another since the early 1800s, it wasn't until the 1970s that it started to enjoy mainstream appreciation or even awareness. The health craze that characterized the 1970s and 1980s provided Evian with an opportunity to redefine the image of water and in the process make it a mainstream product for which people would be willing to pay money.

Evian led the industry and successfully transformed what many people considered a commodity into a differentiated and much sought-after product. In 2006 the bottled water category was estimated to be worth about US$61 billion. The market is forecast to reach some

US$86.5 billion by 2011—a growth of around 42 percent.[4] Not bad for boring water.

Transforming a category that seemed impossible to differentiate into a highly differentiated one hasn't been limited to the water category. When telecom company Orange emerged in Europe in 1994, it was faced with an overcrowded and ruthlessly competitive marketplace. The company chose to eschew the approach traditionally favored by other telecoms, which was to communicate features and attributes. Instead, Orange chose to differentiate itself by opting for a more intangible message: It focused on human values. This approach was, at the time, genuinely disruptive and instantly differentiated the brand from its competitors. While delivering on all the functional product expectations that customers took for granted, it went further and invited them into a relationship. Instead of articulating and promising values, it demonstrated them. Its brand name was unique and disarming, its corporate identity bold and arresting, and its customer language direct and clear. In time, Orange became for its customers the friendly, honest, straightforward, refreshing, and dynamic brand that its values promised it wanted to be.[5] Today, the brand is synonymous with innovative, exciting, customer-centric services.

Instead of selling coffee, Starbucks' brand positioning almost made coffee incidental to the more relevant and compelling experience that differentiates the brand. Starbucks recognized that selling coffee was not the game. That it needed to sell great coffee was considered a given. The management at Starbucks knew it needed to move beyond selling great coffee and create something that was not only differentiated, but also memorable and worthy of repeat purchase and loyalty. They did what no other company had previously bothered to do: They took a critical look at the market landscape, which at the time was divided into only two major categories: instant coffee and gourmet packaged coffee. By adopting a different perspective, Starbucks extended the landscape by adding two more quadrants and in the process quickly recognized where its opportunity rested: in the High Quality/Experience space (see Figure 5.1). In time, that experience matured into what became a credible stake in people's lives: what the company calls "third place,"[6] the first two (according to Starbucks) being home and work.

Singapore Airlines (SIA) provides perhaps one of the most compelling examples of how a generic benefit can be tangibly differentiated. Among the many things first-tier airlines claim and work hard to deliver is "service." Like the hospitality industry, service emerges as a basic

Figure 5.1 The coffee market landscape in the United States in the
early 1970s

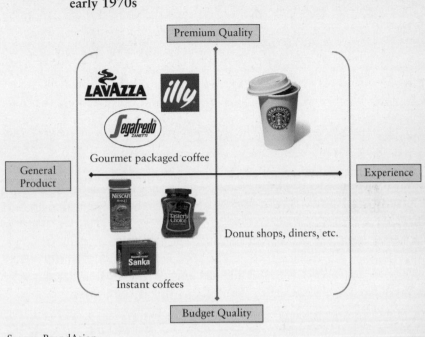

Source: BrandAsian.

given—expected by customers from all airlines. Instead of moving away
from it, SIA chose to adopt a different perspective on the concept of service. Instead of accepting the conventional wisdom that defined good—
or even great—airline service, SIA took it upon itself to define *SIA
service*: It came up with its own interpretation—its own definition—of
service. In consistently delivering something that was effectively different, SIA not only succeeded in converting a generic benefit into one that
was differentiated, but also assumed ownership of it.

So powerful is the association SIA has with exceptional and proprietary service in all three cabin classes, analysts consider it improbable
that SIA could eliminate its first class, as many other airlines have done
in the wake of the 2009 global economic crisis: "It is almost unthink-
able for SIA not to offer first class travel for the major sectors it flies,
since this is an airline—more than any other—that has made luxury
travel a class of its own."[7]

The Strategic Role of Differentiation

Where does differentiation work best? An advertising person will say that differentiation lies in the creative executional end of the process—in other words, the advertising (see Figure 5.2). While this is partly true, the reasoning is mostly flawed as it often fails to recognize that an important formative phase precedes and influences it: the branding phase.

> Differentiation is a strategic imperative. This means it lies in the brand blueprint and is expressed through the brand positioning.

Differentiation is a strategic imperative. This means it lies in the brand blueprint and is expressed through the brand positioning. Further, it is a fixed concept. In other words, the differentiation that counts the most is the enduring type that separates the brand from others at the core identity level. This identity is typically created once, and is consolidated over time. The role of advertising is to harness the essence

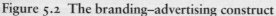

Figure 5.2 The branding–advertising construct

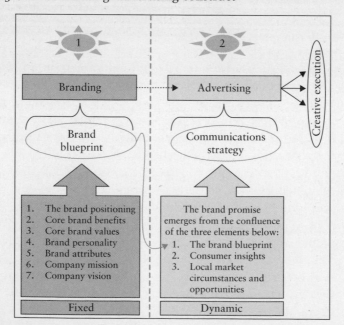

Source: BrandAsian.

of the brand's strategic differentiation and express it in a creative way through one or more ideas that resonate with customers at a local level. Advertising ideas are dynamic and will change from campaign to campaign. Strategic differentiation doesn't change; it is fixed. That is, through constantly reinforcing itself, it becomes stronger and more clearly defined over time.

Summary

Differentiation is not an optional consideration; it is a must-have essential. And as Levitt points out, "Everything can be differentiated, even so-called 'commodities' from cement, to copper, to wheat, to air cargo, to marine insurance, etc. There is no such thing as a commodity, only people who act and think like commodities."[8] But being different for the sake of being different isn't enough. Differentiation must be relevant and credible to its stakeholders (customers, employees, investors), as well as sustainable in the short, near, and long term.

EMOTIONAL DIMENSION

The central, most important component of any powerful brand is differentiation: that which makes your brand unique in a relevant way to your customers. As self-evident as this crucial ingredient is, vast quantities of products and services manufactured and delivered to customers in Asia continue to be facsimiles of what others are already providing. This leads to one inevitable outcome—competition based on price. This is, sooner or later, a death strategy.

Differentiation is not about adding a lengthy list of attributes and features to your product, or shouting the loudest that you are "best." Besides, those features may not always be relevant to or wanted by your customers. Often, they are considered to be overkill by people who are increasingly looking more for complementary lifestyle personal accessories (think the iPod).

The most effective way that brands differentiate themselves is through their "emotional dimensions." The most unique thing about human beings is our involuntary predilection to be emotional. If you doubt this, stop for a moment and critically review a decision that you have made. Perhaps you compiled a list of "must-have" qualities you expect in your life partner: intellect, sensitivity, education, a good background, etc. Or perhaps, when you last bought a car, you decided that it must be safe, reliable, big enough for the family, etc. While those elements played an important role in your assessment, in the end you may have found that your heart ruled. You married the guy your mother warned you about. You chose your car because, well . . . it was just so sexy and you decided you just had to have it. Where decisions pit what we need against what we want, we tend to rationalize the emotional dimension.

I am not a big fan of behavioral models, but I make an exception for Maslow and his "Hierarchy of Needs." Most of us are familiar with the model. It is pyramid shaped and divided into five ascending layers of "needs." The bottom two layers—physiological and safety needs—are markedly separated from the top three—love/affection/belonging; esteem; and self-actualization. The bottom two layers represent, in effect, physical dimensions. The top three represent emotional dimensions. Many of us living in Asia today—though certainly not all—are spared the daunting battle for daily survival. We don't worry about where we will find food, shelter, and safety. We have broader needs and ambitions, as well as hopes for fuller, more meaningful, and more enjoyable lives. Most of our energy is devoted to satisfying Maslow's top three hierarchical needs. We crave affection and love, and we hanker to belong (to a team, a club, a gang, our family unit. . .); we struggle to raise our self-esteem; and many of us have even higher needs—self-actualization, which can come from several sources ranging from religion to self-induced enlightenment. We spend our lives in an emotional crucible searching for a measure of happiness. Being emotional is part of the human condition.

The end-result is: We think with our minds, but—brand owners take note—we act with our hearts.

As already mentioned, a fundamental equation that businesses must master is: brands = promise & delivery. The promise breaks down into two components: the functional (the nuts and bolts of the product) and the emotional (the intangible dimensions of the product).

Attributes and functional product features are very important, but—and this is the critical thing—in today's consumer landscape, they are a *given*. In other words, the increasing minimum expectation by sophisticated, empowered customers who are awash with choices is that your product or service will deliver on its functional promise—and deliver very well: that this razor blade will provide a close shave; that this soap will clean and moisturize well; that this car will get me safely from A to B; that this budget airline will provide low-cost fares. But the extent to which the brand delivers on its functional promise will not, on its own, automatically create preference. It is important to emphasize this point, because the evidence suggests that companies in Asia are not grasping this. Vast numbers of companies are continuing to launch and market an endless parade of brands that are largely undifferentiated. The most prevalent reason for this is a legacy of the old trading mentality: the expectation that, simply because I make stuff, people will buy it.

> Asian brands have lost out to Western brands precisely because they have failed to create emotional relationships with customers. While the Asian business narrative has limited itself to attributes, features, and price, Asian consumers have long been saying: "excite me," "move me," "uplift me."

Why are emotional dimensions in brands so important? Because people are emotional. And because brands help people define themselves emotionally. To the extent that the "definition of self" comes directly and indirectly from a brand—be it an ideology or a wristwatch—the emotional component is certain to be very high. Asian brands have lost out to Western brands precisely because they have failed to create emotional relationships with customers. While the Asian business narrative has limited itself to attributes, features, and price, Asian consumers have long been saying: "excite me," "move me," "uplift me."

The reason for this lies as much in an inability by Asian managers to grasp what emotions in brands really mean, as in an unwillingness to be open to change. Regarding the former, they struggle with the concept because they misunderstand it. The misunderstanding ranges from the misconception that "emotional" equals (almost exclusively) "cool," to the belief that it is at the communication (advertising) end that brands should properly be emotionally expressed. Neither perception is entirely accurate. As for the latter, resistance to change, perceptions of "value for money" strongly influence the persistence of focusing on attributes and features. Ogilvy & Mather's Miles Young suggested yet a third dimension when he wrote that (Asian) "brand owners find . . . the 'emotional' content of a brand . . . difficult, even embarrassing to talk about. . . ."[9] Whether it is due to confusion, stubbornness, or just plain discomfort, this is not good news for the Asian brand.

Emotional Benefits Cannot Be Copied by Your Competitors

"Emotion" in brands doesn't mean, literally, brands that make you cry or laugh. At least, not all the time. Certainly, there are many brands that have become great because they have helped us believe in ourselves, have uplifted us, or simply made us feel good. But "emotion" can also mean a myriad of other very different things, ranging from the user experience that Starbucks' cafés provide, to the kind of fun a visit to Disneyland guarantees, to the self-esteem and confidence an Armani suit delivers, to (and especially so) the reputation a B2B company will have developed over decades. These are the so-called intangibles of a brand.

To better understand and identify emotional connectors, one simply needs to look at great and successful brands: Banyan Tree—intimacy and romance; Nike—inspiration and empowerment; Harley Davidson—American authenticity and a sense of belonging; Vaio laptops—professional cool; The Body Shop—save the world; Virgin—fun, fairness, and anti-establishment; Tiger Balm—Asian authenticity and heritage. And the principle is equally applicable (and more so) to B2B companies: IBM—dependable reputation; Caterpillar—rugged, manly, and professional; Boeing—American know-how; GE—cutting-edge innovation. All these qualities are intangibles that are largely responsible for the lion's share of the decision-making process that prompts people to buy. All of them are unique and virtually impossible to copy. Only Apple can be Apple.

> *"Politicians need a way with words, appeal to the emotions of people and look good on television. . . . If you look cool, calculating all the time, and you can't appeal to the emotions of people . . . viewers say 'Yes, he makes sense, but I don't love him.'"*
>
> Singapore Minister Mentor, Lee Kuan Yew[10]

Why People Buy Apple

The Apple brand was originally built on a powerful emotional platform that celebrated the virtue of being different. That has not changed. Apple's focus on innovation and design only supported a broader vision that was embodied by Steve Jobs: to touch people's hearts, not just their minds. But Apple went further. From the very beginning, it demonstrated a corporate culture that deliberately zigged when everyone else (and in the early days, that meant Microsoft) zagged. And where it zigged, it didn't do so for its own sake—at the expense of substance. It created cutting-edge products with superb functional features across a gamut of categories that captivated its targeted customers (because Apple didn't want to be for everyone) and left them breathless and wanting more. Being different created a "community" where the need

Every time a new Apple product is launched, an event can almost always be expected.

Source: Getty Images.

"**iPad mania hits as global roll-out begins.** Thousands of fired up and sleep-deprived gadget fans mobbed shops in Australia and Japan Friday as Apple's iPad, touted as a revolution in computer use and publishing, began its international launch. A queue some 200 metres long stretched round the block at Apple's flagship central Sydney store, with similar scenes playing out in downtown Tokyo.... In Sydney, security guards had to quell pushing and shoving amongst the media as Mr. Rahul Koduri, who queued for some 30 hours from 2 A.M. Thursday, became the first to buy the touch-screen computer. 'It's fantastic, it was so worth the wait,' said the 22-year-old brandishing two iPad boxes after his long wait.... In Japan, more than 1,000 buyers lined up in front of Apple stores and outlets of its exclusive local partner, mobile phone carrier Softbank, along with big electrical shops. Mr. Kazuki Miura, a 38-year-old freelance technology writer, was the first in line at Softbank's main Tokyo store. Said Softbank president Masayoshi Son, at an in-store presentation: 'Now the time has come for us to hold an iPhone in the right (hand) and iPad in the left—just like the samurai with two swords!'" *Source: Weekend Today*, May 29–30, 2010 (AFP).

to belong provided Apple with its strongest emotional driver. In the process of building a different brand, Apple created a cult-like following.

Ask yourself: Which Asian company has demonstrated and committed to a long-term vision to create outrageously popular products that contribute to outpourings of human emotions that are normally associated with people, not things? Every time a new Apple product is launched, an event can almost always be expected. There is anxiety, excitement, anticipation, and even triumph when someone succeeds in being "the first" or "one of the few" among the throngs of excited early adopters who line up outside stores hours—sometimes days—before the official opening. This is the end-product of a commitment to create a great company—NOT to make money. We need more Asian CEO visionaries with this type of imaginative integrity and a genuine dream.

> The region is not short of companies crewed by highly capable individuals with the expertise and technology to create cutting-edge products of their own. What is missing, however, is the conceptual understanding that separates a product from a brand.

So, where is Asia's Apple? The region is not short of companies crewed by highly capable individuals with the expertise and technology to create cutting-edge products of their own. What is missing, however, is the conceptual understanding that separates a product from a brand. In a 2005 article that announced the launch of Creative Labs' ZenVision:M MP3 player and invoked market leader Apple, the CEO and chairman of Creative Labs, Sim Wong Hoo, flatly stated: "We are not satisfied with the number two slot. We believe that technology not fashion will win through."[11] Hundreds of thousands, and likely millions, of iPod (and iPhone and iPad) owners would disagree with him.

Emotion is a very, very powerful force. Earlier we described how even seemingly mundane products such as toothpaste can, in some measure, define us. The Coke brand provides a startlingly clear example of how a brand that some describe as just "sugary brown water" can galvanize people sufficiently to take extraordinary action, simply because of their emotional connection with the brand.

In 1985 the Coca-Cola Company introduced "New Coke." The launch of this new product eventually evolved into an unmitigated disaster and in the process delivered one of the decade's most significant new marketing insights. Why was it a disaster? And what was the key insight?

In the early 1980s, Coke found itself struggling to maintain its market share. Pepsi had followed up its highly aggressive "Pepsi Challenge" campaign by enlisting the endorsement of Michael Jackson, who was at the time at the height of his career and popularity. Pepsi was successfully developing a younger, hipper, and more sophisticated image than Coke. Already being trounced in domestic supermarket sales, Coke also began to look more vulnerable in fountain sales and the all-important foreign markets. Though the real problems that adversely affected the marketing of Coke were largely internal—systemic structural and management issues—CEO and chairman Roberto Goizueta chose to focus on another issue: its formula. He was convinced that, while the product was not the only source of Coke's lagging market share, changing it would return Coke to its rightful leadership position.

Blind tests carried out over the preceding years had consistently demonstrated significant consumer preference for Pepsi over Coke. This, so the legendary story goes, drove to distraction the tough Cuban-born American, who had long declared that there were "no sacred cows" at the Coca-Cola Company. He ordered his labs to experiment with different formulations until they found one that could consistently beat Pepsi—which they did. In very short order, a massive amount of research to test the new formula was undertaken in the US and abroad. The findings consistently indicated, in very strong terms, that consumers preferred it over Pepsi. With the product issue seemingly addressed, the major challenge that lay ahead was what to do with it. At stake was what essentially amounted to "a global symbol of America."[12]

Cognizant that they were dealing with an American icon, the second round of global research undertaken to probe how acceptable a "new" Coke might be to consumers, and in what configuration, was comprehensive in scale and scope and yet—astonishingly—failed to explore one key crucial question: "How would you feel if we took your Coke away?"[13]

By the time "New Coke" was finally unveiled at a press conference in New York City on April 23, 1985, leak of the big news had already reached Pepsi a few days earlier. Pepsi wasted no time in harnessing its own considerable resources to pre-empt the Coke event. It placed full-page ads that appeared on the morning of April 23 with a headline that screamed: "The other guy just blinked." It was an ominous and inauspicious start to an emerging public relations disaster that continued to accelerate in the days and weeks that followed.

In failing to ask consumers how they would feel if Coke suddenly disappeared not just from the market, but from their lives, Coca-Cola executives—and Goizueta, in particular—failed to realize just how fundamentally emotionally entrenched the brand had become, not just in the fabric of American culture, but in the lives of people from around the world. The reaction was as violent as it had been totally unexpected by the company. "Panic" and "pandemonium" were words used by the media to describe the reactions of some people. The announcement that Coke would disappear elicited feelings of sadness, and even despair and depression, across wide sections of the population in the US and abroad. To these people, the idea that something they had grown up with—that had been so much a part of so many experiences and represented so many emotions—would simply cease to exist was unfathomable: "I grew up with Coke . . ."; "While my father crawled the beaches of Normandy trying to save Europe, Coke was right there by his side. . ."; "Coke is part of the American dream. . . ."

The sheer ubiquity of the brand made its imminent absence incomprehensible. The outpouring was unprecedented: "When the taste change was announced, some consumers panicked, filling their basements with cases of Coke. Some people got depressed over the loss of their favorite soft drink. . . . Protest groups. . . . 1500 calls a day on the consumer hotline. . . . The marketing 'Blunder of the Century'. . . songs were written to honor the old taste. . . 'we want the Real Thing'. . . . 'our children will never know real refreshment. . . .'"[14]

Central to the Coca-Cola brand is the emotional relationship people have with the brand.

And all for what? A brown sugary drink? A soda pop? Central to the Coca-Cola brand is the emotional relationship people have with it. Such is the deep extent of this relationship that when it seemed that the brand might disappear, people reacted passionately.

So passionate was the reaction, so shocked were so many people—and from so many different countries—that New Coke (superior formulation and all) was eventually withdrawn and the "old" Coke returned to the shelves of supermarkets. Such is the strength of the emotional dimension this brand was able to command. The Coke experience demonstrates how potentially powerful emotional relationships can be for all brands.

And what was the significant marketing insight that emerged from this extraordinary confluence of events? Though still debated by marketers to this day, the New Coke experience revealed that companies arguably do not, in fact, "own" brands. Consumers do.

Sources of Emotional Dimensions

The brand blueprint (see Chapter 3) is the key critical frame of reference that allows the company to consider and make strategic decisions.
Within it are the drivers that propel the company forward and provide
it with energy and direction. Emotional dimensions may be found in any
one of several brand blueprint drivers, depending on the company—the
direction it has chosen to follow, and the business strategy it has formulated. Typically, they are manifested in any of four key drivers: core
brand benefits, core brand values, core brand personality traits, and the
company mission.

> *"I lived in Silicon Valley for over three decades. There is one guy
> I take a shine to more than anybody else . . . who has inhabited
> and helped form that Valley of Dramatic Dreams. Steve Jobs.
> Steve is . . . The One Who Really Made the Revolution Happen.
> His company, Apple, was the engine of all else that has followed.
> Here is my favorite Steve-ism:*
>   'Let's make a dent in the universe.'
>   *How sweet that is.*
>   *Most of us won't 'make a dent in the universe.' But . . . every
> one of us has this ability . . . we can at least try.*
>   *It's simple.*
>   *It's impossible.*
>   *It demands your attention.*
>   *Who are we?*
>   *Why are we here?*
>   *How are we unique?*
>   *How can we make a dramatic difference?*
>   *That is the Heart of Branding. Because Branding is ultimately
> about nothing more (and nothing less) than* Heart. *It's about
> Passion . . . what you Care About. . . . There is more to it (of
> course). But if you 'get' this part of BRANDING . . . then you've
> got its . . . HEART."*
>
> Tom Peters[15]

Core Brand Benefits as Emotional Dimensions

What a company "stands for" is always going to be separated by a thin
line that divides the functional from the emotional benefits. As discussed
earlier, companies would do well to limit their core characteristics
(benefits, values, personalities, and attributes) to a small, manageable

number that employees are able to embrace and deliver on. Fewer characteristics that are well delivered are better than many that are badly delivered. Fewer benefits that are consistently better delivered also can, in time, add up to a signature characteristic (e.g. 3M = innovation).

Core benefits should preferably not exceed four in number. Based on their circumstances, which are specific and unique to them (influenced by their core business, business strategy, and vision), companies need to consider and decide carefully which benefits should be functional and which should be emotional. To many people, the core benefits Apple provides are "enduring cool" and "innovation" (and to many others, a sense of "belonging"); Volvo is synonymous with safety, but also with a certain level of luxury; Franck Muller watches offer design and contemporary high luxury, whereas Tag Heuer might perhaps be more synonymous with sporty luxury. The core benefits of Toyota— notwithstanding the unprecedented recalls in 2010—have little to do with luxury (at least of the type one might associate with Lexus or BMW, and certainly with higher pedigrees of the likes of Ferrari). What customers have expected and experienced from Toyota for decades is reliability and value for money. Both functional and emotional dimensions are to be found in all of the core benefits listed above. The balance of what and how much will always be a critical consideration that will, of course, vary from company to company, and brand to brand.

Core Brand Values as Emotional Dimensions

"We intuitively knew that a successful brand was not only about specific product or service features, but about evoking emotional responses from our customers. Through the Banyan Tree experience, which sought to evoke romance and intimacy, we saw ourselves as the facilitators of very memorable and meaningful experiences for our guests. We felt that if we were able to elicit an emotional response from them towards us, it will always remain top of mind, and gives us the advantage of brand loyalty."

Ho Kwon Ping, Executive Chairman, Banyan
Tree Holdings Limited[16]

A great deal has already been said here about the importance of core values. It is manifestly self-evident that a core belief of a company can impact people (both customers and employees) emotionally. As the world becomes a more complex and more endangered place, core brand values are certain to become more relevant leading edges of strong brand identities. This is an important insight that is likely to influence not only the positioning of Asian brands, but also the destinies of many Asian companies moving forward—at least those that recognize the importance and opportunity that exists in plain sight.

Core Brand Personality Traits as Emotional Dimensions

Trailing not far behind core values are brand personality traits—which may surprise many Asian CEOs who may not really understand or care what personality their company or brands have, as long as they sell. When the CEO of Creative Labs, Sim Wong Hoo, stated that "technology not fashion will win through,"[17] he was presumably referring to Apple. It is reasonable to interpret that he meant "fad" when he referred to "fashion." Apple's key strength lies in its emotional appeal, which is hard-wired into the brand. It is classically cool to own and be seen to have an Apple product. Much of that coolness is the direct result of the Apple brand personality. It is young, vibrant, smart, and to some degree, fun. This is neither fad nor fashion.

Virgin, discussed in an earlier chapter, is one of the most brand personality-driven brands on the planet. All Virgin company brands are very clearly defined by the brand's personality (irreverent, fun, provocative, and daring), which is embodied by the personality of its founder, Sir Richard Branson.

> Eventually, all functional benefits can be copied or replicated in one form or another. Brand personality and brand values cannot.

Brand personality delivers the very powerful likeability and trust drivers. Eventually, all functional benefits can be copied or replicated in one form or another. Brand personality and brand values cannot.

The Company Mission as an Emotional Dimension

Like core values, the role of the company mission was discussed in some detail in Chapter 4. It is mentioned again in this context because "purpose" intrinsically owns a high degree of emotional drive. The more compelling is a company's purpose, the more likely it is to move people emotionally. There is a reassuring sense of simplicity and purity in a statement like Disney's "To make people happy." The more socially

The Virgin brand personality

Source: Getty Images.

relevant is the purpose of the company, the more emotional are the relationships with customers likely to be.

Summary

Emotional dimensions in brands are very powerful drivers. They have the capability to move people and, therefore, to trigger action. And, as one might expect, there is a direct correlation between benefit and degree of difficulty. In other words, emotional drivers are as powerful as they are difficult to create (and maintain). They are part CEO vision, part company DNA, and part internal culture. The common denominator that links all three is a brand blueprint's "brand truths." Brand truths are not declarations of "we are the best," or fabricated slogans that mean little to the very people you want to connect with the most—your customers. Rather, they are expressions of "who" your company really is, made to a target audience that is actually willing and wanting to listen. And "who" your company really is goes far beyond the widgets it manufactures.

FOCUSED TARGET AUDIENCE

Almost all great brands recognize the implausibility of a focused, single brand proposition appealing in equal measure across people of different ages, lifestyles, and socio-economic backgrounds. It just doesn't make sense. Still, this obvious fact doesn't seem to prevent most Asian CEOs from going after every single possible candidate customer in an effort to maximize revenues. Too many brands in Asia are hell-bent on corralling as many people as possible, on the assumption that more people means more sales. This is flawed thinking. The irony is that less is often more.

> The combination of a specific brand positioning coupled to a specific customer promise makes a specific appeal that can only resonate with specific types of people. . . .

Brand propositions, by definition, are unique—at least, those that are well crafted. A specific brand positioning coupled with a specific customer promise makes a specific appeal that can only resonate with specific types of people who, in turn, form specific groups. Hence, the term target audiences. What characterizes target audiences is the fact that each is different from the next. There is nothing more elementary than the phrase "people are different." Yet, Asian business decision makers continue to treat not only specific markets, but often the whole region, as if it is populated by entirely homogenous tribes of people. Not only has this rarely been the case, but we are witnessing today increasing fragmentation of population groups as a side-effect of accelerated globalization which is encouraging not just movements of people across geographies on a massive scale, but also the integration of different cultures, value systems, and beliefs as these people meet, form friendships, cohabitate, or marry. The people landscape in Asia has never been more dynamic and fluid than it is today. And this is only going to increase in the near and long-term future. The importance of understanding the needs, expectations, and desires of these different customer groups (and the increasing number of sub-groups that are emerging) has never been more crucial in an environment that is not only becoming much more complex, but also more competitive, than ever. Observes Nichola Rastrick, managing director of Millward Brown Singapore: "The consumer does not sit at the [company] table." This highlights a key critical roadblock: Asian management's poor attitude to research continues to undermine clear understanding of category trends and consumer needs (as well as their unmet needs). This results in a relative absence of insights, which, in turn, minimizes the exploration of new ideas. Ultimately and inevitably, the window of opportunities that are open to Asian companies—particularly SMEs—tends to be smaller. What is even more troubling is that most CEOs are not even aware of this. It is yet another example of CEOs not knowing what they don't know.

According to Rastrick, "Research is almost exclusively seen by [Asian] CEOs as a lot of money that impacts the bottom line, rather than as an investment that is going to build the company. There is a general resistance to risk that is off-set by an innate belief that they know anyway what research will likely tell them—so why spend the money? The biggest client-related challenge research companies face in Asia is client education: what research can do and deliver to a company. It's a battle we fight every day, and the irony is we have to fight to persuade them to do something that should be obvious—something that will profoundly benefit their companies."

Target segmentation provides the company with several important benefits. First, it identifies the universe of customers to which a company can potentially appeal. When we first explored the luxury watch market in Asia and asked senior executives, including the CEO, of a leading watch retail company who they thought their customers were, the answer was consistent across the board: "people who buy watches." By the time we had completed a comprehensive four-market brand audit, we had identified a watch universe with no fewer than seven very distinct target audiences (see Figure 5.3).[18]

Figure 5.3 The retail watch category in Asia

Research undertaken during the course of a comprehensive branding project in 2006 revealed that the luxury watch category in Asia was made up of at least seven separate and distinct target customer segments, each reflecting different and diverse customer needs, expectations, and desires. The seven segments are identified below, along with visual mood boards that provide a pictorial representation of the personality of each segment. To demonstrate the kind of essential customer information companies need to make informed decisions about their overall strategic positioning and marketing, one segment is revealed—"Privileged Ladies of Leisure"—complete with visual mood board and "Y" analysis.

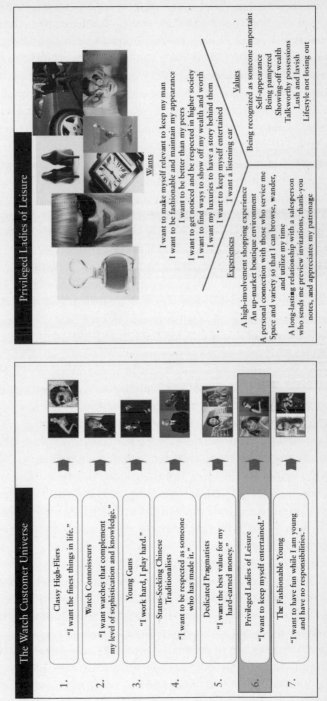

The Watch Customer Universe

1. Classy High-Fliers
   "I want the finest things in life."

2. Watch Connoisseurs
   "I want watches that complement my level of sophistication and knowledge."

3. Young Guns
   "I work hard, I play hard."

4. Status-Seeking Chinese Traditionalists
   "I want to be respected as someone who has made it."

5. Dedicated Pragmatists
   "I want the best value for my hard-earned money."

6. Privileged Ladies of Leisure
   "I want to keep myself entertained."

7. The Fashionable Young
   "I want to have fun while I am young and have no responsibilities."

Privileged Ladies of Leisure

Wants

I want to make myself relevant to keep my man
I want to be fashionable and maintain my appearance
I want to be better than my peers
I want to get noticed and be respected in higher society
I want to find ways to show off my wealth and worth
I want my luxuries to have a story behind them
I want to keep myself entertained
I want a listening ear

Experiences

A high-involvement shopping experience
An up-market boutique environment
A personal connection with those who service me
Space and variety so that I can browse, wander, and utilize my time
A long-lasting relationship with a salesperson who sends me preview invitations, thank-you notes, and appreciates my patronage

Values

Being recognized as someone important
Self-appearance
Being pampered
Showing-off wealth
Talkworthy possessions
Lush and lavish
Lifestyle not losing out

Secondly, segmented customer groups provide key insights about habits, needs, and preferences, as well as other lifestyle cues. This information is invaluable in determining everything from unmet customer needs to what merchandise to stock, to what kind of communications to use in advertising and promotions.

> "Who, specifically—in terms of customers—will help the company deliver its strategic goals?"

Thirdly, and most importantly, target segmentation is a process that examines and identifies which segments are most important to the company in a strategic sense. If a company embarks on a process that defines or redefines its positioning, its core benefits and values, as well as its purpose and vision, the major question it will need to answer is: "Who, specifically—in terms of customers—will help the company deliver its strategic goals?" The answer translates to a task that amounts to an alignment of the company's brand blueprint to its optimal target segments. Some complexity enters the equation when companies are forced to make customer segment considerations based not only on opportunities in the present, but also—by virtue of their articulated vision—those that may emerge in the future.

A typical branding project should comprehensively identify a company's existing customers and then proceed to allocate these to the segments the broader market audit will have revealed. More often than not, companies discover that their existing customers tend to be spread across several, sometimes very disparate, segments. They also discover that their efforts and resources need to be spread equally disparately. This is typically a first sign of inefficiency that company planners need to recognize.

The process of identifying and better understanding a brand's universe of customer segments always proves to be daunting and challenging, because difficult choices will ultimately need to be made. The reconfiguration of a company's essence through its new brand blueprint dictates a specific direction in terms of identity and core benefits. That direction may not necessarily appeal to some—and, in some cases, even the majority—of a company's existing customer base. It is understandable, therefore, that CEOs are often reluctant to reconfigure their businesses' infrastructures if it means risking existing revenue streams. But within this equation lies an important point that these CEOs often lose sight of: Many companies that reposition themselves do so from a position of weakness. In other words, business is bad. These companies are operating in declining trajectories that require some form of major surgery if they are to survive and re-emerge as different and successful companies. Sometimes this means experiencing more pain before the situation improves. It may require consciously moving away from existing target segments that, although may be delivering existing revenue streams, don't promise long-term sustainable growth and profitability. These are the sorts of gut-wrenching decisions that separate "leaders" from "managers."

However, as inferred above, not all companies rebrand from a position of weakness. There are those that may be performing well enough, but where, for one reason or another, the CEO and senior management realize that the company can do much better. This situation characterizes the present and potential future of the vast multitude of Asian companies. Presently, most are performing and most are making money. But the exciting reality is that they could be performing infinitely better, and they are capable of making infinitely more money.

The last category of companies comprises those start-ups that brand themselves properly from the outset. These companies wisely go through formal branding projects for the simplest and most sensible of reasons: to create the best possible road map that will deliver their goals and objectives—from the get go.

Strategic Segmentation versus Tactical Segmentation

Strategic segmentation is BIG-picture segmentation that contributes to and reinforces the definition of the company or product brand. BMW is not positioned for everyone. Most people have a mental picture of the "type" of drivers BMW owners tend to be. This mental picture doesn't exist by accident. It is part of the (fixed) strategic positioning BMW has created for itself. This, however, neither limits the company from targeting a wider range of people, nor prevents people from very different segment groups buying BMW cars. The reason for this is that the brand is aspirational.

If BMW is (strategically) all about 29 to 35-plus year-olds from high-powered, well-remunerated professional backgrounds, with a taste for sporty chic and glamor, the brand's tactical segmentation strategy allows for a much broader demographic group to anchor its overall customer franchise. This is typically done at the advertising level.

Well-conceived and well-crafted communication strategies identify user groups that may be separated by profession, age, lifestyle, and geographies by crafting tailor-made communications that speak directly to them—as long as the message not only does not undermine the strategic target segment definition, but in fact reinforces it. In this way, BMW is able to pursue several (though not all) different female demographic and psychographic segments in places like Idaho, as well as married men from different segments in, say, Florida, as well as emerging affluents in Shanghai and Mumbai. While the advertising will need to tailor make creative executions that directly resonate with these different groups, all will need to reinforce the brand's positioning, which includes its broader strategic (and aspirational) target audience segment definition. For the sake of avoiding confusion, it is useful to say again that several does not mean all segments. Tactical segmentation needs to be tackled carefully. Intelligently implemented, it will stretch the reach of a brand. But there is a limit to elasticity. When stretched too much, the brand suffers.

Tactical segmentation is also very common with brands (usually packaged goods) that adopt a usage-based approach to marketing. One well-known brand of detergent may have a long history and high awareness—and therefore high usage—in one specific market, but be relatively unknown in another, where usage and familiarity with its attributes and benefits will be lower. This situation is typically addressed by creating different advertising executions for different markets—one reinforcing benefits familiar to consumers, the second educating new consumers to the benefits. Once again, there is a caveat: Both efforts will need to share one common characteristic—consistency with the broader strategic positioning.

Not all companies are either capable of or willing to manage the strategic/tactical segmentation relationships properly or consistently; not in the West, and especially not in Asia. As discussed in Chapter 2, Asian CEO attitudes to branding, advertising, and advertising agencies, as well as how agencies accommodate them, must bear a great deal of the responsibility for this.

Summary

In Asia, it is more common for CEOs to aim for mass consumer appeal, rather than to identify and aim for more focused and efficient target customer groups. Part of the reason for this is an overall antipathy to market research in general, as well as to specific research into areas such as customer target segmentation. Much of this aversion is related to a perception that it is an exercise that is too conceptual and intangible on the one hand, and too expensive on the other. Overall, particularly among SMEs, research is perceived as a cost that affects the bottom line in the here and now, rather than as an investment that will build the company in the future.

Strategic target audience segmentation doesn't dictate that the company should limit itself to a single group of customers. While it is essential that a company identify and strengthen its brand's primary audience and always be cognizant of the importance and primacy of that group, it is entirely possible (and sometimes essential) for the brand to have supporting and complementary secondary, and sometimes tertiary, strategic target segment groups as well. Once management has agreed which target segments to focus on, it is vital that all stakeholders in the company be aware of them. This will ensure that efforts are not undermined or cancelled out in home and foreign markets, and, most importantly, that these segments are reflected properly in communication efforts by advertising agencies who must be reminded to work within the strategic umbrellas of their assigned brands.

ABILITY TO INNOVATE AND STAY RELEVANT

"Any time there is change, there is opportunity.
So it is paramount that an organization get energized
rather than paralyzed."

Jack Welch, former CEO, General Electric

The premise of this book is that brand and branding must emerge as the strategic leading-edge drivers of the 21st-century Asian company. There is, however, one other powerful driver sharing almost equal importance: innovation. And it is in this area that Asian companies are so visibly wanting. The ability to move quickly and nimbly—an increasingly powerful hallmark of strong Asian companies—will not make up for the essential equal need to think and act differently. World Intellectual Property Organization figures record only 3,882 patent applications originating from India in 2007, 160,523 from China compared to 409,952 from the United States.[19] In a *BusinessWeek* cover feature, Dexter Roberts explores China's power brands and concludes that the "mediocre record of Chinese companies in innovation is a liability. It's rare for Chinese companies to meet the international norm of spending 5% or more of revenues on research and development."[20]

Unless Asian companies learn to think—and act—disruptively; unless they are able to invoke more creativity into the products and services they make; unless they are willing to adapt their internal processes to better deliver their offerings to customers; unless they succeed in influencing internal culture by encouraging employees to think freely and openly with no shadow of risk or penalty—Asian companies will struggle to deliver on the great promise that political commentators such as Kishore Mahbubani and others are predicting: the great rise of Asia and the "irresistible shift" of power to the East in the 21st century.[21]

It is extremely tempting, not to mention fashionable, to look at the aggressive ascents of China, Singapore, Taiwan, and Korea, among other countries in Asia, and declare that a new world order is imminent. To be sure, the indicators are there. The shift may well be inexorable, so it is no longer a question of "if" but "when." But the signs are trending to later, rather than sooner. And a lot of it can be traced to the famous or notorious (deserved or not) Asian resistance to change.

There exists a relationship between change and innovation. If resistance to the former exists, the latter will be affected. As change is taking place all the time and at high rates of velocity, companies wanting to keep up must create mechanisms built into their cultures that automatically trigger responsive behavior to new developments—either to exploit them or defend against them. The inability or unwillingness of any organization to react to the disruptive type of change that is taking place every day will, in time, render it irrelevant. Beyond irrelevance lies stagnation and, ultimately, extinction. It is that simple.

While change is a major catalyst for innovation, it doesn't constitute its sole source. Beyond responding to external forces, an organization must embrace a culture that seeks to rejuvenate itself in order to stay fresh, vital, and, ultimately, competitive.

> *"If you don't like change, you're going to like irrelevance even less."*
>
> General Eric Shinseki, US Army

Although Asian CEOs use the term "innovation" on a regular basis, most of them will admit to struggling with the concept, finding it mysterious and daunting. Consequently, across the board, innovation remains an area that is relatively under-explored and under-exploited by most companies in Asia—and particularly by SMEs.

Five Factors that Discourage Innovation

Why is there such a relative paucity of innovation in the region, compared to in the West? With the exception of companies such as Infosys, Samsung, and Taiwanese phone maker HTC—and many more, of course, from Japan—Chinese and other Asian companies are doing an abysmal job of creating, mostly because they are still spending too much time either replicating or outright copying. Is it a lack of creativity, or of competence, or of confidence? In their book *Inspire to Innovate*, De Meyer and Garg suggest the latter, describing many Asian CEOs as having an "underdog mentality" that triggers vicious cycles within Asian organizations that end up convincing management that their companies don't have "sufficient capabilities to innovate."[22] In their book, they go further and invoke a term that Mahbubani coined in his own book, *Can Asians Think?*: "mental colonization." This term refers to the efforts many Asian companies make to come across as more Western, lest their Asian pedigree prove to be a liability. This, many hold, is a legacy of the region's former colonization by Europeans.

In his latest book, Mahbubani revisits the subject of Asians and "thinking," but from a more specific Chinese context. He states that as far as the "freedom to think . . . Chinese society may appear to be at a disadvantage: China remains a politically closed society." He goes on to explain cryptically that there exists in the minds of the Chinese a distinction between the freedom to think and the freedom of expression (unlike Westerners, who "see these two freedoms as two sides of one coin").[23] Although he doesn't explain what that distinction actually amounts to, Mahbubani concedes that, like its cousin, "freedom of expression remains limited."[24] Though the point he tries to make is unclear and his context is political, one reasonable interpretation is that the Chinese are either prohibited or discouraged from expressing themselves. This prohibition manifests in everyday life in China—including in business. It has also migrated out to most Asian societies, where it has found expression (no pun intended) within modern Asian companies and emerged as a cultural characteristic of the region.

> . . . innovation cannot take shape when people are unwilling to engage.

Whether because of the psychological traumas Asians have endured through colonization, or their inability or unwillingness (or prohibition) to express themselves, innovation cannot take shape when people are unwilling to engage. This is part of the reason why most Asian companies default to a business strategy that uses or combines competitive pricing with rapid replication (sometimes with some modifications or new features). As already mentioned, too many Asian CEOs eschew research in general, and customer research in particular. It is difficult to innovate when you are unwilling to better understand your own market or listen to your customers.

Secondly, there exists a genuine dearth of sophisticated marketing experience and expertise within Asian companies. Anachronistic practices and philosophies adhered to by CEOs are being blindly adopted by lower-rank managers who themselves lack critical skill sets. Thirdly, the practice by some governments of giving preferential treatment to local companies (resulting in unfair competitive advantages) has discouraged investment and effort being put into innovation. Fourthly, the continued widespread disregard of intellectual property protection (particularly in China) has also played its part in discouraging innovation investment.[25] A final, and perhaps most damaging, cause is CEO mentality. The circumstances that most CEOs create in their companies simply inhibit innovative thinking. Such circumstances range from narrowly defined job descriptions that prevent or discourage interaction among employees from different functional departments, to truly medieval policies that penalize employees who volunteer an idea or suggest an initiative that, for one reason or another, fails to deliver.

Whatever the problem or the source, the future generation of Asian CEOs will need to overcome the barriers that are arresting innovation within their organizations. Further, they will need to demonstrate a comprehensive understanding of the different types and manifestations of innovation, as well as how to nurture and weave them into the fabric of their companies' culture. Present perceptions are limited to the narrow band of newer, better products and services (through better technology and control of costs) that traditionally come from bigger investments in research and development. While this is one important area of innovation, it is not the only one. For progressive Asian companies, innovation might be expressed through newer, better, more disruptive processes, systems, and business models. In 2000, after physically separating its OEM (original equipment manufacturer) business from the Acer consumer brand name, Acer made a "counter-intuitive" decision. At a time when Dell dominated the landscape by selling desktops direct to business clients, Acer zagged and went the other way; betting that the market would turn, which it eventually did, it focused on selling laptops through partners and retailers.[26]

Another, perhaps more significant source of innovation might prove to be even more challenging to CEOs: adopting different management philosophies and mindsets. One powerful example of this is the willingness of companies to share more strategic information with more employees, and a larger willingness to empower more employees with increasing levels of trust and authority. During a visit to the 3M headquarters in Singapore, labor chief Lim Swee Say commented on the pressing importance of innovation and how it would directly impact the nation's declared goal of dramatically increasing productivity. He pointedly debunked the persistent myth that only engineers and technologists could deliver innovation, and rhetorically asked whether it could include "the people in sales and marketing, the people involved as rank-and-file workers." He added: "Anyone can innovate so long as the right processes and support are in place."[27]

Summary

CEOs need to demonstrate leadership. Innovation cannot be delegated to others in the company or farmed out to external consultants.

The non-stop dynamic nature of modern-day relentless change requires innovation from companies if they are going to survive. Managers wonder out loud: "How can we innovate?" "Which consultants should we appoint?" "How much money do we need to spend?" They are asking the wrong questions, and they are looking in the wrong places. They need to begin by looking *inside* their companies and addressing themselves to five key issues:

1. CEOs need to demonstrate leadership. Innovation cannot be delegated to others in the company or farmed out to external consultants.

2. CEOs need to take greater risks. They should start by placing more trust in their employees.

3. CEOs need to encourage and engender an internal culture of learning and creativity. Talking about it, and pressing their employees to deliver it, will not be enough. CEOs will need to initiate and approve implementation plans that involve concrete action.

4. CEOs themselves, therefore, need to be more creative in their approach to innovation. They could, for instance, introduce new subjective metrics for performance appraisals of employees, such as "creativity" and "idea generation." This would include convincing their employees that they will not be penalized if they experiment and fail.

5. CEOs need to reconfigure their management philosophies. They could start by encouraging employees from different functional departments to communicate more and cross-pollinate in a manner that is more effective and, most importantly, more creative.

What will separate the future Asian corporate landscape from the present one will be—in the words of a brand that embodies innovation—the willingness to "think different."[28] And leading this effort personally, and from the front lines, will be the CEO.

CEO INVOLVEMENT AND LEADERSHIP

Chapter 2 pulled no punches and identified what I believe are some real shortcomings and personal challenges many Asian CEOs need to recognize and deal with if they are intent on building great brands and great companies. To the CEOs who are reading this book, I would like here to speak to you directly and bluntly, but with respect. I am going to tell you what I think you need to hear, not what you want to hear, or what a lot of people around you will tell you because they think that it is what you want to hear. Too much of that happens in business in Asia every day, and if you don't feel patronized by that and actually welcome it then you might as well toss this book into the nearest trash-can.

As far as building great brands is concerned, Asian CEOs are their own worst enemies. They are faced with three major obstacles that the facts show they are simply unable to overcome:

(a) Lack of knowledge;

(b) Misconceptions about branding, and therefore about what is needed;

(c) An abundance of providers willing to exploit (a) and (b).

The combination of lack of knowledge of and misconceptions about branding creates a particularly high hurdle that can trip up almost everyone who gets involved, which is one reason why middle managers rarely speak up or contradict their CEO. The issue of "face" almost always gets in the way. Trying to explain what branding is, and what a strong brand is capable of delivering, to a tough-minded chief executive who has fixed ideas about what he wants in a branding project (and what he is prepared to pay) has a very low chance of succeeding. Almost invariably, the CEO's interpretation of what the consultant is saying is: "You are clueless." From that point on, it doesn't matter a whit how cogent the consultant's argument is, or how diplomatically the message is communicated; there is no going forward. It is therefore paradoxical that these same CEOs are often susceptible to less-professional providers who play to these characteristics and simply promise to deliver whatever the CEO expects (particularly on the price point). In most cases, this results in a complete waste of effort and resources. It goes without saying that the brand the company is intent on building never gets built properly.

CEOs who are aiming to capitalize on the unprecedented opportunities this century is offering Asian companies will need to recognize this weakness in themselves and deal with it in one way or another. This book is aimed at the CEO who wants to know what he or she doesn't know, in order to know where changes need to be made. Now, I am far from being an oracle of knowledge or wisdom, but I do know a few valuable things about the relationship between branding and CEOs. This is what I will share with you.

To be brutally honest, most of you are clueless. As brilliant an entrepreneur as you are, as ambitious and hard-working as you may be, you may still have no real clue about brands and branding, and about their role within your organization. More to the point, you may have no understanding of the real benefits that branding can deliver to your business. My intent in saying the above is not to offend; rather, it is to shake up some people and make them aware of a condition that should *not* exist. The redeeming aspect of this condition—if it is of any consolation—is that you don't know that you don't have a clue. The question is: Are you willing to listen?

I will try to temper what many will argue are generalizations by relating an actual case study that is currently taking place in one particular Asian market. What I am about to describe is like a scene from a play I have seen a dozen times. What this particular company is doing is happening every day in other boardrooms in many Asian cities, despite the absurdities that will become quickly apparent as I relate the story. The full picture is simply not visible to the protagonists in this particular story—the directors and senior executives who are participating in it in real time—just as they are not apparent to other companies behaving in very similar ways every day in other parts of the region. From the outside, however—that is, from your vantage point as a reader— the view should be quite revealing.

A Case Study

This story is about an organization that approached us for what was identified as a "branding project." Our first meeting brought us face to face with five capable and smart senior executives, including the president. They explained in broad-stroke terms what the vision of the project was and how it would physically roll out. Our contribution—which is always more or less the same with first meetings like this one—was to ask several key, probing questions designed to reveal whether the decision makers we would be dealing with had a clear understanding of the challenges they would likely face, and the opportunities from which they might benefit. Often, clients focus only on the latter. Our objective is to look for real red flags; "real" in the sense of those things that might compromise the integrity of the project or even paralyze it, either before or once it was underway. Typically, these manifest as a wrong mindset, unreasonable demands, and unrealistic expectations. We consider that a meeting has been successful when either no red flags emerge, or the other people at the table recognize and acknowledge them as such and begin to experience small revelations or even epiphanies that persuade them that their original expectations might need some reconsideration.

We reached a point in this particular meeting where it was clear to everybody in the room that this project faced far more critical challenges than had been originally anticipated and planned for. Digging further, we also came up with our first potential red flag: their Board of Directors. Everyone in the company, including the president, effectively reported to the Board. And as we explained the kind of strategic permutations a project like theirs would likely need to address, they knew instantly that their Board would not relate and would opt instead for the low road that offered short-cuts and compromises. And to their credit, they told us so. Red flag confirmed.

We did not have a second meeting. Instead, via a telephone call, we— along with four other consultancies—were invited to present a "proposal" to the Board of Directors who (a) were not willing to meet with us to answer key questions that would shape the scope and scale of the proposal, and (b) had specified that presentations should take no more than 15 minutes. It wasn't difficult to decline the invitation, and I will explain below why we did so.

The typical Asian CEO that I have identified in this book is replaced, in this particular story, by the Board of Directors. The difference isn't particularly material, because the subject at issue is the authority and power to make (bad) decisions that end up having (worse) consequences. This story takes place in the medical/health, as well as hospitality, categories. This is a significant variable on its own, and the reason why will also become apparent.

The company that approached us is an organization that was cobbled together by an entrepreneurial group of doctors who saw—to their credit—a potentially significant opportunity in integrating the services of three distinct entities—a hospital, a medical center, and a hotel—that would all be physically connected to one another in the same locality and offer integrated services. They would, together, service the needs of "customers" at home and from abroad who would require medical treatment as well as hotel accommodation while being treated. This is a multimillion-dollar enterprise with construction that has already broken ground (as of 2010) and an aggressive estimated date of completion of only a handful of years away.

The first briefing with the organization was revealing. The five senior executives we met with presented us with a snapshot of the "big picture." And in spite of the major investment already made and yet to come, a great number of the details had simply not yet been considered or identified. The executives candidly admitted that no business strategy of any substance existed. The "big idea" was restricted to: (a) a commitment to build three operating units: the hospital, the medical center, and the hotel; and (b) a public launch of the overarching corporate (brand) name that had already been created for the project. The mention of "brand names" provided us with our first opportunity to identify for them some of the complexities (and important strategic choices) that lay ahead. Did they realize that, given the default circumstances, the corporate brand name was playing the role of "master brand"? "No," they replied. Did they know what a master brand was? Again, the answer was "no." Had the Board of Directors realized, or made allowance for, any of this? "Absolutely not," was the instant reply. Red flag. What kind of relationship did the business strategy suggest the brands should share? Blank stares. Another red flag.

And it is at this point that the brief literally ends and the requirement is stated: quite simply, "brand this organization." This would have been a straightforward exercise had we been provided with a brief containing comprehensive details of the role and goals of the master brand and the three individual businesses, and of how all four elements would need to relate to one another. But we were not given those details, quite simply because none of these issues had been considered. Yet, the expectation was to launch a "branding project." I asked the president, quite seriously: "Brand *what*—exactly?" My question was critical in terms of the issues raised by and the implications of the project. The "vision" as expressed in the company's otherwise impressive website is longwinded and provides little hint of what might differentiate the concept beyond merely being a hospital, medical center, and hotel in physical proximity to one another. The absence of a mission statement also precludes any reasonable speculation over the purpose the investors might have had in mind in creating an integrated operation in the first place.

The issues

Was the idea to build three separate businesses or one integrated concept (from a branding point of view)? The question is not as easy to answer as one might think, because the effort and costs involved in building one master brand differ significantly from those involved in building four separate brands: the hospital brand, the medical center brand, the hotel brand, and the umbrella master brand. Expressed differently, and notwithstanding the fact that the three operating units already had their own brand names, was the intention to build a business based on the Virgin model or the Procter & Gamble model?

The implications of one brand versus multiple brands

The first obvious and very major implication was the probable need to build not one, but multiple brands. This effectively meant four separate brand blueprints: one for each of the operating units, and one for the master brand. This, in turn, comes close to meaning multiple branding projects (or a multi-faceted major single project)—not the straightforward, rapid effort that had been the expectation of the executives we met with and, no doubt, of the Board of Directors as well. While the market audit for the hospital and medical center could arguably have been combined to reduce effort and investment, the hotel lies in a separate category and would require its own audit. And all audits would involve primary and secondary research of some kind to assess the market landscape in terms of growth and opportunities, analysis of "customers" (their needs, desires, and expectations), and analysis of competitors (in both the medical and hospitality sectors). Beyond the data collection was the analysis and the essential workshops that would use the synthesis of the analysis to construct the basis of the multiple brand blueprints that would eventually be crafted. This methodology is not only standard for building brands (particularly those that are created from scratch), but the need for it is—or should be—self-evident if considered from a logical perspective. It was clear that the Board of Directors lacked that perspective.

Impacting further on how all of the above would be conducted was the central critical question of brand architecture, as alluded to earlier. So, I asked my question again: "Brand *what*—exactly?" The executives had no answer. They also clearly indicated that the Board was not aware of the issues and implications we had identified, and was unlikely to engage in any exercise aimed at addressing them. Big red flag.

When the phone call came to invite our company to present a proposal, I was advised—as mentioned earlier—that we would have only 15 minutes to present a proposal that theoretically would influence the destiny of a multimillion-dollar project. Fifteen minutes to provide a comprehensive overview of the proposed activity on four separate brands, plus an explanation for the recommendations, plus a further explanation for the costs involved—all of these involving line-by-line items. Fifteen minutes to then introduce (briefly, of course) the concept of brand architecture and explain the likely options for the portfolio of brands they planned to create. Lastly, fifteen minutes to then introduce the concept of "internal alignment" (see Chapter 7), which is really about implementation and execution—what separates strong planning from failure.

It was clearly unrealistic to expect us to do all of the above in the time allocated. But that wasn't even the issue. The most problematic issue was that the members of the Board didn't have a clue about what lay ahead in terms of building a strong brand for the business they had in mind. If they did, common sense alone suggests that they would have acted very differently. But they thought they knew, and we were told they would not entertain any suggestions that deviated from the course they had embarked on.

So, rather than be part of a train wreck, we withdrew.

The project will go ahead

Consider this further probability. Our decision to withdraw will likely make no material impact on the process. What do I mean by this? There will always be a provider willing to deliver whatever it is that the client wants. And when the client doesn't have a clue, that is easy to do; the provider will just make up stuff. In this case, my experience suggests that a provider will quickly recognize what the Board is looking for, which I suspect is a visual corporate identity: a bunch of logos, designs for ads and promotional materials, and a media plan, all concocted by the provider and centered on a message that involves a "big idea." The idea will probably have some glamor or reflect some important but generic insight that will please the Board. And all of this will come in on budget (minuscule relative to carrying out an effective branding effort, but about right for a cosmetic veneer).

This is a story that won't have a happy ending. The budgeted cost will result in one ironic outcome: "output" that won't serve the needs either of the company or of its four brands. In fact, the "recommendations" made by the provider may well damage the brands in some measure in the longer term. So, the entire investment will not just be wasted, but may well result in a negative outcome. In effect, no action would have been more prudent—not only from a cost point of view, but also, more importantly, from a brand point of view.

The Bottom Line

As visible as the absurdities are, they remain invisible to the protagonists of this and hundreds of other similar stories taking place all over Asia on an ongoing basis. This is no way to build great Asian brands. Things need to improve, but this will involve management being willing to change their mindset. And for that to happen, the CEO will need to involve himself—completely, totally, and with an open mind.

> You are, as CEO, the main protagonist in your own brand story.

You are, as CEO, the main protagonist in your own brand story. You are central to the creation and maintenance of what should be a great—not merely a good—brand. If you don't champion it, your employees won't support it and customers won't buy it. You must not delegate or abdicate this responsibility, which is entirely yours. A great brand and a great company starts with your simple realization that (a) your brand is everything, and (b) you must be the catalyst for leading the process that builds it.

You must lead, and that means you will need to embody the brand. You must be the:

- Chief brand strategist
- Chief brand catalyst and evangelist
- Chief brand ambassador
- Chief integrator of brand and business strategy.

The championing of the brand by the CEO means getting up on a soapbox and evangelizing, in a genuine and sincere way, about the virtues of the brand to external audiences (customers) as well as internal stakeholders (employees). The former chairman and chief executive of Disney, Michael Eisner, publicly declared: "We all know that the Disney brand is our most valuable asset. It is the sum total of our seventy-five years in business, of our reputation, of everything that we stand for."[29] To him, there was nothing more important and more sacred than the Disney brand.

You must believe in the brand—and belive that, in a fundamental way, it represents the destiny of your company. It is only when this happens that the right kind of policies (aligned to the brand)—ranging from organizational structure to people management to marketing—will emerge. It is also only when that happens—when you believe—that execution takes place and things get done. Nothing happens—especially in Asia—unless you sign off on it.

There is no shortage of brand and branding seminars, workshops, and conferences in most markets in Asia that provide education and insights that can help a company like yours begin to recognize and exploit the benefits of a strong brand. Having delivered papers at dozens of these events myself, it is a source of concern to me that only about 5–9 percent of those who attend are senior managers, 90 percent are middle and lower managers, and less than 1 percent are people like you—the CEOs. The vital messages that are being shared at these conferences are not making their way up to you. As a result, Asian CEOs like yourself tend to be the most uninformed individuals in your own organizations on the subject of brand and branding. This is absurd.

One of the first things you can choose to do, immediately, is to educate yourself. Go to a seminar, or commission one for you and your senior executives. Read a book on branding, and then another. Don't allow what you don't know to deprive you and your stakeholders of something that is truly invaluable and perhaps even inspirational. Avoid at all costs the fate of "the Board of Directors."

At the risk of repeating a key point covered in Chapter 2, it is worth highlighting a characteristic of Asian management: It is typically directive, with the CEO ruling largely without the benefit of consultation or consensus. This has implications, as discussed in that chapter. To recall some of the more pernicious ones: It leads to uninformed or misinformed employees, information bottlenecks, inefficiencies within functional departments, poor integration between departments, poor corporate culture, and low morale. Clearly, I am not a fan of the directive style of management. In today's business climate, it is obsolete and, frankly, self-defeating.

It is reassuring to see exceptions. There are some signs that more inclusive and open management styles are creeping into some companies headed by CEOs who are not wedded to conventional wisdom. In an interview with Banyan Tree's CEO Ho Kwon Ping, he provides a hint of an unconventional management style that has resulted in the creation of a highly differentiated brand delivered by engaged and empowered employees: "I admit I'm still a bit of an iconoclast—Che Guevara was my hero when I was a student—and do not particularly like to accept something simply because it's accepted wisdom or because somebody says it must be so."[30]

You now have an opportunity to be one of these exceptions. Seize the opportunity.

EMPLOYEE INVOLVEMENT AND COMMITMENT

The ability of any brand to be good, or great, lies in combining employee involvement with commitment. The two are not only linked; they are dependent on one another.

Employee Involvement

Whether a company's brand blueprint evolves over time or is delivered out of a formal branding exercise, employee involvement will be crucial and common to both. The elements contained within the brand blueprint reflect the company's core truths. Core truths cannot be manufactured or brainstormed or dictated by the CEO and his management team. Core truths reflect the strengths and characteristics that define the company and its brands—in a real way. They are largely innate. They are crafted and articulated by those best placed to recognize them in the first place: the company's employee population—from the lowest ranks to the CEO. This is why formal branding projects adopt a methodology that stretches primary research from the external to the internal; from consumers to employees. While the insights that need to be collected from the marketplace are critical to the mix, even more essential is an internal reality check: What do employees believe are the real strengths of the company? What are its more glaring weaknesses and deficiencies? Where do they see opportunities? What do they really think of the company and how it is managed? Do they believe their own advertising?

The answers to these questions help define a company's character. Without character, a consumer message is not likely to be successful because the promise the company makes to its customers will be either half-baked or inconsistently delivered.

Why are employee contributions so important? Employees, like everyone else, reflect Maslow's Hierarchy of Needs. Once their very basic needs are satisfied, they yearn for fulfillment of a higher kind: belonging, achievement, self-esteem, and pride in themselves as well as in what they are doing. Those needs are not parked at the factory entrance or in the office lobby when employees clock-in, and then collected again when they clock-out. They are ever-present needs that, in scores of companies across Asia, are simply being ignored or, worse, suppressed. This is particularly true of the more developed markets such as Taiwan, Korea, Hong Kong, and Singapore. The absence of consistent quality, leading-edge innovation, commitment, and loyalty—the intangible costs—translates into lost value in multiple areas: revenue, market share, prestige, and competitive advantage. A food and beverage veteran of an Asian hotel chain working in its Los Angeles property described his contribution to the hotel's growth as follows: "For 30 years they used my hands only when they could have had also my brain and my heart."[31] Companies should be harnessing this essential need people have to contribute and do something meaningful. Failure to do so cheats not only employees contribute and of self-actualization, but also companies of greatness.

The Brand-Centric Company

"Managing brands is going to be more and more about trying to manage everything that your company does."

Lee Clow

Once it has been created from within, the brand blueprint is sustained from within. For brands to develop and grow in a strong and sustainable way, the CEO must accept and adopt a business philosophy that dismisses the obsolete notion that only the marketing team is responsible for marketing and recognizes that everyone in the company—either directly or indirectly—is responsible for building the brand.

A brand blueprint acts as a frame of reference that guides and helps management in making decisions that influence and impact all facets of the business. Core benefits, for instance, will certainly impact the communications strategy, but they will also influence sourcing, quality management, delivery, and even accounts receivable, among other things. And each of these will have a supply chain of its own that supports it. What is included or discarded within that chain is likely to be influenced in no small measure by the core benefits the company has chosen to adopt: Is this supplier, or that ingredient, or this particular level of quality consistent with helping deliver the core benefits? If the answer is yes, it stays. If the answer is no, it goes.

Core values will also influence the brand's communications strategy. But they also have a major impact on a myriad of other things, for the simple reason that values influence behavior. One of the more visible of these manifestations will be found in a company's human resources (HR) policy. Beyond skill-sets, expertise, and experience, candidates' values will also be increasingly scrutinized: "What do you believe in?" "What is important to you?" "What do you value?" The answers to questions such as these help in determining how well the candidate's values match with the culture of the company. What is the point of employing even the most capable individual with the highest qualifications if his or her personal beliefs conflict with the values the company is actively trying to build? A conflict of values creates dissonance at the people level. Some simply call it "bad chemistry."

The same formula applies to the other elements of the brand blueprint—those that already exist, as well as those that will be created in the times ahead; they all impact on every facet of the organization. Those things that are judged to help deliver the brand blueprint stay; those that do not, should go.

When the brand blueprint is allowed to impact and influence everything that goes on within the company, that company can be said to be brand-centric. A brand-centric company does away with traditional silo organizational models that encourage independent and isolated activity from different departments and focuses instead on working, evolving, and—most importantly—delivering to the customer together. To achieve this, the brand needs to be literally positioned at the center of the company where it is in a position to affect every operational department, as well as every strategic consideration (see Figure 5.4).

Figure 5.4 The brand-centric company model

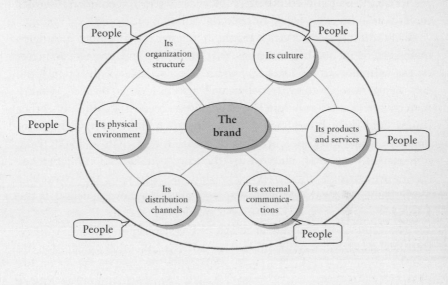

A brand-centric company converts every single employee into a positive brand ambassador.

A brand-centric company converts every single employee into a positive brand ambassador. This is important, because the modern organization now has to deal with multiple touch-points that go beyond the advertising and the product experience: Brand perception is influenced, for instance, by how a customer's telephone call is answered; by how the customer service department treats requests and addresses complaints; by how transparent the finance department is with the financial community; by how socially responsible the sourcing department or manufacturing unit is, and so on. And this provides the company with infinitely more opportunities to connect positively with customers than ever before.

But the flip-side of that same coin also serves to expose the company and its less-than-desirable practices to the scrutiny and judgment of the outside world. The recent tragic suicides of some 13 employees within six months at the Shenzhen plant of Taiwan-based Foxconn highlights another key touch-point that is increasingly visible to the outside world, and especially to customers: how employees feel they are treated by their companies, and how they behave as a result. A combination of exceptionally long working hours and relatively low salaries is alleged to have contributed to the spate of suicides at the plant. Regardless of what caused the employees to take their own lives, significant damage to the Foxconn brand image might be reasonably expected. Further, B2B brands such as Foxconn create "collateral" damage when they come under pressure. Global consumer brands such as Apple, HP, Dell, and others that source some of their products from Foxconn, also get tarred with the same brush. As Scott Davis and Michael Dunn point out in their book *Building the Brand-Driven Business*: "Every time an employee gets to touch a customer or a customer gets to touch a brand, that company gets the opportunity to either reinforce its brand promise or totally denigrate it."[32]

Employee Commitment

> *"[Our employees'] passion and devotion is our number one competitive advantage. Lose it, and we've lost the game."*
>
> Howard Schultz, Chairman and CEO, Starbucks[33]

We often see advertisements and product literature that proclaims, "The customer is no. 1." And companies often boast that they understand their customers and their needs better than anyone else. But to what degree do companies deliver?

The reality is that many companies got to be successful by implementing a strategy that effectively relegates the customer to the No. 2 position. For companies such as Starbucks, where the "what?" is indeed to serve customers well and give them a unique experience, the "how?" involves a management philosophy that propels employees very much to the forefront of the organization. Starbucks prioritizes employee attitude ahead of the desired end-deliverable: customer satisfaction. But this is for a reason that makes eminent sense: Only employees can deliver customer satisfaction.

In the brand-centric company, all employees—not just those who interact with customers—are responsible for "delivery." Employees on the assembly line contribute to the company's ability to deliver its customer promise as much as do those who work in HR, finance, administration, and all the other functional departments within the organization. The logic applies equally to B2B and business-to-consumer (B2C) companies. This is why Jack Welch emphasized that "the head of human resources at every company should be at least as important as the CFO."[34]

As obvious as that sounds, this elementary equation is, for the most part, lost on a lot of Asian companies, where the prevailing attitude is: "Employees are expected to do as they are told, because they are paid to do so." News flash: More often than not, employees—in one way or another—do as they want. And rarely does that align optimally with customer expectations. The result is companies that fail to deliver on their promises, and customers who are disappointed and often alienated.

Brands are not built by television and press ads—at least not to the extent believed by client CEOs and claimed by advertising agencies. Though this belief is popular and persistent, it is, nevertheless, a half-truth at best. People—employees—build brands: Employees deliver the brand promise by providing consistent, positive customer experiences. Ads are simply vehicles that communicate a brand's proposition in a relevant and—ideally—compelling manner. The best advertising campaigns are those whose "big ideas" reflect powerful consumer insights but which are guided by the core truths of the brand. Those core truths come from within the company. They lie within the brand blueprint.

If employees believe in your brand, so will customers.

People—employees at all levels, from the janitor to the CEO—are the only ones capable of bringing to life a genuine truth about a company or a brand. They are all, in their different jobs and roles, involved in what amounts to an interconnected process that acts like a chain reaction. What happens at one level of the company affects another, which in turn affects another level, and so on. Everything is connected. If employees' hearts and minds are not aligned with what the advertising promises, products won't get made well, or arrive on time, or last as long as they should. In the service sector, customers won't be treated properly.

Genuine truth is the physical expression of a company's soul—in other words, what employees think and how they behave. When was the last time you thought about your own company's "soul"? If the very question sounds odd, then chances are you have a lot of colleagues who are probably indifferent to—or at best, ambivalent about—the company you work for and the products you sell. If you have any doubts about this, ask anyone at Apple how they feel about working at the company, and they will tell you—if they are typical of most Apple employees—that they live, breathe, and eat Apple. Apple has soul. The end-result is a culture of sustained innovation that churns out products people want to make a part of their lives. Take a walk around a Harley Davidson factory floor and you will notice that every third person or so sports a Harley Davidson tattoo. Do you love your job enough to carve your company's logo onto your arm? When employees worship a brand like some sort of religion, customers find the brand promise of authenticity credible. If your employees believe in your brand, so will customers.

Engagement

"With its in-house play areas, Google's staff at Kirkland stay in when they need a break.... Google employees famously get free gourmet meals. They also work in one-of-a-kind offices . . . that [include] a rock-climbing wall in one of the three buildings on the so-called campus . . . a wellness centre and gym, soda fountain, fireplace, a mini-kitchen stocked full of food, cafeteria, dance room, massage room and doctor's office."[35]

While the above amount to amenities that are tangible and relatively easy (though clearly costly) to implement, it is the intangibles that really contribute to Google receiving up to 3,000 job applications a day. The intangibles are entirely embedded in its management philosophy and include unfettered internal communication, freedom from supervision, and across-the-board employee empowerment, among many other things. The most powerful of these—for Google and all companies—will always be the core ideology-related intangibles listed below, which are some of the very things many Asian companies are either reluctant or fearful to implement.

Key components that contribute to employee involvement and commitment include:

- **Vision**: "Where is my company going? I want to know . . . (a) because I want to know, and (b) because it allows me to figure out how I can help it get there."

- **Mission**: "What is the greater purpose of our company, beyond making money for the bosses? What makes others want to come here and me proud to belong here?"

- **Values**: "What does the company really believe in? And are these things consistent with my own value system?"

How do you get employees to engage? "Engagement" is the key word. Without it, there is no willingness on the part of employees to do more. It is that incremental "more" that separates mediocrity from excellence. Engaged employees at all levels will do their jobs better, will willingly volunteer opinions that improve their functions and how they interact with others, will engender an environment of internal discussion (which leads to creativity and innovation), and, ultimately, will deliver the promises the company makes to its customers.

Asian companies looking to engage their employees have a range of options they may consider. Before any of these can be implemented, the CEO himself must formally and visibly adopt a new mindset. To make the effort stick, the CEO will need not just to involve himself, but to lead.

Employee engagement can best be created and sustained by focusing on the following five strategic areas:

- The CEO declaration.
- Bringing alive the brand blueprint.
- Giving power to the people.
- Accepting that failure is always an option.
- Being accountable. (A "winner" company is one that is accountable.)

The CEO declaration

While this infers a single act, the CEO declaration is in fact an ongoing process whereby the CEO communicates with and makes himself available to his staff, inviting their feedback, ideas, and suggestions. One of the most common complaints and sources of employee frustrations a brand audit uncovers is the near-total absence of any communication by senior management with the middle and lower ranks of employees. Most often absent from view is the CEO. If this situation doesn't change, any effort made in the direction of brand building is likely to be stillborn. This means that the Asian CEO is going to have to go from being, to all intents and purposes, invisible and make the effort to be everywhere and to talk to as many people as possible. He will need to reach out, tell his people he is listening, and then act on some of the things he hears. Further, the CEO will need to gather his troops and formally declare that the company is committed to its guiding principles and core ideology: its vision, mission, and values.

Bringing alive the brand blueprint

Once the CEO has publicly declared his intention to lead the process, he must then create a process that will address each element of the brand blueprint in turn, and identify initiatives that will bring each of those elements alive. It is important to understand that this phase often results in significant change management, which may be disruptive and costly. As a result, many companies that go through a formal branding process and craft a brand blueprint then falter and fail to execute it. One of the leading reasons companies fail to follow through is the loss of momentum that can occur between the end of the branding project and the beginning of the internal alignment process. If the gap is too wide—which is often the case—CEOs and managers get distracted, and employees become demoralized (or, worse, cynical). Any trust and confidence the CEO might have gained from employees during the first phase is thus lost, making it harder to secure in the future.

Giving power to the people

More empowerment of more employees is absolutely essential in a globalized arena, where companies are venturing far from their home turfs to establish operations in other markets. Empowerment provides individuals with the authority to make decisions on their own—particularly those who are posted to foreign markets. This is essential where fast-moving markets, and the need to make quick decisions, preclude consultation with head office. Delays in communication and decision making translate instantly into lost competitive advantage. Companies have the choice of being either nimble or dead.

Empowerment enhances employees' self-esteem and encourages them to do more—that same more that separates mediocrity from excellence. Most people welcome responsibility, seeing it as an opportunity for personal growth. Every realized opportunity to grow delivers personal satisfaction and the innate need to sustain it.

> *"Nothing strengthens the judgment and quickens the conscience like individual responsibility."*
> Elizabeth Cady Stanton

There are several possible reasons why Asian CEOs appear reluctant to empower more employees with greater levels of authority. Earlier we identified the anachronistic issue of obsessive secrecy. Another important, and perhaps more practical, reason is the risk that some CEOs believe is inherent in allowing important decisions to be made outside of head office. The basic concern revolves around the issue of individual unpredictability. Specifically, how likely are empowered officers in offshore markets to make decisions that are in line with management expectations? This is indeed a legitimate concern, but it only persists if these companies fail to build an internal frame of reference that is known to and is clearly understood by every member of the organization. That frame of reference is, of course, the brand blueprint. A brand blueprint provides not just a road map for planning; it also acts as a common oracle that all employees can refer to for routine decision making, as well as for those decisions that need to be made during periods of crisis. It encourages consistent and relatively predictable personal judgments.

More ambitious, more aggressive, or more visionary companies that are willing to take empowerment one step further can convert risk taking—when used as a strategic tool—into a powerful competitive advantage. Risk taking is a highly risky strategy, but it need not be a reckless one. Equipped with a robust brand blueprint, responsible company officers who have demonstrated inordinate insight may be given sufficient authority to act on their own and take greater risks. This is like granting James Bond a license to kill. It amounts to a calculated bet that can provide very high returns.

Accepting that failure is always an option

"*. . . learn from mistakes and listen to feedback.*"

Sir Martin Sorrell, Chief Executive Officer, WPP[36]

One of the most noticeable characteristics shared by many Asian workers across all seniority levels is their unwillingness to express an opinion or to volunteer an idea or to criticize another's point of view—at least publicly—lest they be subjected to ridicule, censure, or even termination if they are proved to be wrong. Even when a team is charged with getting something done, or solving a particular problem, getting started is always a challenge because few members of the team will be willing to take the initiative. The Western expression "too many chiefs" finds no context in Asia. Instead, the reality is too many followers waiting to be told what to do.

While some may argue that the above is a generalization, many more will agree that this is very much part of the reality in Asia today, and is a major reason why Asian companies are not living up to their potential. The origins of this mindset are as complicated as they are controversial and contentious. They cover an extremely sensitive landscape that starts with culture and values and goes off in multiple directions that include political governance and its associated extensions: freedom of speech, personal liberty, and others. All of these find expression throughout most of Asia. Social psychologists have a great deal of territory to cover if some sort of measurable impact can be expected to affect its root causes in the near term.

Meanwhile, the "problem" affects not only individuals, but also their companies. People who are unwilling to express an opinion or provide a point of view directly impair a company's competitive advantage. These individuals are a dead weight to the organization, and can even drag it down. A notable exception is the Taiwan-based brand, HTC. Explains John Wang, the company's "chief innovation wizard" (CMO): "We have an organization that is designed to fail. . . . It takes close to 1,000 ideas to turn up a few projects that are worth running."[37]

Asian companies are operating like bad football teams (see the accompanying box). And if they win the occasional game, their response is not only disproportionate to the effort and the win, but also inconsequential in terms of the more important wider picture. "Picture," here, is a euphemism for real potential (bigger wins). The absence of perspective, or the wrong perspective, prevents many Asian companies from recognizing how successful they could otherwise be. If these same companies are managing to generate high revenues and deliver strong profits with disengaged employees who are incapable of or unwilling to contribute critical thought, then they are doing "well" despite themselves. Infinitely higher revenues and profits would materialize if the CEO's efforts were supported by those of engaged and proactive employees. To return to the football analogy, they would score many more "goals" if they simply played like a team. Further, this significant benefit amounts to low-hanging fruit. It can be immediately capitalized on and could, in very short order, demonstrate strong returns. But this doesn't happen all that frequently—mostly because, again, too many CEOs simply don't know what they don't know.

Business is like a football team

A good analogy for business lies in football. Beyond the rules, most people understand how the game is played and recognize the logic of the broad strategy that is used. For the purposes of the analogy, goals are to football what revenues and profit are to business.

Consider any champion European football team. While players will run all over the pitch, they are generally configured in an inverted "V" formation in a vector that pushes forward and aims directly for the goal posts. How they ultimately score goals is important: Every player knows his position; every player knows the position of his teammates; every game has a strategy which is known to all players, and when players are aware of the strategy they know who to pass the ball to and when. Inexorably the ball moves forward from one player to another until it reaches those in the forward lines—the strikers. The strikers will either create opportunities or wait for them to materialize before capitalizing and scoring. And when they do score, it will mostly be the result of team effort.

Now consider the Asian equivalent—the Asian company as the football team. In this football team, while most players know their position, they are wedded to them in such a fixed manner that it excludes interaction with other positions (the "that is not my job. . ." mentality). Instead of an inverted "V," we have players literally all over the field; some are even facing the wrong way. Because they lack initiative, they won't go after the ball and will only interact with it if it happens to come their way. When it does, they generally don't really know what to do with it, because (a) the objective of the game hasn't been made clear to them (it's a secret known only to the top players—the C-level guys/strikers), and (b) they are not interested or encouraged to play together. So they lose possession easily and often. So clueless are some of the players that occasionally one will run off in the wrong direction and end up scoring an own goal! But the worst outcome of this team's "strategy" is that the heavy lifting is done only by the two or three strikers up front (the CEO, COO, and CFO), since they can't or won't rely on the rest of their teammates. The capability of this team to score goals (to make higher revenues and profit) is significantly handicapped by its players, who are unaware of the objective and unwilling or incapable of playing together.

This Asian "football" team analogy illustrates how a lot of Asian companies do business. Do these companies make money (score goals)? Many do. Could they make more money (score a lot more goals)? Absolutely.

Asian CEOs need to overcome those specific cultural influences and prejudices that translate into regressive management styles that limit the potential of their companies. CEOs are a major reason why employees choose to decorate meeting rooms like mute trees. At the same time, too many Asian CEOs are notorious for loving the sound of their own voices. They are driven by a profound conviction that they know what is right and what works, so they end up dictating, rather than consulting or listening. To make matters worse, many go a step further: They penalize people who get it wrong. Unfortunately, this approach is replicated by their subordinates and then filters down and across all levels of the organization to become part of the company's culture. The result is as inevitable as it is catastrophic to the organization: Nobody says anything—ever. The fear of failure is pervasive. The company—without its CEO noticeably realizing it—doesn't move forward.

> *"Our company has, indeed, stumbled onto some*
> *of its new products. But never forget that you can only*
> *stumble if you are moving."*
>
> Richard P. Carlton, former CEO, 3M Corporation

The absence of active contributions by employees renders the company effectively dead in the water. When people are unwilling to express a point of view or an opinion, merit-less ideas that are floated by senior managers or the CEO, or by hired outside consultants, don't get challenged and often survive to graduate to policy. The harm that is born out of bad ideas that are implemented is dwarfed only by the real damage created by the lack of any dynamic internal input. The most common, and costly, result is a paucity of innovation—of any type. In fact, the hotly debated subject of the lack of innovation in Asia exists in the first place only because of widespread institutionalized employee timidity, insecurity, and anxiety brought about by a management philosophy that discourages employees from expressing themselves and voicing new ideas, and penalizes them for making mistakes or getting it wrong when they take initiatives. In the meantime, the best examples will continue to be set by Western companies doing business in Asia. A technical manager from 3M's Singapore office commented: "Sometimes I disagree with my boss . . . and she doesn't say 'no' to me immediately. She says: 'Why don't you try it out and let's see from here where we can go.'"[38]

> *"Be unafraid of failure."*
>
> Sir Richard Branson, founder and CEO, The Virgin Group

Instead of penalizing failure, companies should be considering doing the exact opposite. A certain measure of encouraging, and even celebrating, failure makes a great deal of sense. *BusinessWeek* devoted a cover story to doing just that. Its July 10, 2006 covery story, "Eureka, We Failed!"

BusinessWeek devotes a cover story to celebrating failure

Source: *BusinessWeek*, July 10, 2006.

revealed the extraordinary number of world-famous brands that resulted from initial blunders or failures. It provides case studies, and even personal accounts by accomplished marketers of their "favorite mistakes."[39]

Allowing—even encouraging—employees to "fail" sends the important message that the company understands that it is only through mistakes and failures that people learn—not just how to do their jobs properly, but new things; that it is only through risk taking that breakthroughs happen; and that it is only through trying that ideas eventually emerge. Commenting on the spectacular failure of Virgin Cola in the US and later Virgin Credit in Australia, Richard Branson said: "There is no better way to learn how to succeed in business than to learn from mistakes—yours or someone else's."[40] Failure from experimentation should always be an option for creative companies looking to improve constantly and build better brands.

A "winner company" is one that is accountable

The curious thing about employee relations across many companies in Asia is that while there is still minimal recognition of the productive partnership role employees can play, there is an equal reluctance to institute performance-driven cultures. As a result, many companies suffer from an over-abundance of mediocre human resources at virtually all levels of operations. As mentioned above, a management philosophy that fails to engage employees by not consulting with them or training them properly certainly contributes to the problem. But this doesn't diminish the role of another fragile pillar that threatens the integrity of the company edifice: low employee proficiency. Most Asian companies are carting around overweight levels of unproductive and underperforming employees. Most of them glide under the radar on a daily basis. Nobody notices or, apparently, cares. As a result, an almost Dilbert-like attitude pervades a lot of Asian companies: "I did nothing today and I still got paid."[41]

A central component of any company's brand strategy must be the stated aim to perform strongly. It must also have a corresponding appraisal system for employee measurement that actually works. While most senior managers might argue that they agree with this, the facts on the ground suggest they only give it lip service. Although most companies do have in place some sort of employee appraisal system, in the vast majority of cases, the wrong things are measured; or when serious deficiencies are detected, little or no action is taken. Further, not enough senior managers are involved in the process, leaving most of the effort in the hands of HR personnel who, alone, are not empowered to effect the important changes that need to be implemented to deliver high operating performance. This results in making the organization vulnerable in one vital area—people.

High achievers are generally drawn to companies that have developed a reputation for high performance—for winning. Why? Because these people—who are special—generally want to be part of something successful. They want to be winners. Winning, to them, is what a well-managed company with strong leadership does. They are attracted to companies like McKinsey and Google and Disney, because they are perceived to encourage excellence and celebrate success. For many of these high achievers—certainly those that share classic alpha-type personalities—winning is exhilarating. It is also a source of profound personal satisfaction that can satisfy many important psychological needs: self-esteem, pride, confidence, achievement, and many others. As Jack Welch put it in his book *Winning*: "I think winning is great. Not good—*great*. Because when companies win, people thrive and grow. There are more jobs and more opportunities."[42]

> "... the important thing is the passion and intensity among your people to go out there—day in, day out—and find ways to win and stay ahead. Our success has helped us attract more high-quality people to fuel the passion to carry on successfully."
>
> Pat O'Driscoll, Vice President, Shell Retail, Europe

High achievers are the people—other things being equal—that companies should be aiming to recruit and—importantly—retain. Motivated people who are committed to winning need an environment that encourages success. If that environment is filled with other like-minded and motivated colleagues, the company is likely to drive forward and upwards with reliable and dependable human resources. Conversely, high achievers will in time become demoralized by an environment cluttered with people who are either not up to the tasks they are responsible for, or are simply not suited to them. Workers who—for whatever reason—cannot deliver end up slowing down those who can. In this environment, high achievers don't last long. Eventually, they leave.

The only way to deliver a high-performance culture and keep high achievers from leaving is to implement a transparent policy that measures the performance of all employees on a regular basis and relative to a declared benchmark. The idea is to communicate a message to all employees that the company's goal is to deliver excellence to the best of its collective ability; that its "ability" lies in actively measuring the contributions of all employees: rewarding those who excel, and—for a specified time—helping those who are encountering difficulties or even struggling. But at the end of the day, all individuals need to deliver to the declared benchmarks. This means that those who cannot deliver, even after being given additional opportunities to improve, simply need to go. Staying doesn't do them or the company any good.

An essential component of any brand's strategy is having the right people, on whom delivery of the brand proposition is entirely dependent. To deliver it successfully, they will need to be motivated; and oftentimes that means feeling proud to be part of a company that is universally perceived to be a great company. To many, that means a winning company.

INTELLIGENT BRAND ARCHITECTURE

> "... most Asian groups have not defined their long-term business priorities, nor have they invested in the skills needed to assure success in a more competitive environment. Some are too diversified, and are wasting resources and management effort on businesses that may offer near-term gain but have little long-term potential. ... Building core businesses: The corollary of world-class performance is the need to focus on selected businesses. Superior performance is possible only in a few areas, where funds, skills, and management passion are concentrated."

T.C. Chu and Trevor MacMurray[43]

One of the great defining characteristics of Asian business is entre-preneurship and a vibrant, enterprising mentality. Over the past two decades, we have seen small, mostly family-owned businesses grow aggressively into large concerns not only in their own countries, but also across other Asian markets. The opportunities of the 1980s and 1990s were abundant and the circumstances favorable.

One of the drivers of the "Asian Tigers" era was (and continues to be) a business operational philosophy that is best described as "opportunity-driven." Two very visible manifestations of this philosophy are diversification, and mergers and acquisitions (M&A). Because the only motivating drive for both is usually the possibility of generating incremental revenues, rarely are detailed and comprehensive assessments made of the desirability of additional product lines, on the one hand, or the strategic fit of a target company in an M&A, on the other. This reflects an absence of an overarching strategic vision. It tends to result in companies distracting themselves from their core businesses in order to pursue the manufacturing or marketing of products and services that are outside their usual areas of experience or competence. As a result, a not insignificant portion of the Asian business landscape today is com-prised of highly diversified but less than efficient companies.

Apart from some notable exceptions (such as computer maker Acer Inc.), the concept of "core business" is not strongly valued, or even fully appreciated, in Asia. Rather than see focus as a means to generate an enduring competitive advantage (category leadership and economies of scale), it is effectively seen as risky and opportunity costly. Whether this is true or not, CEOs in Asia are failing to ask themselves fundamental ques-tions before making decisions that effectively move their companies away from what they know best. First among these is: "What, really, is our core business?" The question may seem straightforward, but so many Asian companies have expanded so arbitrarily, and in so many directions, over the past two decades that management attention and priority will likely have shifted back and forth between different businesses several times in that period. (Think of Lenovo going into investment banking in 2004.) If management cannot adequately answer this first question, it will struggle with this next one: "How should we allocate existing financial and human resources among our brands to grow shareholder value?"[44] And this ques-tion is important for the simple reason that resources are scarce and finite.

> *"We've got one stock that investors buy.*
> *We need one brand."*
>
> Larry Bossidy[45]

If you, as the CEO, together with your management team and your workforce, are unfamiliar with a business you are contemplating diversifying into or buying, don't do it. Beyond the likelihood of underperforming in the new business, the move invites distraction from what you do understand and do well, and from the dependable revenue streams that are associated with it. Many business analysts argue that one of the main reasons for the spectacular growth of the Coca-Cola Company in the 1990s and its wide lead over Pepsi was the company's decision to refocus on the core business of beverages after selling off its Columbia Pictures division in 1989. That point of view was certainly promoted by the company's then CEO, Roberto Goizueta. Paraphrasing Goizueta, David Greising described the legendary leader declaring "that the day of the conglomerate was over. Businesses of the future must focus on their core areas of expertise and ruthlessly realign operations whatever those core capabilities might be."[46]

While increasing numbers of companies in the West are moving away from the conglomerate model and selling off units inconsistent with their core businesses or mission statements, the model—notwithstanding Goizueta's firm conviction—doesn't lack legitimacy *per se*. And it remains popular in Asia. But this doesn't mean it is always created for the right reasons or is managed effectively. Managing diversification of products and services, or the integration of new brands via a merger or an acquisition, requires that the CEO and his management have a fundamental and profound understanding of the concept of brand architecture. In fact, next to brand positioning, brand architecture emerges as the single other most important brand and business dynamic managers must understand and master. Brand architecture is an involved area that deserves a book on its own. For that reason, I will limit my observations to a brief overview.

> *"GM has 33 brand names. BMW has one.*
> *Both are valid brand architectures."*
>
> Amy Campbell[47]

Brand architecture clarifies the strategic relationship between all brands in a company's portfolio. It describes the way in which a company organizes, manages, and goes to market with its portfolio of products and services. Brand architecture is to a company's portfolio of brands what teamwork is to a baseball team: critical. To avoid brand conflict on the one hand, and to deliver brand synergies on the other, a company's brands need to "play" together.

Figure 5.5 The brand architecture for GAP Inc.

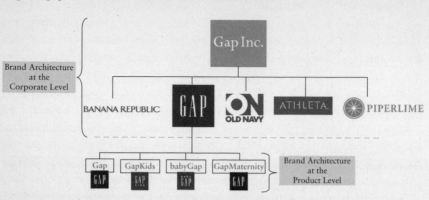

Brand architecture finds expression in two major and often connected ways: (1) at the corporate level, and (2) at the product level. The corporate level reveals the relationship different businesses belonging to the same holding company have with one another. The product level reveals the relationships different brands within the same company share among themselves. Figure 5.5 provides an example of how both can reside within the same corporate entity. GAP Inc. is a holding company that operates six separate stand-alone businesses. Each business is managed independently and may also market its own portfolio of brands. GAP Inc. is a good example of a company that has multiple businesses that are all part of the same core business—apparel.

The way in which a company organizes, manages, and goes to market with its brands refers to its CEO's choice of brand architecture from among four basic alternatives. There is no "right" or "wrong" architecture option *per se*. The "correct" choice is dictated by the company's business strategy. This is a critically important point. If the business strategy is unclear or nonexistent, the brand architecture strategy will be seriously flawed. Everything is connected.

Brand Architecture Alternatives

The four brand architecture alternatives are:

- Master branding (also known as "branded house")
- Invisible branding (also known as "house of brands")

- Co-branding
- Endorsement branding.

Master branding

Master branding leverages the equity of the corporate brand across all divisions and/or products. It is monolithic and provides a single brand identity. Familiar examples of companies that use a master branding strategy are Virgin, Boeing, and GE (see Figure 5.6). Advantages include: (a) elevation of the master brand's profile, adding immediate legitimacy to all its product brands and effectively delivering a halo effect if the master brand has positive brand equity; and (b) the ability to build a corporate brand name quickly. The main disadvantage of a master brand approach is the inability to build stand-alone brands that provide flexibility in several areas, particularly access to multiple mutually exclusive customer segments.

Figure 5.6 The brand architecture for Virgin

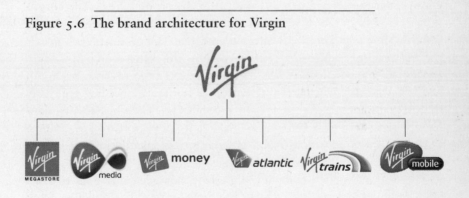

Invisible branding

Invisible branding is usually used by holding companies. The individual business/subsidiary/product brands are developed and promoted as separate entities. Familiar examples of companies that use an invisible branding strategy are Procter & Gamble (P&G) and Viacom (see Figure 5.7). Advantages include: (a) the ability to target distinct market segments; and (b) more flexibility when launching new products or services, as they don't rely on the image of the master brand. Disadvantages include: (a) the need for significant investment to build each brand; and (b) the inability to cross-leverage positive equity across the different brands.

Figure 5.7 The brand architecture for P&G

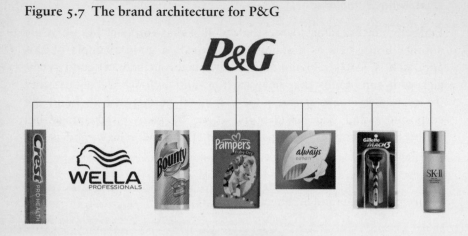

Co-branding

Co-branding is used when two corporate or product brands are given equal weight. The companies are (usually) engaged in a joint venture or a merger. Each brand benefits from the existing equity of the other. Familiar examples of companies that use co-branding strategies are MasterCard and Sony Ericsson (see Figures 5.8 and 5.9). The main advantage of this approach is that it allows for the transfer of desired brand associations/personality traits (and equity) from one brand to the other. Disadvantages include: (a) the possibility of failure if a poor selection of the partnering brand is made; and (b) customer confusion if the reason for the alliance is unclear or if the businesses seem incompatible.

Figures 5.8 and 5.9 The brand architecture for MasterCard and Sony Ericsson

Endorsement branding

Endorsement branding focuses on the subsidiary/product brand, while another brand acts as a stamp of approval. A good example of this approach is 3M (see Figure 5.10). Advantages include: (a) good synergies with sub-brands that have existing and well-defined equity; and (b) leveraging on the strengths of individual brands to help build the corporate brand and broaden its scope. Its main disadvantage lies in the fact that it takes longer to build if the endorsing brand is not well known.

Figure 5.10 The brand architecture for 3M

Which Strategy Is Best Suited to My Company?

It is worth repeating: The company's overarching vision and choice of business strategy provides the basis for two very important strategic decisions: (a) the choice of whether to focus on the core business or to diversify; and (b) the choice of brand architecture (see Figure 5.11).

Figure 5.11 Brand architecture flowchart

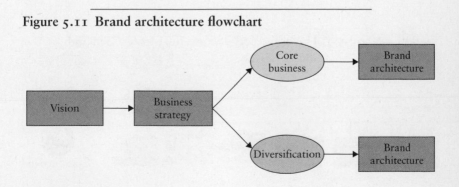

> Whatever the company does, the master brand must always be protected.

Whether a company stays in or strays from its core business, the right brand architecture framework will be essential for effective management and growth of all brands in its portfolio. The absence of an intelligent brand architecture strategy will almost certainly result in portfolio underperformance and, in many cases, outright damage to many brands. Another even more dire potential consequence is the dilution of the master brand, the very thing that holds the company together. This must never be allowed to happen. Whatever the company does, the master brand must always be protected.

Companies need not limit themselves to one or even two brand architecture alternatives. Hybrids are common, as the Marriott hotel group illustrates (see Figure 5.12). One good look at their operations provides some insight into the group's business strategy and, by extension, its brand architecture strategy.

Figure 5.12 The brand architecture for Marriott

On the surface it seems that Marriott has chosen to manage its expansion through organic growth and acquisitions that are consistent with its core business—hospitality. It operates some 16 separate hotel brand names in all price and quality points of the category.[48] In this way, Marriott is able to target virtually all customer audience segments in the markets in which it does business, through a strategy that in some cases leverages its master brand.

Marriott has adopted a business strategy that divides the entire category into five separate, contiguous segments that offer services and accommodation at virtually all levels. Though perhaps an oversimplification, the five categories can best be understood within the popular hotel "star" system.

The Marriott corporate website provides detailed descriptions of each of its hotel brands. Based on the differentiated service each hotel delivers, it is possible to create a matrix chart that identifies and positions each brand relative to the others within the "stars" framework. For the purpose of this exercise, we have used only a small selection of the Marriott brands.

Marriott's presence in the market allows us to infer several things about its business strategy. Among these are: (a) a broad reach of customers across all socio-economic levels: luxury, mid-price, and value for money; (b) psychographic customer segmentation, with some brands designed to appeal mostly to business executives while others favor leisure and holidaymakers; (c) geographical distribution: while some brands are deployed "locally" (in the US), other brands are operated on a global basis; and (d) a presence across different hospitality segments: from hotels to serviced apartments.

Marriott's business strategy, even the little that is visible, appears to be sophisticated and robust. The company appears to be aiming for most, if not all, segments of the hospitality category. And there is little wrong with that, as long as the appropriate brand architecture is adopted and different operating units managed by different executive teams are created to manage the brands.

The Marriott Brand Architecture

In an effort to maximize its presence right across the category, Marriott is using a combined master brand/invisible/endorsement brand architecture strategy. The starting point is the master brand itself—Marriott Hotels & Resorts. Given a business strategy that aims to occupy virtually all hospitality segments, how might this master brand—which owns a generally solid "premium" association—best be harnessed and leveraged?

At the luxury end of the category are two very exclusive hotel groups: The Ritz Carlton and EDITION. Marriott's decision not to associate its name with either of these two brand names (invisible brand strategy) makes a great deal of sense. The reason is that Marriott may be premium, but it is not six-star über-luxury. With virtually everything else, Marriott does add its name to the brand—to better effect in some instances than in others.

As a premium master brand, it is appropriate, logical, and possible to stretch the "Marriott" name upwards into the five-star category. And the founder's initials—JW—play a role in clearly separating it from the more mainstream (less luxurious) Marriott Hotels & Resorts. Occupying the five-star luxury segment is the master-branded JW Marriott network. This works by setting the experience as visibly "higher" and better than the mainstream brand. At the four-star level, Renaissance is a stand-alone brand, probably because the customer experience standard is close or identical to that of Marriott Hotels & Resorts, which also has a presence at this level. The brand name was an acquisition in 1997 and, owning valuable equity, it was likely decided to operate it apart and independently so as to increase the group's overall presence in this segment level. While this is probably the strategy—and it is quite a reasonable one—there will always be some cannibalization, since the Renaissance brand doesn't compete just with other competitor brands but also with its Marriott cousin as well. The existence of Marriott Executive Apartments is also obvious and logical. Offering a level of quality comparable to that its sister network is known for, this brand provides an alternative apartment option for executives with longer-stay needs.

It is really at the three- and two-star levels that questions can be raised about the company's choice of architecture. The main argument one might speculate for the company's decision to add the Marriott master brand name is, most likely, brand awareness and the halo effect it provides. That said, the decision deserves closer scrutiny. The key question that all companies need to ask themselves before venturing to volunteer the master brand for anything is: Will stretching the brand that far damage it? Far too often, this question isn't asked; instead, the focus is solely on the anticipated benefits. When the stretch is too great, the "rubber" snaps and all the brands suffer—especially the master brand, which must always be protected.

Summary

The Marriott experience provides a useful case study for Asian brand owners. It reveals both the opportunities that can be pursued, and some of the more obvious elements of a deliberately thought-out strategy for pursuing them. Right or wrong, the Marriott example provides a blueprint for decision making. In Asia, brand portfolio strategies are too often driven by emotion or gut instincts. In the years ahead, as Asia attracts more and more attention and investment, both the opportunities and the competitive pressures will increase. If they are to exploit the former and manage the latter, Asian CEOs will need to guard against four typical mistakes that tend to affect the portfolio architecture process:

- The tendency to make brand architecture decisions for emotional, rather than data-related, reasons;
- The tendency to focus on individual products or brands; independently of how they might impact the master brand or the broader portfolio of brands;
- The tendency to politicize brand architecture so as to define turf and authority;
- The failure to use brand architecture as a forward-looking strategic tool.

Furthermore, CEOs will need to be clearer about what it is their companies do best, and whether it is really in their interest to expand into new areas that are removed from their existing core competencies. The trend adopted in the West of focusing on one's core business merits careful consideration by Asian CEOs. The arguments that support it are compelling and relevant in an age of fast-moving innovation, fierce competition, and increasing commoditization. All three dynamics impact the allocation of crucial company resources: people and money. Companies that elect to focus on their core business, like the Marriott Group, will need to look at how their related brands—some of which may or may not rely on the master brand—deliver synergies while avoiding dilution of the master brand.

On the other hand, where diversification is sought and justified, brand architecture models will also need to be carefully considered and adopted. They will need to be based on an overarching vision of where the company is going and how its portfolio of (different) businesses and brands will help get it there. The indicators for this will be found in the company's business strategy.

Once again, it bears repeating: There is no good or bad architecture choice—just the right one that will correspond with and deliver directly to the company's unique circumstances and objectives. Whether a company is looking to expand its existing line of brands, add new ones, or even add new businesses to its portfolio mix, it should consider this: Strong master brands are like geese that lay golden eggs. Intelligent brand architecture provides the means for the goose to keep on laying eggs. Shortsighted, opportunistic decisions that stretch master brands into categories where they have no "permission" to go will only end up cooking the goose.

CSR: THE NEW BRANDING IMPERATIVE

"Integrity in business is the ultimate competitive advantage. . . .
Without it you have nothing."

Attributed to Roberto Goizueta, former CEO,
The Coca-Cola Company[49]

If ever there was a phenomenon that threatened to disrupt the current paradigm of global business in the new century, it is the concept of corporate social responsibility. CSR is an area replete with complex arguments that cloud the very definition of the concept. In addition, different people—ranging from company executives, to representatives of non-government organizations (NGOs), to private citizens—have not only different views on the subject, but also vastly different expectations of actions and outcomes. These gaps and disparities create both major risks that CEOs need to be clearly aware of, and huge opportunities that are already changing the way business is conducted.

The first challenge lies in the very definition of CSR. Historically, and as late as 2005, the popular perception of CSR continued to revolve around the "good" a company can contribute to society. In some quarters, this still means treating your own employees well, at one end of the spectrum, and donating time, effort, and money to charities, at the other end. More or less reflecting this perception, an article entitled "The Good Company," which appeared in the January 2005 issue of *The Economist*, described CSR as "the tribute that capitalism everywhere pays to virtue."[50] The discussion in the article centered around the genuineness of companies that were systemically reforming themselves in a manner that demoted profitability in favor of social contributions. Regardless of what side of that debate merited credit, no mention was made of the issues that are today more closely associated with

CSR: the environment and sustainability, and how business impacts both. But that is changing very quickly.

The evidence suggests that the planet is warming and that, as a result, we can expect a multitude of consequences ranging from climate change to elevated sea levels, along with all the implications of these changes. The problems will only continue to get worse unless action is taken to arrest and reverse the causes of global warming. But, who is responsible for fixing the world, and what does this have to do with business?

In 1970 the economist Milton Friedman wrote a famous article for *The New York Times Magazine* entitled, "The Social Responsibility of Business Is to Increase its Profits."[51] Addressing students at Yale University, 22 years later in 1992, Coca-Cola's CEO Roberto Goizueta presented the opposite viewpoint: "While we were once perceived as simply providing services, selling products, and employing people, business now shares in much of the responsibility for our global quality of life."[52]

Today, it is Goizueta's viewpoint that is attracting overwhelming favor. Businesses are increasingly being seen as part of a new mainstream reality that is continuing to evolve. This reality is also galvanizing people—who are also consumers—to demand more from governments, and even more from business. Much of this is, no doubt, the result of the huge amount of media coverage devoted to global warming, its causes, and the Doomsday scenarios predicted by some scientists.

Findings from a 2007 McKinsey global survey, "Assessing the Impact of Societal Issues," identified major—and, in some cases, overwhelming—shifts of opinion across several key CSR metrics among company executives when compared to 2005 numbers. Top of mind for most respondents, and scoring the highest percentages over other stated concerns, were environmental issues, including climate change. On a regional basis, the numbers varied only a little, to reflect mostly local priorities: In North America the environment was slightly behind the concerns of health care and employee benefits. In Europe the environment was perceived to be the most pressing issue by a very large margin—almost doubling the second-placed issue. In China, some might be surprised to learn, the environment also scored first. And in India, the environment was just pipped at the post by privacy- and security-related issues, with a difference of only 1 percent. Summing up, the survey declared: "Executives seem well aware that action on the environment will be important for many companies if they are to earn the public's trust."[53]

Among consumers the picture is similar. Findings from the Synovate/BBC global study on climate change concluded that "concern for the environment has gone mainstream." The study found that "more than two-thirds of respondents said they were very or somewhat concerned" and would not "purchase products that have been made through a process that has increased poverty, harmed [the] environment or destroyed wildlife."[54]

The picture is very similar regarding attitudes to another equally important CSR metric: sustainability. According to Edelman's 2009 "goodpurpose" study, which polled 6,000 people aged 18–64 across 10 countries (including emerging and developing countries such as Brazil, India, and China): "61% have purchased a brand that supports a good cause even if it wasn't the cheapest brand . . ." and "83% [were] willing to change consumption habits if it [would] help make the world a better place to live."[55] An *MIT Sloan Management Review* study, also conducted in 2009, revealed almost identical findings: "People were willing to pay a premium for products perceived to be ethically produced. . . . The bottom line of the survey was that it pays to be good and that consumers increasingly want to support companies which are socially responsible and products which were not made by exploiting nature or people."[56]

As a result, companies around the world are fundamentally reassessing their roles in society and, by extension, are reviewing how they do business. At the center of the transformation is the realization and acceptance by companies that their activities create a carbon footprint. In other words, many companies are recognizing that they are (at least in part) responsible. And consumers not only agree, but are constantly reminding them of this.

The writing is on the wall: Consumers want to make the world a better place and will absolutely support companies they believe are sincere about helping that happen. And companies are beginning to respond: "The most progressive [ones] are talking about a triple bottom line— profit, planet and people."[57]

Effective CSR must be supported by genuine conviction and a visible and credible plan for implementation if companies are to avoid accusations of greenwashing (see the accompanying box).

Be careful what you promise: BP's "Beyond Petroleum"

It is not surprising to see some companies begin to experiment with CSR initiatives while others venture bolder commitments. While the general public as well as NGOs generally welcome genuine demonstrations of good intent, some of the transformations have generated immediate controversy and suspicion.

In 1997 Lord John Browne, CEO of the giant oil company British Petroleum (BP), delivered a seminal speech at Stanford University. He surprised his audience by announcing that BP recognized the link between carbon emissions and environmental degradation. This was major news. Some considered it comparable to a tobacco company admitting that cigarettes cause cancer. He went further and said that, as a result of recognizing the link, "BP had decided that it was time to go beyond analysis to seek solutions and take action."[58] His speech was a precursor for the now famous—many vigorously insist, infamous—2000 global advertising campaign that communicated the company's then new positioning: beyond petroleum. In his book *Beyond Business*, Lord Browne explains that the new positioning meant to communicate a brand "that represented what we were—and that was more than oil and petroleum." He argued that, while "the image of the industry was that it was old-fashioned and dirty, and still secret and manipulative, [that] was not the reality. We wanted our image to reflect what we believed BP now stood for. It was to be a competitively profitable force for good, which valued top-class safe operational performance, innovation, progress and environmental leadership."[59] On its website, BP's advertising agency, Ogilvy & Mather, explained that "the newly re-branded, global BP sought to position itself as transcending the oil sector . . . while remaining . . . environmentally responsible."

The universal external understanding, fair or otherwise, was that BP was going green.

Ten years later the facts underscore the importance of a fundamental construct of strong branding: Be careful what you promise. Between 2000 and 2010, BP has experienced at least three accidents of catastrophic proportions that have resulted in loss of life and massive environmental damage. In 2005, 15 workers were killed at the Texas City refinery. A BP report concluded that there had been "apparent complacency towards serious safety risk."[60] In 2006, an oil spill at Prudhoe Bay was described as the largest to damage Alaska's North Slope. The cause was determined to be pipe corrosion, and in 2007 BP pleaded guilty to negligent discharge of oil. And more recently, the explosion at the Deepwater Horizon rig in the Gulf of Mexico on April 20, 2010 resulted in the deaths of 11 men and the biggest oil spill in North American

(*Continued*)

history. An estimated mindboggling 35,000 to 60,000 barrels of oil were discharged into the sea every day for some 87 days. At an average of 45,000 barrels per day, this works out to a staggering 3.9 million barrels since the explosion. By way of comparison, the 1989 *Exxon Valdez* spill resulted in the discharge of some 257,000 barrels in total. Beyond the human toll, the devastation to marine life, as well as to the livelihoods of people living in those southern states that border the Gulf, has only just begun to be measured.

Immediately after the launch of beyond petroleum and in the years since, BP has been relentlessly accused of greenwashing. Whether the critics have been vindicated or BP has been unfairly treated remains something that might be better assessed in the future. But this experience clearly demonstrates how sensitive people become when a company makes a big promise of the type BP made in 2000 and then fails to deliver on it convincingly.

The Edelman study finding that 83 percent of people would change their consumption patterns if it would help make the world a better place is nothing short of staggering. It also serves to remind errant CEOs—particularly in Asia—about the power of a company's mission statement and core values. A persistent CEO mentality that considers "making money" to be the sole purpose of a company will ultimately alienate both employees and consumers, who are simply not interested in goals that are both so patently self-serving and display indifference to a growing and visible communal need. Employees will be demotivated and will do their jobs less effectively, and consumers will walk away in droves. Those CEOs of Asian companies who do recognize the value and importance of a mission that helps the world become a better place may find that the starting point for their efforts lies within their core values. These will need to be more than just window dressing. Core values will underpin the mission the company commits itself to, and provide the reason for people—employees and customers alike—to "believe." And to be effective, CSR needs to be believed. It needs to act in a manner that is relevant—which is to say, in a way that minimizes or compensates for the damage companies create. And it needs to do this in a sincere manner.

The Opportunity

Companies that still think of CSR as merely good management practices or contributions to worthy causes are in serious denial. They neither understand the dynamics (and potential consequences) of evolving circumstances, nor recognize the opportunities. Corporate social responsibility—the act of responding responsibly in terms of the impact a company has on the planet—is emerging as the most significant vehicle for differentiation and customer loyalty since the invention of the USP (unique selling point). It not only taps into a swelling global concern, but does so via the most powerful brand dynamic: the emotional dimension. Increasingly, people in their hundreds of thousands, and soon millions (witness the increasing numbers of demonstrations and moratoriums on global warming around the world each year), will add environmental responsibility as a characteristic that helps them define themselves: "I care, therefore I am." Responsible brands that prove themselves to be part of the solution, and not the problem, will be the first these consumers will adopt as part of their effort to feel good about what they themselves are doing to help solve the world's problems.

While this opportunity is unique and significant, its exploitation will not be tolerated. Greenwashing, a new term that has entered the social and business lexicon, refers to cynical efforts by companies with no real conviction or genuine concern to jump on and benefit from the CSR bandwagon. Although NGO groups are ever vigilant and ready to pounce on and denounce such companies, it is the risk of generating contempt among consumers that will ultimately bring them down.

Moving forward, CSR will be about companies acting with governments, and sometimes unilaterally, to do good in a way that is consistent with the business they are in. Relevance of action will increasingly overshadow random acts of philanthropy.

In Asia the CSR learning curve is likely to mirror that of other learned business disciplines: It will be short. Research to date points to similar and, in some cases, higher levels of conviction by Chinese and Indian consumers compared to those in the West. Everywhere, CSR will emerge as an opportunity for strong differentiation. Key to making this happen in a sustainable way will be the recognition by leaders that all initiatives will need to be anchored by genuine conviction and be "deeply embedded in the core DNA of the organization." In Asia, where branding practices remain weak, CSR will not just represent a branding imperative; it promises to deliver nothing less than a silver bullet to smart and responsible companies.

SUMMARY

Contrary to the expectations of many who look for formulas, brand strategy can be an amorphous thing. It can stretch from the solid and elementary brand positioning building blocks (differentiation), to internal culture drivers (employee engagement), to management style (CEO involvement), to controversial and polarizing issues that test new boundaries (CSR). In reality, brand strategy is extremely elastic and can cover a multitude of areas, depending of the category where the product or service lies. If the brand lies in the motor vehicle category, safety might well emerge as an element of brand strategy; if it lies in the toy category, child education may be relevant; if it lies in the airline category, on-time departures for business travelers may represent an essential ingredient. All brands do business in unique universes. Each will exhibit unique characteristics that may well find their way into brand strategy plans.

Having said this, the eight brand strategy drivers discussed in this chapter constitute those that are common to most brands in most categories. They are elementary in as much as they are essential and pivotal in any effort that aims to create competitive advantage.

If there is one factor that perhaps trumps everything in importance and, at the same time, provides relevance to all brand strategy drivers—especially the elementary eight identified in this chapter—it is the mandatory need for decision makers to make choices. The common habits of aiming a brand at everyone, or stuffing a product with every conceivable feature in the absence of a defined purpose, or experimenting with different benefits to see which "stick," betray signs of a company that lacks conviction in terms of its values and is mercenary in its mission. This doesn't translate well with consumers, who are increasingly holding brands (and their companies) to ever-higher standards. In an environment characterized by a sea of choices, it is mostly those that are more difficult to make that ultimately serve to define the company and, in the process, provide relevance to customers.

NOTES

1. Paul Temporal, *Asia's Star Brands* (Singapore: John Wiley & Sons (Asia), 2006), p. 128.
2. www.brandassetvaluator.com.au (Financial Returns).
3. Theodore Levitt, *The Marketing Imagination* (Collier Macmillan, 1986).
4. *Bottled Water—Global Industry Guide—New Research Report on Companies and Markets*, July 7, 2008, www.companiesandmarkets.com.

5. Orange website, www.orange.com/en_EN/group/brand/our_values/.
6. Howard Schultz and Dori Jones Yang, *Pour Your Heart Into It: How Starbucks Built a Company One Cup at a Time* (Hyperion Books, 1999).
7. Liang Dingzi, "The Spark That's Needed to Fly High," *Today*, June 10, 2009, p. 17.
8. Levitt, *The Marketing Imagination,* op. cit.
9. Miles Young (O&M Asia), in De Meyer, Mar, Richter, and Williamson, *Global Future* (Singapore: John Wiley & Sons (Asia), 2005), p. 287.
10. Singapore Minister Mentor Lee Kuan Yew, *Today*, November 6, 2009, p. 4.
11. Stuart Miles, "THE BIG INTERVIEW: Creative CEO Sim Wong Hoo," *Pocket-lint.com*, December 9, 2005, www.pocket-lint.com/news/2075/creative-zen-vision-mp3-player.
12. David Greising, *I'd Like the World to Buy a Coke* (John Wiley & Sons, 1998), p. 120.
13. Ibid.
14. The Coca-Cola Company website.
15. Tom Peters, *Re-Imagine* (Dorling Kindersley, 2003), p. 163.
16. "CEO Interview with Mr. Ho Kwon Ping, Executive Chairman, Banyan Tree Holdings Limited, 2009," *My Small Business & Medium Business*, http://mysmbcommunity1.com/component/content/article/34-ceo-interviews/18-ceo-interview-with-mr-ho-kwon-ping-banyan-tree-holdings.html.
17. Miles, "THE BIG INTERVIEW: Creative CEO Sim Wong Hoo," op. cit.
18. *Brand Audit, 2006*, BrandAsian. All rights reserved.
19. Ernst & Young, Redrawing the Map. *Globalization and the Changing World of Business* (2009).
20. Dexter Roberts, "China's Power Brands," *BusinessWeek*, November 8, 2004, p. 50.
21. Kishore Mahbubani, *The New Asian Hemisphere* (Public Affairs, 2008).
22. Arnoud De Meyer and Sam Garg, *Inspire to Innovate* (Palgrave Macmillan, 2005), p. 117.
23. Mahbubani, *The New Asian Hemisphere, op. cit.*, p. 139.
24. Ibid.
25. Professor Arnoud De Meyer, "Asian Firms Must Innovate More," *The Business Times*, August 6, 2004.
26. Ashlee Vance, "Acer's Everywhere. How Did That Happen?" *The New York Times*, June 28, 2009.
27. Lim Swee Say, "Take it from 3M, All Staff Can Innovate," *Today*, February 26, 2010, p. 12.
28. "Think Different" is an advertising slogan created for Apple in 1997 by the Los Angeles office of advertising agency TBWA/Chiat Day.
29. Tom Peters, *What is Brand Equity?*, www.tompeters.com/dispatches/007577.php.
30. Adeline Chong, "Ho Kwon Ping—Rooted in Romance," *brandchannel*, January 31, 2005.

31. Employee comment, Carlyle Brand Consultants Brand Audit, Hospitality sector, 2002.

32. Scott M. Davis and Michael Dunn, *Building the Brand-Driven Business* (Jossey Bass/Wiley & Sons Inc., 2002).

33. Schultz and Jones Yang, *Pour Your Heart Into It,* op. cit.

34. Jack Welch with Suzy Welch, *Winning* (HarperCollins, 2005), p. 2.

35. Leslie Yee, "Singaporean Workers Want More than Just Money," *The Business Times*, November 9, 2005.

36. "How We Do it: Three Executives Reflect on Strategic Decision Making," *McKinsey Quarterly*, March 2010.

37. Miguel Helft and Laura M. Holson, "With Google Phone, HTC Comes Out of the Shadows," *The New York Times*, September 23, 2008.

38. Lim Swee Say, "Take it from 3M, All Staff Can Innovate," op. cit.

39. Jena McGregor, "Eureka, We Failed. How Smart Companies Learn from their Flops," *BusinessWeek*, July 10, 2006.

40. Richard Branson, "Nothing to Fear but Fear of Failure," *Today*, August 5, 2010, p. 22.

41. "I Did Nothing Today and I Still Got Paid," www.dilbert.com/blog/entry/cubicle_toys/?Page=4.

42. Welch and Welch, *Winning*, op. cit.

43. T.C. Chu and Trevor MacMurray, "The Road Ahead for Asia's Leading Conglomerates: As Regional Growth Blossoms, Past Approaches to Strategic and Organizational Success May No Longer be Adequate," August 1993, http://mkqpreview1.qdweb.net/Strategy/Globalization/The_road_ahead_for_Asias_leading_conglomerates_24.

44. Petromilli, Morrison, and Milion, "Brand Architecture: Building Brand Portfolio Value," *Strategy & Leadership*, May 30, 2002, p. 22.

45. Larry Bossidy and Ram Charan, *Execution: The Discipline of Getting Things Done* (New York: Crown Business, 2002).

46. Greising, *I'd Like the World to Buy a Coke,* op. cit., p. 181.

47. Amy Campbell, "Brand Architecture: A Method to the Madness," *Infoworks! Information Design + Content Strategy* (1999), p. 1.

48. www.marriott.com.

49. Greising, *I'd Like the World to Buy a Coke,* op. cit., p. 304.

50. Clive Crook, "The Good Company," *The Economist*, January 22, 2005.

51. Milton Friedman, "The Social Responsibility of Business Is to Increase Its Profits," *The New York Times Magazine*, September 13, 1970.

52. Greising, *I'd Like the World to Buy a Coke,* op. cit., p. 294.

53. "Assessing the Impact of Societal Issues: A McKinsey Global Survey," *McKinsey Quarterly*, 2007.

54. MKT, "The Business of Giving," Marketing Interactive.com, January 15, 2007.

55. 2009 Global Edelman goodpurpose™ Study.

56. Chua Mui Hoong, "For MNCs, It Pays to be Good," *The Straits Times*, October 10, 2009.
57. Richard Stengel, "The Responsibility Revolution," *Time*, September 21, 2009, p. 28.
58. John Browne, *Beyond Business* (London: Weidenfeld & Nicolson, 2010), p. 77.
59. Ibid., p. 194.
60. Andrew Simms, "The Rise and Fall of BP," www.guardian.co.uk, June 14, 2010.

6

METHODOLOGY INSTEAD
OF MYTHOLOGY

*"The best and most effective brands of the future
will be built around knowledge."*

Lord Puttnam, CBE

Asians are always in a hurry. Whether you are talking about Indians
in Mumbai or the Chinese in Hong Kong and Singapore, or Malays in
Kuala Lumpur, or Koreans in Seoul, they all demonstrate a common
characteristic: high velocity. They are dynamic, energetic, and filled with
the vitality that comes from their confidence in the potential of their
entire region.

This buzz and energy is evident on the streets of most major Asian
cities. But it's not all positive. Many in Asia fear being left behind or
missing out on opportunities—what Singaporeans call *kiasu*.

Speed is also manifested in business (as is the business equivalent
of *kiasu*). In fact, next to bargaining down supplier prices to the lowest possible levels, short-cuts are celebrated to the point that they are
almost strategic tools. In the minds of many, short-cuts minimize the
chances of missing out.

The entire branding process suffers from this "short-cuts" mindset. In
Asia, where the goal of making money has been elevated to an art form,
time and money spent on branding is seen as a disruption to the primary
business of making money—and is thus kept to a minimum. Combine
this mindset with misconceptions about or outright ignorance of branding at the highest levels of the Asian corporate organization and the

result is an undermining of the branding effort within Asian companies before it even begins.

Central to the problem, and impacting everything else like a domino effect, is the rarity of the CEO's involvement in the process. Reflecting his perception of the task's lack of importance, he delegates it—often to mid-level managers who have neither the experience to critically consider the parameters of the process, nor the authority to make decisions of any consequence that might get it moving in the right direction. Inevitably, the process is flawed from the outset. The CEO (or, in some cases, the board of directors), who participates only at the end to make a decision, is usually presented with a set of alternative "proposals" that invariably don't reflect the key issues or unique circumstances that affect the company. By the time the proposals reach the key decision maker, they will have been revised many times over to reflect minimum project time frames and minimum investment. This is a key point.

All companies are affected by unique circumstances. These circumstances must impact on any branding proposal. This renders the proposal directional, not generic. But these critical contributions are usually not made, for the simple reason that mid-level managers are unaware of these issues—or of their importance—in the first place. The Petronas Towers in Kuala Lumpur are a magnificent example of great engineering. Construction of the towers clearly required consideration of circumstances unique to Petronas's needs. In this case, specially formulated reinforced concrete (among other materials) was essential to support the great height of the towers. Ordinary concrete wouldn't have been up to the task. Similarly, branding proposals become just useless bits of paper that can potentially do more harm than good unless the company's special circumstances and unique needs are integrated into the recommended solution.

Proposals are in some cases undermined even further by submissions from unethical or unqualified providers who are only too eager to deliver exactly what the CEO (who doesn't know what he doesn't know) demands. The caliber or philosophy of some providers is revealed in the debates in which the industry occasionally engages. Often these include personal definitions of the branding process, how well clients are being served by providers, and who is qualified to serve them. In one such debate conducted in 2009 in the pages of a trade magazine, different "experts" put forward their views. On one side of the spectrum, a "former head of brand strategy" argued that traditional brand development processes (presumably those delivered by the strategy-centric consultancies—see Figure 2.3 in Chapter 2) were "smoke and mirrors" that don't fool "savvy marketers." This "expert" went on to deride workshops (a central tool of the brand development process) as "completely off the wall where nothing really gets sorted." The piece concluded with additional remarks attributed to him: "The smarter clients are now seeing the process for what it really is. They've realized that they can actually truncate the whole thing . . . in[to] a much shorter time frame."

The other side of the debate was represented by the creative director of "one of Asia's biggest branding and product design firms . . . who declined to be named." While conceding that the development process could be accelerated, the creative director went on to express a diametrically opposed point of view. He said: ". . . too many marketers don't know their brands well enough to make the right decisions about their brands . . ." The impact of the recession, he said, contributed "to a dumbing down of branding and product design in the region."[1] Rounding off the piece was a full-page ad by a "leading global brand and communications agency." The ad's headline identified this company's "Top Five Brand Moves." The fifth "move" counseled marketers to "Develop a *flexible* brand positioning statement" (the emphasis is my own).[2]

Comprehensive branding processes do not amount to "smoke and mirrors."

Asian CEOs interested in building great brands and great companies would do well to reflect on the three differing points of view reflected above. Though compressed within a couple of pages of an article and an ad, some key contradictions and dangers that exist within the broader branding universe are revealed. At the risk of clouding the picture even further, I will add my own summary point of view, much of which has already been explained in the body of this book:

1. Comprehensive branding processes do not amount to "smoke and mirrors."
2. The majority of Asian marketers are not brand and branding savvy.
3. Workshops are critical and central to the development of a brand proposition (and the delivery of other elements of the brand blueprint).
4. The time required to complete branding processes can be reduced, but with a serious caveat that the process maintain minimum levels of strategic robustness.

5. I agree that the branding process has suffered a dumbing down (see points (1) and (3) above).

6. Brand positionings are most definitely not flexible statements. On the contrary, they are as fixed as the Rock of Gibraltar. Beyond being just plain wrong, this statement borders on the irresponsible (see "The Positioning Statement" and Figure 3.6, "The Branding–Advertising Construct," in Chapter 3).

CEOs who fail to educate themselves about a process that literally has the potential to change the trajectory of their companies, and who instead order ill-qualified subordinates to provide a direction based on incomplete thinking (not to mention unrealistic budgets), will fall prey to their own ambitions as well as to predator providers in the marketplace. The latter will often echo like parrots what CEOs want to hear and have no genuine interest—regardless of what their shiny brochures say—in the welfare of the company and its ability to communicate effectively with its stakeholders. Some readers may consider my comments harsh. Be that as it may, they nevertheless reflect the reality of the situation. And Asian business is not well served by this. Asian CEOs ought to reflect on this brutal truth if they are genuinely interested in building great companies.

> Branding is a process, and a clearly well-defined and relevant brand is the result of that process.

Like most important things that deliver critical results, brand development and brand building are not straightforward. This is not to say, either, that they are complex or complicated. But contrary to the damaging misconceptions of far too many Asian CEOs, branding doesn't amount to creating a logo or a tag line, or expressing products and services through catchy advertising. Branding is a process, and a clearly well-defined and relevant brand is the result of that process. This chapter will deal with the critical steps of a mandatory process that leads to the formulation of a sound brand blueprint.

POSITIONING OR REPOSITIONING?

Strong and well-defined brands ultimately deliver value to the company: brands that customers can relate to, or depend on, or feel safe with—or define themselves by. Central to the company's core mission should be building a brand that its stakeholders will find compelling enough to bring into the orbit of their lives. Positioning does that. It positions the brand in a specific way, with a specific set of associations that, in time, attracts certain groups of people. It follows that the positioning process is crucial to any company intent on entering (and staying) in the lives of its customers.

What separates positioning from repositioning is not to be found within the process itself. The process for both is largely identical. Rather, the difference more accurately reflects where along the development stage the company finds itself. Positioning is a proactive initiative a new company embarks on as part of its overall roll-out and growth strategy. Existing companies that choose to launch new products also go through positioning exercises. It is about consciously creating something from the beginning.

Repositioning is when an established company—typically on a declining trajectory—takes the major step of reinventing itself in an effort to appeal either to altogether new customers or to existing customers who have new expectations or have been disappointed in the past. Repositioning a company or a product brand amounts to a very serious decision. The effort is more risky and more challenging than positioning because, in its efforts to create a new identity, the company must find ways to overcome existing prejudices already associated with it. If the existing associations are too negative and too entrenched, repositioning efforts are often fruitless. Such is the power of branding.

Companies that make the strategic decision to position or reposition themselves recognize that the effort must be systematic and comprehensive—devoid of short-cuts. It must be not only holistic, but also honest. Different strategy-centric companies offer proprietary methodologies that share common characteristics. The differences lie in small areas or additional (often, optional) deliverables. But the essence of the process is common across the board.

PREPARING FOR A (POSITIONING OR REPOSITIONING) BRANDING PROJECT

A branding project is a major milestone, and what is at stake goes beyond the time, effort, and money that will be invested in the effort. What is really at stake is the very future of the company—its viability and destiny.

If you are a CEO considering a positioning or repositioning branding project, you will need to tick-off a three-point checklist before leaping into the process:

1. Do you know why you are considering this project?
2. Have you identified a consultant whose strengths and specialization match your needs (see Figure 2.3 in Chapter 2)?
3. Are you prepared for the project period ahead? (That is, are you and your key executives aware of the branding basics?)

As already mentioned, a project proposal should not be written in a vacuum. To ensure that a sound and relevant proposal is submitted in the first place, you as the CEO will need to ensure that a number of important steps are taken.

Once you have identified the key objectives of your project, you will need to select a short-list of appropriate consultants/providers that demonstrate experience and specialization in the areas relevant to your project's needs. You will do yourself a great disservice—and risk wasting more than just time—if you approach too many companies that specialize in different areas of the continuum. Limit your short-list to like-type providers. Once you have identified them, have a preliminary meeting with them. What happens between that first meeting and the final meeting before the decision to appoint is made is summarized in four key steps, as outlined in Figure 6.1. It is essential that the final decision is

Figure 6.1 Choosing the right brand consultancy to partner with

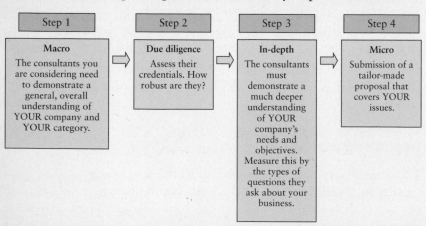

Source: BrandAsian.

based on how well the provider has delivered on each of the steps. That decision is your responsibility.

Step 1: General Interest

All too often, representatives of consultancies approached will arrive at the initial meeting with a company having made no effort to explore—at even a general level—what it does. I know this because clients will often express their general satisfaction at the end of their first meeting with us by complimenting us on the quality of questions we have asked or our general preparedness. That expression is almost always coupled with another: their disappointment that many providers arrive with no inkling of what their business is about and leave without asking questions they feel are important. I have seen this myself in collective briefings, where a client will go through a full PowerPoint presentation with no one asking questions that probe or challenge the thinking or expectations in the brief. Common sense would suggest that a minimum effort be made—particularly when the internet provides ample information at the click of a mouse. A consultancy hoping to make a good first impression will have done some research, and its representatives will have prepared pertinent questions to ask.

Step 2: Due Diligence

This step involves some effort on your part. Step 1 should have yielded a hardcopy credentials document from each company invited. Your interest in the providers' capabilities should not be restricted to this document. You will need to have the spectacular credits and achievements claimed in that document checked. More important, however, is getting first-hand impressions from senior executives and CEOs of past projects delivered by the provider. Their opinions will provide unique and reliable insights that will be invaluable when it comes time to decide on a provider.

Step 3: Real Interest

This is probably the most important of the four phases and the one most often overlooked by CEOs. Your branding project will explore key issues that are mostly relevant to your business: facts, as well as internal and external perceptions, that revolve around your market share, your business strategy, your customers (as well as those who are

not) and your relationship with them, your mission, vision and values, your internal infrastructure, your organizational chart, your key
markets, your goals for growth, your distribution strategy, your
competitive environment, your individual products and services
(perceived existing perceptions, strengths and weaknesses), your
employees (How are they recruited? How do they feel about the
company? How motivated do they seem to be?), and many other questions. It may well be that you cannot answer some of these questions,
but those that you can answer will help the consultants shape a more
effective proposal.

You should expect—and appreciate—a request from the providers you have approached for a session (normally lasting between one
and two hours) that allows them to better familiarize themselves with
your business and to ask the questions identified above. Make yourself
or a very senior and knowledgeable member of your management team
available for that session. It is inconceivable that any branding project
(regardless of whether it costs $80,000 or $800,000) should proceed in
the absence of a comprehensive proposal road map. This would be akin
to a doctor recommending treatment for a patient without first making a diagnosis. Yet, many CEOs do exactly this, either because they
are unaware of the importance of this input (because they are unaware
of the branding process in general), or because they are unwilling to
engage, or both. This is a major mistake.

The quality of the questions asked by the provider at this session, not
its promises and glossy brochures, will reveal whether it is a suitable
potential partner. As for those providers who don't ask for the session
in the first place, your decision on how to proceed should be clear.

Step 4: Professionalism and Truth

It is with this step that everything is either won or lost—both for the
company considering the process, as well as the consulting company
offering to provide it. A proposal that is tailor-made to the needs and
circumstances of your company will identify relevant project scope
action items. These are essential for the efficacy of the project and the
long-term success of your company.

If the CEO has not performed proper diligence, which includes the
very important step 3, it is likely that he will not understand the relevance or context of the suggested scope line items in the proposal or
the rationale provided that supports them. Not "getting it" will automatically make the CEO defensive and resistant to anything he doesn't

understand. This creates a ripple effect across everything. He (or you) will ask suspiciously:

- "Why should the scope extend to these markets? Why survey these target audiences or stakeholders (especially employees)? Why use three (or six) research groups? Why do research at all?
- "Why does the branding project need to tie in with our company vision and strategic objectives?"
- "Why do we need to 'validate' the positioning alternatives we have created?"
- "Why can we not just say what our customers want us to say?"
- "Why do we need to change our organizational structure?"
- "What does 'culture' have to do with anything, and why is HR suddenly so important?"

In short: "Can we take short-cuts here, or here, or there?"

The CEO who doesn't "get it" will be unaware that guiding principles, for instance, are important building blocks for the delivery of the brand proposition. He won't understand the need to talk to his employees, as well as his customers, to gain insight and "truth." In fact, he is very likely to resist any type of research, as well as any discussion about possible organizational restructuring of his functional departments. This CEO expects the consultants to talk mostly to him, because he has most of the answers and knows what he wants.

Often, the risk to an ethical and professional consulting company lies in its willingness to tell the truth.

Often, the risk to an ethical and professional consulting company lies in its willingness to tell the truth. A proposal submission that identifies the difficult things a company must do is often the one that Asian CEOs immediately dismiss. These CEOs don't want hard; they want easy. And in their minds, "easy" is easily available in the form of alternative submissions that provide the solution they are looking for. You should not fall into that trap.

Here's the thing: Every well-constructed proposal will have a number of scope items that are non-negotiable, key steps. Failing to recognize their importance and dismissing some or all of them will almost certainly risk compromising the integrity of the project. Simply stated, project integrity is the bare minimum threshold below which the project will be compromised. Any effort that fails to meet or exceed this threshold won't have sufficient critical mass to deliver a solution that is meaningful or robust. Theoretically, even reaching 90 percent of the threshold level still won't be enough to guarantee effectiveness. The reality is that most efforts that go by the name of branding projects in Asia reflect 50 percent and below critical mass threshold levels. This means that the majority of these projects have no project integrity and the companies would have been better off simply doing nothing, instead of something that is half-baked. As the CEO, your challenge is to figure out approximately where that threshold lies in your proposal.

THE STRATEGY-CENTRIC BRAND DEVELOPMENT METHODOLOGY

I will provide below an explanation of a "generic" version of the type of methodology used by most reputable, strategy-centric brand consultancies. This methodology is linear and multi-phased. All the phases, with the possible exception of the validation phase, are compulsory. Central to its efficacy are two key pillars: (1) the use of qualitative research; and (2) the use of workshops. Figure 6.2 provides an illustration of the

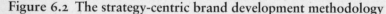

Figure 6.2 The strategy-centric brand development methodology

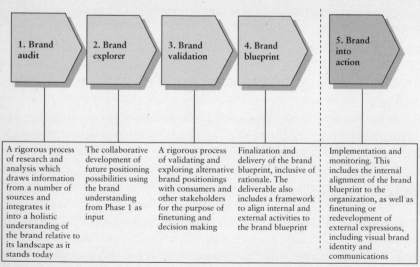

1. Brand audit	2. Brand explorer	3. Brand validation	4. Brand blueprint	5. Brand into action
A rigorous process of research and analysis which draws information from a number of sources and integrates it into a holistic understanding of the brand relative to its landscape as it stands today	The collaborative development of future positioning possibilities using the brand understanding from Phase 1 as input	A rigorous process of validating and exploring alternative brand positionings with consumers and other stakeholders for the purpose of finetuning and decision making	Finalization and delivery of the brand blueprint, inclusive of rationale. The deliverable also includes a framework to align internal and external activities to the brand blueprint	Implementation and monitoring. This includes the internal alignment of the brand blueprint to the organization, as well as finetuning or redevelopment of external expressions, including visual brand identity and communications

Source: BrandAsian.

methodology's four main phases. The fifth phase is all about implementation and amounts to a separate project. It will be discussed in detail in Chapter 7.

One very important thing needs to be said about this "full-bodied" approach from the outset: Its very comprehensiveness makes it effective, but at the same time intimidating to smaller Asian companies—particularly SMEs. The thoroughness of the process typically translates into what CEOs consider to be two problematic side-effects: (1) projects can take some time to complete: anything from three months for a project that requires a two- or three-market coverage, to one year or more for projects that are multi-market/multi-regional; and (2) projects can be relatively costly: anything from US$200,000 to US$1 million or more, depending on the scale and scope of the effort.

Consequently, typical "full-bodied" projects have not enjoyed great popularity among mid-sized and smaller firms in Asia over the past decade, because they have neither the financial resources nor the motivation that larger companies may enjoy. Most feel too pressured by competitive challenges and the burden of daily uncertainty to engage in a time-consuming and (to them) nebulous process they additionally don't quite understand. This resistance has reshaped the Asian brand landscape and contributed directly to the development of alternative "fast-track" methodologies. While some of these provide sufficiently robust processes, many others do not and so caution must be exercised. Those that do will usually ensure that the two indispensable key pillars of efficacy (primary research and workshops) are adopted in some measure. While the end-product (the brand blueprint) won't be as robust as what might have been created using a more full-bodied approach, it will be directional and provide a sufficiently accurate solution that can be extrapolated.

Notwithstanding the emergence of alternatives, full-bodied projects continue to offer the most desirable approach, particularly for medium and larger-sized organizations that have made the strategic decision to leave no stone unturned in understanding their markets, their customers, and their own staff, and in harnessing this intelligence to create differentiated and enduring brand blueprints.

Phase 1: Brand Audit

The brand audit is easily the project's longest and most intense phase. In some cases, it can take up as much as 50–60 percent of the total project time frame. It is a critical phase on which all else is dependent and from which all else is built. The brand audit is best characterized as rigorous (primary and secondary) research and analysis carried out in order to understand and deliver insights into four key areas of business:

- The brand's perceived image, strengths, and weaknesses;
- The desires, needs, and aspirations of key target audiences;
- Market analysis: size, trends, opportunities, threats, and barriers;
- Competitors' position, image, strengths, and weaknesses.

> *"We are suffering from a plethora of surmise, conjecture and hypothesis. The difficulty is to separate the framework of fact—of absolute undeniable fact—from the embellishments of theorists and reporters."*
>
> Sherlock Holmes in Arthur Conan Doyle's, "Silver Blaze"

Though what exactly is explored will differ from company to company, all branding projects will cover internal as well as external analysis (see Figure 6.3).

Internal analysis

Internal analysis is, by far, the element that gets the most push back from CEOs. Many don't recognize its relevance and, therefore, its importance. Others feel that it amounts to an invasion of company privacy. Overall, there always seems to be a general discomfort with outside consultants talking directly to employees at all levels or "poking their noses" into sensitive company business.

Figure 6.3 Phase 1: The brand audit

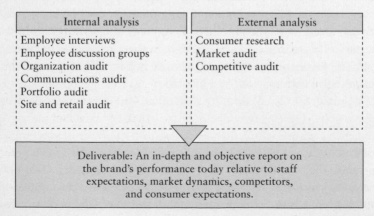

Internal analysis	External analysis
Employee interviews	Consumer research
Employee discussion groups	Market audit
Organization audit	Competitive audit
Communications audit	
Portfolio audit	
Site and retail audit	

Deliverable: An in-depth and objective report on the brand's performance today relative to staff expectations, market dynamics, competitors, and consumer expectations.

Source: BrandAsian.

However, internal analysis is critical to the mix, as it provides an internal employee perspective that can be measured against external customer attitudes and real market dynamics. Further, as Chapter 5 identified, the involvement and commitment of employees is essential to the successful delivery of the brand's proposition to the customer. It is, therefore, clearly important to assess how they feel about the company they work for and the brands they help create and market.

Exploring the attitudes and opinions of staff requires group discussions with lower and mid-level employees and one-on-one interviews with senior managers. Wherever possible, the sessions are videotaped so that they can be reviewed at a later time in greater detail by the consulting team before the tapes are destroyed. A standard condition that CEOs need to agree to before the start of work is that the contents of these tapes will not be made available to unauthorized members of the company. That basically means everyone, including the CEO. Honest opinions and insights can only be hoped for if respondents feel reassured that their comments will remain confidential and won't penalize them or come back to haunt them in any way. While exact and attributable expressions are not provided to management, the analysis of the collective sessions is. How many group discussions and interviews need to take place is an important consideration and a scope line item that deserves close scrutiny by the CEO. The number needs to be representative of the general employee population both at home and in markets abroad.

Employee group discussions tend almost always to deliver significant surprises, and even major revelations, to senior management and the CEO. This is because a gap *always* exists between what management and employees believe. To ensure that employees feel sufficiently comfortable to be honest and forthcoming with their thoughts and opinions, two things must happen at the recruitment stage: (a) only employees of the same level should be grouped together; and (b) senior managers should not be anywhere near the employee sessions. They certainly should not participate. The reason is obvious: With senior colleagues or managers present, employees are not likely to venture honest opinions or volunteer any meaningful information. Yet, as obvious as this need (and likely outcome) is, many CEOs continue to insist that senior managers be present at the sessions. Other offenders in some parts of Asia include government agencies whose senior managers insist on the right to view the confidential videotapes. Needless to say, reputable providers won't agree to compromise the confidentiality promised to employees. Apart from being a betrayal of trust, it is self-defeating. Employees know when Big Brother is watching. As a result, the process will deliver no insights of any value. This should be self-evident to managers, yet to many it is not.

Separate from the talk sessions are the communications and organization audits. The visual touch-points of the company play an important role in communicating the strategic elements of the brand blueprint—whether they are brand values or brand personality cues, or other drivers. Another key goal of all communications material should be consistency. Inconsistency of visual material confuses customers and leads to brand erosion. The audit should involve a comprehensive review of everything that visually communicates the company: from the corporate/product brand identity to its advertising. This will include the corporate logo, the corporate mark, primary corporate colors, the website, and the brand identity guidelines manual, as well as the ways in which these are applied. With advertising, it will also include a critical review of print ads and television commercials (where relevant and applicable).

Work-site analysis contributes to visual touch-points. If the company operates a retail business with outlets in one or more markets, the interior look and feel of each outlet plays an essential role in the delivery of the customer experience. "Site" also refers to an office work environment or the environment of a manufacturing plant or assembly line. The interior and exterior designs of Google's offices around the world reflect the company's quirky brand personality but at the same time inspire one of its most important values: innovation. Color is liberally splashed everywhere, and employees are encouraged to express their own individuality in shaping and decorating their own workspaces and in dressing in any way they find most comfortable. The Google approach is not "right" *per se*; it is simply right for that company. The objective of communication and site audits is to identify strengths, weaknesses, and, importantly, dissonance where inconsistencies are identified.

To complete the internal analysis, an audit of the company's portfolio of brands should also be undertaken. Emphasis should be placed on how product brands relate to one another and how all relate to the master brand. Analysis should also identify whether the brand architecture in place is consistent with the objectives of the company's business strategy.

External analysis

The external analysis component of the brand audit delivers a real-time snapshot of important consumer/customer, market, and competitive insights essential for ongoing planning and operations. With B2C projects the focus is on end-consumers. The research adopted is qualitative and, usually, focus-group based. One of two challenges is deciding what kind of respondent profile best addresses present as well as likely future brand needs. This results in identification of the consumer segment universe. The other challenge is determining the optimum number of groups needed to deliver sufficient insights that are representative of the broader customer community.

With B2B projects the focus is on key decision makers of customer companies. To better understand these individuals, the best approach lies in the use of one-on-one interviews. As with the consumer focus groups, a key challenge is determining who to speak to and how many individuals will provide a representative sample.

Whether talking to end-consumers or interviewing customers, this exercise provides an opportunity for gap analysis. As with the internal employee group discussions and employee interviews, profound revelations are almost guaranteed to occur (see Figure 6.4). While many of these may be positive and provide pleasant surprises, others may be negative. Not knowing is clearly not a good thing, and this exercise delivers an extremely useful amount of intelligence that is not only relevant to the branding project, but can also be deployed immediately to improve the company's ongoing operations.

A very valuable bonus provided by the external analysis effort is the delivery of a detailed and accurate report on market conditions and development, which includes the disposition of competitors. To many Asian companies that do business in the complete absence of market data (market size, market share, growth, developments, etc.), this information is nothing short of a boon. Independent of the role this analysis plays within the context of the branding project, it separately

---

Figure 6.4 Gap analysis

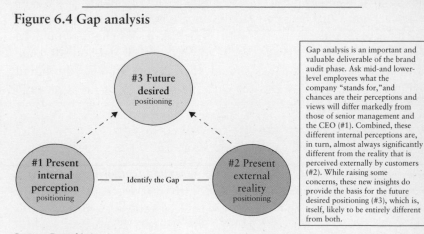

Gap analysis is an important and valuable deliverable of the brand audit phase. Ask mid-and lower-level employees what the company "stands for," and chances are their perceptions and views will differ markedly from those of senior management and the CEO (#1). Combined, these different internal perceptions are, in turn, almost always significantly different from the reality that is perceived externally by customers (#2). While raising some concerns, these new insights do provide the basis for the future desired positioning (#3), which is, itself, likely to be entirely different from both.

Source: BrandAsian.

provides the CEO and his management team with critical market intelligence that, if used appropriately, can deliver measurable competitive advantage—often immediately. The competitive audit is particularly valuable. It needs to be detailed and comprehensive. It needs to identify all the players in the market, their relative shares, their sources of competitive advantage, and their overall strengths and perceived weaknesses. Differentiation of a company's brand is difficult to do in a vacuum. A clear understanding of the positioning of all competitors is more than useful; it is essential in providing a concrete frame of reference.

The brand audit phase provides the CEO with a set of vital tools: comprehensive data and insights about the market, competitors, and employees. This provides not only an invaluable window into knowledge, but also into possibilities.

Summary of brand audit outcomes:

1. Internal people perspective on a range of issues and subjects;

2. A better understanding of the organization's infrastructure;

3. Exposure of problems that may be systemic in nature;

4. External perceptions of the brand;

5. Gap analysis of internal versus external perceptions of the brand;

6. Internal and external awareness and understanding of the corporate vision, mission, and values;

7. Assessment of existing culture(s);

8. Drivers and barriers to establishing a stronger corporate culture;

9. Gap analysis between projected image, desired image, and communications;

10. Comprehensive competitors' analysis;

11. Overview of the company's brand portfolio strategy.

Phase 2: Brand Explorer

*"It was funny. Just by thinking of a couple of unrelated issues,
out came a simpler design."*

Stephen Wozniak (from *Return to the Little Kingdom*,
by Michael Moritz)

The brand explorer phase marks the beginning of defining creative solutions. The brand blueprint, for all of its strategic dimensions, is the product of a creative process. If the process is delivered technically well and undertaken with open and imaginative minds that are willing to consider issues that in the past might have been thought of as unrelated or unlikely, disruptive thinking is likely to emerge. The more disruptive the solution (everything else being equal), the more unique and differentiated (and therefore, the more effective) it is likely to be. The vast quantity of information collected and synthesized in the brand audit phase will have revealed challenges and opportunities. These will form the basis of the discussions and debates that will take place within the full-day workshops that are part of this phase. The workshops are moderated by the consultants but are populated entirely by a select group of senior managers who are representative of the company's operational departments and the geographies in which the company does business. For the workshops to be effective, no more than 25 or so individuals (who are then divided into five or six teams) should participate. Too few participants and the quality and quantity of the ideas generated will be compromised. Too many, and the workshops promise endless long-winded debates that can become academic at best, or acrimonious at worst.

The workshops are characterized by a process that is collaborative by design. They aim to harness the experience and expertise that exists within the organization. By injecting the intelligence collected in the brand audit phase, a forum is created for open and creative thinking that will influence the company's future. Almost as importantly, the workshops enhance commitment by participants to the future expression of the brand. The workshops are an important and integral part of the overall brand blueprint development process.

The workshops (which can number between two and four) typically make use of a sophisticated "tool-box" that includes exercises that require discussion, debate, and decision making from the individual teams. When positions are reached, team leaders present them to the broader group. This approach distills the information collected in the brand audit and, with the completion of every exercise, translates it into articulated drafts of each of the eight strategic brand blueprint elements: the positioning statement, the core brand benefits, the core brand values, the core brand personality traits, the core brand attributes, the company mission, and the company vision. Of these, the showcase deliverable is the positioning statement. Typically, up to four iterations of one or more positioning statement ideas will be drafted nearing the conclusion of the phase. At that point, some brand development methodologies will deploy a version of a "positioning continuum" (see Figure 6.5).

Figure 6.5 The positioning continuum

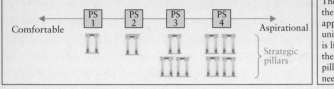

The further to the right the positioning appears, the more unique and exciting it is likely to be; but also, the more "strategic pillars" the brand will need to address.

The different brand positioning alternatives are plotted on a continuum to reflect the distance the brand has to "travel" from its present associations (those discovered in the brand audit) to its future positioning. The implementation of the positioning option on the far left (positioning statement #1) promises the least amount of change or general disruption to the company, either because the mandatory initiatives the company will need to adopt—the strategic pillars—will be relatively painless and straightforward, or because the positioning is likely to be quite close to existing associations the company already owns. Usually, it is a combination of both. "Strategic pillars" amount to those minimum changes the company must adopt as a prerequisite if the positioning statement is to emerge and develop. The further to the right the positioning appears, the more unique and exciting it is likely to be; but also, the more strategic pillars the brand will need to address.

Achieving new positionings isn't easy and doesn't happen on its own. The company must consciously identify the changes and initiatives that will need to be implemented throughout its organizational and operational processes to give the positioning and the rest of the brand blueprint a chance to emerge and, in time, become a credibly firm association that all stakeholders have with the brand. Much of this forms part of the internal alignment phase, which is discussed in Chapter 7. What makes a brand blueprint robust and strategically sound is the CEO's commitment to implement each of the strategic pillars. No shortcuts are permitted here. Failure to implement any of the pillars will rob the brand blueprint of internal support and external credibility. This will deprive the company of long-term sustainable growth and success.

The brand explorer phase will also be the first opportunity senior managers will have to discuss the brand audit findings on the state of the company's portfolio of brands—specifically, the brand architecture strategy in place. As discussed in Chapter 5, brand architecture is a critical business and brand strategy component. So important is this area that it deserves focused attention. Any branding project that creates a new brand or repositions an existing brand will upset the balance of an existing portfolio of brands. Once the branding project at hand is completed, attention should immediately be directed to recalibrating the company's brand architecture strategy.

The purpose of the brand explorer phase is to explore brand positioning alternatives, as well as the other strategic elements that form part of the brand blueprint. This is an information-based process that relies on collaboration of senior individuals. To be successful, the process requires an attitude that suspends resistance to and denial of unexpected or unpleasant insights resulting from the research. It also requires collaboration, open-mindedness, and imagination that disregards conventional wisdom in favor of disruptive innovation.

Summary of brand explorer outcomes:

1. Draft brand positioning alternatives that are relevant, compelling, differentiated, and sustainable;

2. Brand positioning statements' continuum;

3. Draft brand blueprint elements;

4. Target audience segmentation universe;

5. Draft overview of a revised brand architecture strategy.

Phase 3: Brand Validation

This phase is the only one that is arguably "optional." Brand validation involves taking the short-listed draft positioning statements (which typically include mood or video board expressions that provide a visual interpretation), as well as the other strategic brand blueprint elements, back to customers and employees for their opinions and feedback. The goal is to validate. It is a research-driven process aimed at evaluating and assessing the positioning alternatives with external and internal stakeholders for their relevance, credibility, differentiation, and commitment, while, at the same time, identifying their strengths and weaknesses. The brand validation phase identifies and refines the "winning" idea and defines the necessary modifications needed to arrive at the final recommendation.

The reason why this phase is optional: Given the (legitimate) view of many that a brand blueprint dictates the very destiny of their company moving forward, it makes eminent sense for committed CEOs to cover all their bases and benefit from as much feedback as possible before making final decisions. On the other hand, many argue that the comprehensive brand audit process is exhaustive in its effort and scope. Indeed, a frequent and common outcome of that phase can be information overload. In addition, the brand explorer phase exposes the insights of the brand audit to the smartest and best-informed executives in the company. On the basis of these two points, many CEOs (around 40 percent) conclude that they have more than sufficient information to make a well-informed final decision. Everything considered, this view is reasonable. It must be remembered that, although desirable, going back into the market across multiple geographies to reach out to customers as well as employees is time-consuming and costly. But if the time and funds are available, it remains a desirable option.

Objectives/deliverables:

1. To individually assess each positioning statement;

2. To identify possible challenges or opportunities relating to each;

3. To evaluate key brand blueprint elements—specifically: brand benefits, brand values, and brand personality traits for their relative strength and appeal;

4. To evaluate the draft mission statements for relevance, appeal, credibility, and sustainability;

5. To identify possible barriers or challenges for the adoption of the mission by employees.

Phase 4: Brand Blueprint

The brand blueprint should—theoretically—provide companies with a vital and invaluable tool. It simultaneously anchors the company while providing it with direction and a road map to operational consistency. It is, without question, the single most important strategic document the company should have at its disposal. However, in Asia, there is an alarming absence of brand blueprints—or at least ones that are well crafted and coherent. This is not only a shame; it is an absolute waste. Opportunities that are hiding in the open are being ignored or missed by some of the brightest and most ambitious CEOs, because they are moving too quickly to notice them and are taking too many short-cuts.

As stated earlier, there are no short-cuts to developing an effective, robust, and directional brand blueprint. With the possible exception of brand validation, the three phases that precede it ensure that the groundwork needed to deliver the brand blueprint is in fact done.

Like much of the first phase, the brand blueprint phase is almost entirely in the hands of the consultants. With the draft elements and statements (validated or not) completed, the consultants withdraw to review the considerable output generated in the workshops. From this they will craft a master document that will reflect not just the final iterations of the selected elements—the brand positioning statement, as well as the "core" brand benefits, the "core" brand values, the "core" brand attributes, and the "core" brand personality traits—but also, critically, a rationale that supports, explains, and provides clarity and context for each. This rationale typically accompanies the final expression of the brand blueprint when it is transformed into a strategic document for existing and future employees, as well as customers, or is expressed in forums such as the company website. The document will also include the company mission statement and a draft expression of the CEO's vision moving forward.

While the rationale that accompanies the brand blueprint is revealed visibly in open and public forums, the master document prepared by the consultants for senior management contains far more critical and sensitive information that need not have such broad exposure. In addition to the brand blueprint and its supporting rationale, the final master document will provide comprehensive information, insights, and conclusions on key operational and marketing areas, such as:

- Clarification (sometimes, the reformulation) of the company's business strategy.
- The strategic pillars: organizational processes, structures, and resources that the company will need to put in place to deliver on and support the brand positioning.
- Identification of the target audience universe, as well as the selected primary and secondary key audiences on which the brand will focus. The choice of segments will be supported by a rationale.
- Brand architecture strategy: a review of where the brand fits in the present company brand portfolio inclusive of recommendations that could lead to incremental or wholesale changes.

COSTING THE PROJECT PROPOSAL

A question Asian CEOs are lightning quick to ask about any branding project is: "How much is it going to cost me?" And while the question is legitimate and understandable, it is often asked as if branding projects are comparable to the relatively straightforward act of buying a car or an apartment, where most people know more or less what they are doing—and what they are getting. This isn't usually the case with branding projects. CEOs who ask this question—often even before a proposal has been formally crafted—are usually unaware of what goes into the process and what it is capable of delivering. Consequently, the "answer" is, in reality, neither here nor there, because it is provided without the benefit of context. Where $100,000 may be too expensive to some, others may perceive $500,000 as being reasonable and affordable.

The importance of perspective

While all dimensions of branding projects (inclusive of cost) require and deserve close scrutiny and due diligence like any other business initiative, it is important to recognize that this specific endeavor is not, in fact, like any other business initiative. It is unique and special and requires perspective. There are three important lenses through which to assess the cost and value of a branding project to a company. If these three elements are considered in their proper perspective, the cost element becomes a decision that is made with confidence and without hesitation:

- Project scope line items;
- Anticipated near-, mid-, and long-term enhanced revenue streams;
- Anticipated long-term company valuation.

PROJECT SCOPE LINE ITEMS

CEOs make a serious mistake when they compare projects based solely on price. They make an even worse mistake when they make a decision based on price. In Asia this happens all the time, especially with mid- and small-sized companies. It is also very characteristic of how government (branding project) tenders tend to be decided, as the decision makers who preside over the process are bureaucrats keen to show they are capable of controlling costs. As a result, a debate has raged for some time in certain markets over whether it is even worthwhile for consultants and ad agencies to participate in what tends to be a time-consuming and costly process that frequently ends in disappointment.

It is also not uncommon for multiple providers to submit proposals for the same project that differ greatly in cost—often by as much as 100–200 percent. While this reveals a problematic issue among providers, it is mostly the result of very poor, confused, and contradictory briefings by the requesting companies. Whatever the reason, CEOs will usually gravitate immediately to the lowest-priced projects. When this is done for the wrong reasons, it causes untold damage to Asian brands.

Competent and ethical providers often run a real risk of putting themselves immediately out of contention if they submit a proposal that includes individual scope line items that they consider essential, but which are interpreted as costly by CEOs. Who is to say that exploring two markets in which the company does business will be less effective than exploring, say, five markets? Who is to say that four focus groups representing multiple user and non-user profiles are better than two? Who is to say that comprehensive customer segmentation analysis is critical to the brand strategy? The "who" clearly needs to be an informed CEO. A mistake in this area is not simply measured in terms of a more or less expensive project cost; a mistake potentially impacts the integrity of the project. If CEOs are unaware of what they need to be aware of, they will dismiss the line items as unnecessary and consider the proposal expensive. Out the door goes not only the provider, but in many cases, also the scope the company needs most. While not all scope line items are always needed or relevant, they nonetheless remain the basis for considering and comparing project proposals.

NEAR-, MID-, AND LONG-TERM ENHANCED REVENUE STREAMS

"57% of consumers would give the most reputable companies across the globe the benefit of the doubt in a time of crisis."

Reputation Institute, "Global Reputation Pulse 2009" study

The cost of a well-crafted branding project will always amount to a negligible amount in relative terms when compared to the kind of customer attention the company can expect to attract in the near, mid, and long term if the brand blueprint is implemented properly. The distance between no (or a confused) identity, and one that delivers a clear and compelling reason to a customer to buy, should be obvious to any CEO. It translates immediately into invigorated or altogether new top-line revenue streams.

Intangible benefits that are just as important also manifest themselves externally via better and more effective relationships with suppliers and other stakeholders, and internally in terms of better efficiencies and stronger morale.

The more visible benefits a strong brand can reward a company with are summarized below. These benefits need to be taken into account when considering the cost of a strong and well-crafted project proposal:

- Trust and reputation;
- Ability to command a premium price;
- Ability to develop more stable demand;
- Ability to establish barriers to entry;
- Ability to leverage its brand equity when introducing new products;
- Ability to incur lower sales conversion costs;
- Ability to obtain more favorable supplier terms;
- Ability to generate lower staff acquisition and retention costs;
- Ability to secure capital at a lower cost.

LONG-TERM COMPANY VALUATION

> *"The total worth of the 250 most valuable global brands is more than France's gross domestic product."*
>
> John Gerzema, interview with Bloomberg

Brands are not only about image or warm and fuzzy feelings. Ultimately, the value of brands lies in the tangible and measurable benefits they deliver to a company and its shareholders. One of the major differences that separate many large and successful Western companies from large and successful Asian companies is valuation. Some of the largest corporations in the world, such as Coca-Cola and McDonald's, owe as much as 50–70 percent of their total market capitalization to the intangible contribution of their brands.[3] Why is Coca-Cola valued so highly? The most common answer is that it is expected to be operating as profitably 20 years from now as it did 20 years ago, and 20 years before that. What financial analysts (and, importantly, prospective acquirers) factor in is the power of the brand name to generate revenues and profits not just in the present, but into an estimated future period as well.

Viewed through the position that the brand represents the very destiny of the company, the cost of a branding project arguably becomes almost irrelevant.

The cost of any branding project is important and should be representative of the scope of work that needs to be covered. But CEOs should not focus exclusively on the cost. A strong branding culture is not a nice-to-have; it is among the most important company must-haves. In this context, the question of affordability becomes a relative one. Some CEOs who really "get it," go further. To them, branding is as indispensable to their company as air is to the human body. Viewed through the position that the brand represents the very destiny of the company, the cost of a branding project arguably becomes almost irrelevant. The issue of affordability doesn't revolve around the absolute cost of the project itself, but rather the cost of its absence. In other words, given what is at stake, one could make the powerful argument that companies cannot afford *not* to engage in a branding project.

NOTES

1. "No Guts No Glory," *Marketing*, July 2009, p. 44.
2. "STC's Top Five Brand Moves," company advertisement, July 2009, p. 45.
3. "Visual Depiction of Brand Contribution to Market Capitalization," slideshare.net, www.slideshare.net/DannielleBlumenthal/the-financial-value-of-a-brand-an-open-source-presentation, slide 15, from Interbrand/JP Morgan league table 2002, *BusinessWeek*.

7

BRAND INTO ACTION: DELIVERING AGAINST YOUR PROMISE

BE CAREFUL WHAT YOU PROMISE

"Most often today the difference between a company and its competitor is the ability to execute."

Larry Bossidy and Ram Charan, *Execution: The Discipline of Getting Things Done*

A common trap for companies is falling victim to the over-promise syndrome, despite the ever-increasing levels of leverage and empowerment enjoyed by consumers in these times of unprecedented competition. The better informed consumers are, and the more control they enjoy, the less tolerant they are of companies that disappoint them. One of the fundamental rules that underpin branding projects is: "Be careful what you promise." Why? Because you will need to deliver it—every time.

Many CEOs, on completion of a branding project, rush to communicate to the market their new positioning, new values, and updated core benefits. While their haste may derive from their genuine enthusiasm for their new identity, their companies may not yet be ready to face the world. Rebranded companies usually require time to digest their new brand blueprints and find ways to live up to their new characteristics *before* telling the world. This means recognizing that many things within their companies will change, and providing their employees with the motivation, opportunities, and time to make their new brand blueprints come alive. In each case, this amounts to an implementation project—what we refer to as the brand-into-action phase (See Figure 6.2, Chapter 6).

A brand will never live up to its potential, and in most cases will actually flounder, unless conscious efforts are made to make it real—that is, to go from the talk to the walk.

A brand-into-action implementation program is analogous to the follow-through of a tennis swing. It delivers power and accuracy with a sense of conviction. Without it, the stroke will be weak, off the mark, or out of bounds. As important as the brand blueprint is, it is a mean-ingless and useless (and wasted) document unless it is formally imple-mented. A brand will never live up to its potential, and in most cases will actually flounder, unless conscious efforts are made to make it real—that is, to go from the talk to the walk.

In meeting rooms across Asia where branding proposals are being presented, the disclosure many brand consultants are reluctant to make (mostly because they know that CEOs are loath to hear it) is like the proverbial elephant everyone pretends not to see: that the process of for-mally building a brand requires two projects, not one. Everything that leads to the creation of the all-important brand blueprint amounts to a single self-contained project: the branding project (project #1). Brand-into-action amounts to project #2. It is, as has been discussed in this book, difficult enough to persuade Asian decision makers to consider committing to this one process, without adding an additional complica-tion that may further undermine their willingness to proceed.

Instead of full disclosure, two much less desirable things are taking place. On the one hand, in the hopes of securing the brand develop-ment project quickly and simply, no disclosure is made. It is only later that the CEO realizes that even more time and funds will be required for implementation after the brand blueprint is created. Whether this is considered disturbing news will depend entirely on whether—disclosure or no disclosure—the CEO would have been willing to go through this additional process in the first place. The fact is, many are not.

The partial disclosure approach, on the other hand, is where the CEO is aware that some formal action will be needed following the craft-ing of the blueprint, but makes it clear to the consultants that when the time comes he will want it done quickly and painlessly. And in spite of the fact that this is the follow-up project, he wants to know the cost up front—before the branding project begins. The result is predictable. Again, in an effort to ensure that the main (brand develop-ment) branding project is secured, a relatively superficial assessment of implementation needs is made and at a low cost that is likely to meet the threshold expectations of the CEO.

Neither of these two approaches is very helpful or likely to deliver effective outcomes.

Any effort to determine the parameters of a brand-into-action project proposal at the same time that a brand development proposal is crafted will fall short, for one very simple reason: It is the brand development process (project #1) that reveals where a company stands and where it needs to travel to. In other words, the scope of the second project at that point in time is an unknown. It is impossible (not to mention unwise) to ask for or accept a half-cocked brand-into-action project proposal before the brand development project is completed. It simply doesn't make sense, yet it happens all the time. Inevitably, as there are more unknowns than knowns, these proposals are not going to reflect accurate and effective initiatives or just how much should be invested. Invariably, what ends up being identified in these submissions amounts to cosmetic changes and tactical initiatives related to the logo, website, collaterals, and advertising—not the substantive issues, which are the most critical factors in validating the brand development process: operationalizing the brand blueprint internally (via infrastructure or organizational change), employee education, and, very importantly, exploring ways to dimensionalize (bring alive) key elements of the blueprint (such as the positioning and/or core values).

What does "brand-into-action" mean? For one thing, it means an additional project. A newly repositioned company or product brand will aim to impart a new identity to customers and other stakeholders. The new identity—the brand positioning, as well as the other strategic drivers of the brand blueprint—will result in a measure of change that will need to be introduced to the organization. As Figure 6.5 in Chapter 6 illustrates, all positionings can be plotted on a continuum that identifies corresponding strategic pillars. These pillars spell out the minimum amount of change a company must be prepared to adopt if it hopes to successfully live up to that positioning. Some of these changes will be relatively cosmetic—for example, refreshing or overhauling the corporate visual identity of the brand (colors and logo, among other things). Or changes can be more involved and complicated, often requiring a change management program.

. . . the CEO and his management must adopt a mindset that is open to new ideas and from sources normally not heard from (such as lower-level employees). They will not only need to accept this, but should encourage it.

Secondly, it means that the effort is time sensitive. Ideally, it should start very soon after the branding project is completed. There are several reasons why sooner is better than later, but one of the more important ones is maintaining momentum. Losing project momentum is like getting the wind blown out of your sails: People get distracted, interest in the process deflates, the credibility of management's commitment takes a hit, and the hoped-for project effectiveness is jeopardized. In describing the reinvention of the State Bank of India that began in 2006, chairman Prakash Bhatt observed that moving quickly to educate employees about the "need for ongoing change" was an imperative: "In 100 days, we covered everybody. Any slower, and the skeptics might have overwhelmed the conversation."[1] Lastly, it means commitment. Beyond kicking off in a time-effective manner, the CEO and his management must adopt a mindset that is open to new ideas and from sources normally not heard from (such as lower-level employees). They will not only need to accept this, but should encourage it.

MAKING THE BRAND COME ALIVE

A properly conceived brand-into-action program focuses on creating the solutions, processes, standards, and tools for implementing as well as measuring the impact of the brand blueprint both internally and externally. The former amounts to the internal alignment of the brand blueprint across as many operations of the business as possible. The latter ensures that all external expressions of the brand also reflect the essence, if not the letter, of the brand blueprint. A third dimension—brand metrics—also plays an important role in measuring how selected key branding drivers perform over a period of time (see Figure 7.1).

The deliverables of all three dimensions result in procedural, behavioral, physical, and visual applications that are consistent with, and support and reinforce, the brand positioning and other elements of the blueprint.

Internal Alignment

If the CEO and his senior team are committed to transforming the company and making it brand-centric, they will need to be open to the idea that the internal alignment process will result in the introduction, change, or replacement of anything (and everything) that helps to operationalize the brand.

Figure 7.1 Brand into action

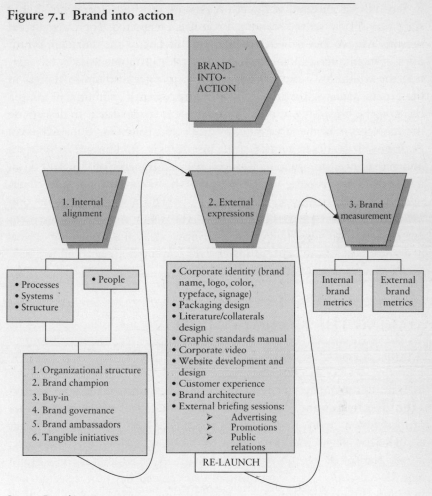

Source: BrandAsian.

Aligning the new brand blueprint internally involves and results in many changes. Very often some of these changes can be profound and significant, impacting processes, systems, and structure, as well as people. The former grouping has traditionally been associated with more tangible and measurable business practices and disciplines: TQM, ISO9000, and Six Sigma, to name a few. The latter grouping—"people"—is more closely associated with "softer" functions and constructs, such as human resources and corporate culture. Both contribute to change management. If the CEO and his senior team are committed to transforming the company and making it brand-centric, they will need to be open to the idea that the internal alignment process will result in the introduction, change, or replacement of anything (and everything) that helps to operationalize the brand. This will not only provide the physical means to bring the brand alive, but will also deliver internal credibility to sometimes skeptical employees who are used to seeing "initiatives" come and go.

Change management is a complex discipline. A whole industry has been built around it, with dozens of companies providing expert specialty services catering to all kinds of change connected with all aspects of business. It is therefore disingenuous to claim that even the most professional and credentialed brand consultant could provide comprehensive advice and services that address all aspects of change. What the better consultancies can do is provide change management advice that specifically empowers employees to think and behave in ways that breathe life into the brand blueprint, transforming a collection of words into a visible, tangible, and credible reality.

Internal alignment involves essentially six main areas of operations and initiatives:

1. Review of the organizational structure;
2. The role and goal of the brand champion;
3. Motivating and persuading employees to buy into the new brand blueprint;
4. Establishing a brand governance structure;
5. Appointment of brand ambassadors;
6. Finding tangible ways to bring each of the brand blueprint strategic elements alive. This last initiative anchors the entire internal alignment effort.

> *"Howard [Schultz] beamed with pride. At every level of the company, Starbucks employees understood the complexity—and ultimate power—of the brand positioning."*
>
> Scott Bedbury, *A New Brand World*

It is important that the emphasis of the six initiatives be collaborative and explored and developed as much as possible by employees at all levels. A bottom-up process is desirable because the participation it offers people facilitates buy-in.

1. Review of the organizational structure

One of the benefits of a comprehensive brand audit (from project #1) are the insights it delivers into company structure and the kinds of relationships that exist between employees. An organizational structure that may be too hierarchical or inflexible, or simply dysfunctional, will not lend itself to operational efficiencies or build a positive internal culture. One of the first things most companies that have completed a branding project find themselves needing to do is restructure (at least part of) the organization in a manner that facilitates the delivery of the brand blueprint.

The brand audit will have identified a range of issues that may reflect strengths as well as weaknesses: internal efficiency of individual departments; or the effectiveness of interdepartmental collaboration; or the presence or absence of specific processes or systems needed for existing operations or growth; or the absence of key rank and line functions that may compromise the effectiveness of some key individuals (or, indeed, the presence of redundant functions whose disappearance would benefit the company). The list is long.

Problems uncovered by the brand audit should not be addressed in isolation. Instead, the company's organizational structure as a whole needs to be reconsidered and, if necessary, reconfigured in a brand-centric way that helps people live and deliver the brand.

As discussed in Chapter 5, a brand-centric organization views virtually everything—and organizes itself entirely—through the prism of the brand. So, in restructuring, the company needs to recognize that efficiency and effectiveness need to be goals that are assessed in terms that are relative to the delivery of the brand blueprint. That means revising processes and systems, as well as changing employee mindsets in each functional department, so that the brand blueprint is used as a key frame of reference for all operations.

2. The role and goal of the brand champion

For the internal alignment process to succeed, the chief executive must actively fulfill the role of the brand champion. Apart from leadership and direction, employees must see that the CEO and, therefore, the organization are truly committed to delivering on the promise the brand will make to its customers.

> *"The best brand-building efforts are a form of leadership, showing your internal audience where you want them to go."*
>
> Lou Gerstner, former CEO, IBM

It is essential that the CEO take his role as brand champion seriously and with the utmost sincerity. This cannot be learned; ultimately, it must be felt. The CEO must genuinely believe that it is within the brand, and the belief of all employees in the brand, that greatness lies. To this end, he will make great efforts to lead physically. He will be present at seminars, he will participate in workshops, and he will make himself available to the brand council (see point 4 below) at all times. His goal will be to inspire others: Only when the CEO believes in the brand with his heart and soul, will others have the confidence and motivation to follow.

3. Motivating and persuading employees to "buy" into the new brand blueprint

Each and every employee plays a part in the delivery chain. In a world where product, technology, and design can be easily copied, it is the delivery by people that creates long-lasting differentiation. For employees to deliver positive customer experiences and perceptions, they need to be inspired by the company—what it stands for and what it does. Just as with customers, the brand needs to be persuasively "sold" to employees as well. What they need and deserve is the opportunity to know what is going on and to participate in the brand's journey.

Message to employees: "Your opinion matters."

Typically, the act of motivating and persuading employees is in one direction, from the top down. Attempting to motivate others by "telling" them how to behave, how to think, and even how to feel is doomed to failure. Yet, it happens all the time—and not just in Asia. Instead, people need to feel that they are part of the process and have some ownership in it. This is one of the major reasons why the brand audit phase of the brand development project involves as many employees from as many divisions and markets as possible. Beyond the collection of critically important insights, the invitation to employees to participate—from senior managers to factory-level workers—communicates an important message that reveals a sub-text: "Your opinion matters." Research consistently confirms that being consulted—being made part of a process (to come up with a new idea, or to solve a technical problem, or to resolve a dispute)—matters highly to employees. It contributes to their sense of self-worth and self-esteem. By inviting employees to be part of the development process, they become stakeholders with vested interests in the solution. When it then comes time to align that solution internally, they don't have to "buy" into anything. They belong to the team of original authors and can actually claim credit for its existence.

But, clearly, not all employees can participate in the brand audit phase of the branding project. In fact, most will not. A major and sincere effort by management will need to be made to align those who don't participate with the solutions identified in the brand blueprint. This will be achieved partly through communications and partly through interactive initiatives that achieve three things simultaneously: (1) it educates employees on the role and importance of a brand; (2) it shares with them the newly crafted positioning of their own brand (and the implications of implementation); and (3) it solicits opinions and observations on the finished work. This is best achieved by means of seminars that, over a short period of time, reach every individual in the organization. The key aim of these sessions is to psychologically prepare employees for the anticipated changes, as well as to encourage them to emerge as catalysts of change. A separate objective is to identify and train suitable employees to be qualified "brand ambassadors" (see point 5 below).

The seminar sessions need to address the following areas:

- The value and importance of brands and branding;
- Their own brand DNA: understanding their own brand blueprint;
- What the new brand blueprint should mean to employees;
- The critically important role that they will play as employees in delivering the brand positioning, as well as the other strategic elements of the brand blueprint;
- How the company will move forward to physically implement the brand, and some of the changes that will take place within the organization (see point 6 below).

The seminars will need to adopt a tone that avoids being clinical and impersonal, and is instead warm and purposeful. *All* employees need to attend these sessions, which means a time and cost investment. And the CEO should attend as many of these sessions as possible, if only to welcome attendees and introduce the subject matter.

4. Establishing a brand governance structure

Brand governance is an important function that provides the structure and tools necessary for managing the brand. It will involve the creation of a "brand council" that is assigned the responsibility to monitor the flow and expression of the brand. The council will be the "address" for all employees who have questions, as well as ideas and initiatives that help to implement, improve, and promote the brand over time. The council is charged with appointing and managing the brand ambassadors.

> "... *every member of the organization down to the janitor is an ambassador [for the brand]...*"
>
> Singapore Yellow Pages executive

5. Appointment of brand ambassadors

Change doesn't happen on its own. If left to themselves, people's natural tendency is to maintain the status quo. Therefore, catalysts are needed in order to stimulate change and encourage brand-centric behavior. One such catalyst is brand ambassadors. In the broader definition of the term, all employees are brand ambassadors—either knowingly or unwittingly. What they say and how they behave influences what people think of the company or the company's brands. But in the context of an internal alignment process, formally appointed brand ambassadors need to be first among equals—those individuals who provide an example to all other employees.

Ideally, brand ambassadors are passionate and committed, with an infectious enthusiasm for and emotional connection to the brand. As catalysts they encourage brand-centric behavior in the organization, and facilitate the brand implementation program. This means entrusting them with the responsibility of continuously finding ways to strengthen the brand by introducing new ideas on the one hand, and "policing" the brand on the other—ensuring that the brand in all its iterations is expressed consistently and is not compromised in any way. Clearly, these people don't grow on trees. The most likely candidates need to be identified and then encouraged and nurtured to represent the brand. Outside of personal passion, these individuals will also need to be motivated in a practical manner. This is going to require the consideration of incentives and rewards that must reflect the importance and responsibility of the role, as well as the expectations and confidence management and the chief executive have in this group.

One way to identify potential candidates is to hold a workshop, moderated by senior management, where the company's best and brightest, as well as volunteers who are attracted to the potential responsibility, are invited to get together to discuss a wide range of issues. The CEO should attend.

The workshop will have several objectives. First, it will aim to stimulate discussion, obtain in-depth insights, and generate a base of ideas that can be taken forward for brand implementation; secondly, it will encourage employees to (among other things) eventually use (and know when to use) the terms "on-brand" and "off-brand" to identify, respectively, behaviors that are aligned with the brand and those that are not; thirdly, it will, through a process, select those individuals best suited to be brand ambassadors, and determine—in a collaborative manner—the parameters of the role and purpose of brand ambassadors. In other words: Where will their roles begin? What kind of responsibilities and authority will they have?

One argument favors that the brand ambassador team be exclusively made up of the rank and file. This would engender a bottom-up approach (like the broader internal alignment process) that would encourage ownership and engagement. However, given the command-and-control management style and the silo-like organizational structure that characterize so many Asian companies, brand ambassadors made up exclusively of rank-and-file employees would likely achieve little. Instead, open-minded and progressive senior managers need to participate, to provide guidance and encouragement while at the same time resisting the inclination to manage. Overall, a bottom-up effect is desirable: Brand ambassadors report to the brand council; in turn, the brand council is answerable to the brand champion, the CEO.

One of the key factors that influence the success of this important function is the level of authority ambassadors are entrusted with in a region that is characterized by hierarchical management structures. Just how much empowerment the individuals are given will not only impact their roles as ambassadors, but likely trigger a chain reaction of internal change that must be closely monitored and managed.

6. Finding tangible ways to bring each of the brand blueprint strategic elements alive

The preceding five operational initiatives pave the way for what is probably the most consequential of all initiatives: creating the physical environment that will tangibly facilitate the delivery of the brand blueprint.

The strategic pillars identify in broad terms the scope of gaps that exist between the existing reality and the desired identity and customer promise the company will aim to deliver in the future. Its ability to do so will depend as much on the willingness of employees to engage and be part of the journey, as on the infrastructure that facilitates their ability to do so. Expressed differently, it is difficult, if not impossible, for employees of, say, a fruit juice company—generally perceived to deliver an "average" product—to promise consistent premium quality and a unique taste if no changes are made at the sourcing level, or to the manner in how the juice is produced, or to how quality control is managed. Each of these (and other) touch-points provides opportunities for the physical introduction of "tools" that can lead to measurable improvements.

The brand blueprint reflects not only the core characteristics that the company already has, or wants to improve on or deliver from scratch; it also provides an articulated definition of each characteristic.

Consider the formal branding exercise Singapore-based Snorre Food commissioned in 2009. Following the completion of that project, managing director Frank Arne Naesheim moved quickly to translate the desired identity that had been collaboratively crafted by management and employees into an operational reality. His internal alignment program examined ways to improve the company's organizational structure, as well as interdepartmental communications and interaction, to deliver higher levels of efficiency. To complete this process, all employees were exposed to seminars that shared the new company identity and direction. From these seminars, selected individuals were invited to an offsite workshop to discuss and agree on ways and initiatives that would bring each of the brand blueprint elements to life.

One of the four core benefits the Snorre branding project identified was "quality." To ensure that the company didn't fall into the trap of gravitating to a generic expression of quality that offered no differentiation or advantage, the rationale that was crafted to support the benefit defined, in specific terms, what "Snorre quality" would mean to employees as well as customers (see Figure 7.2).

As an importer of fine and premium seafood with a pre-existing reputation for excellence, Snorre decided to express its commitment to quality explicitly, and provide context for its own brand of quality: the CSCT construct. Its decision to focus on North Atlantic sourcing also provides an additional dimension to the fabric of its quality claim. The key challenge at the employee off-site was to get all participants to dimensionalize the expression of Snorre quality, and identify (conventional, as well as disruptive) vehicles that would deliver it consistently. Ideas ranged from introducing new warehousing operational protocols, to implementing enhanced quality control systems that would go beyond industry standards, to the more disruptive game-changing catalyst of launching a state-of-the art, direct-to-the-public facility that would showcase the company's unique range of delicacies. The output of that session would then move one step closer to actual implementation.

In describing his internal alignment exercise, Mr. Naesheim revealed just how central employees were to delivering the company's mission (which strongly reinforced the quality core benefit): "To me everything and everyone is important. When we talk about Snorre quality, I don't want to just import the best possible product to Asia, I also want my people to believe that best quality is something that they themselves will

Figure 7.2 The Snorre brand blueprint

"**Snorre Core Benefit: Quality**
Snorre is an established company that has built a solid reputation of premium fish and sea-food quality that is in large part assured by our Norwegian origins. Our product consistently delivers CSCT—Color, Shape, Consistency and Taste. We ensure that all of our seafood caught thousands of miles away in the pure and unspoilt waters of the North Atlantic is always immediately frozen. This guarantees freshness and Snorre quality to our Asian customers."

only settle for. A feeling that only comes out of natural pride. Doing this is not easy. They need to want to do this. And my job is to create the environment that will help make this happen and be the best example I can be. And in this I can't compromise."

Every company intent on bringing alive its brand blueprint needs to ensure that the appropriate environment that facilitates its delivery exists and is allowed to develop. The best source for ideas that will define that environment will always come from inside the company—those that have a stake, or come to believe they have a stake, in it. While a workshop process provides a useful vehicle to explore and identify the relevant initiatives—the expression of the strategic pillars—it is the CEO's will to implement that makes all the difference. He must not only demonstrate the intent to act, but must also do so within a relatively rapid time frame if he is to maintain credibility and employees are to remain engaged.

External Expressions

Externally communicating the brand is an exciting process because it reveals in often graphic, dramatic, and sometimes entertaining ways much of what, up to that point, has been endless research, analysis, and workshop discussions. It is the phase that transforms much of the theory into reality—much of it visual. It is what some describe as the "sexy" side of the business. But, as was discussed in Chapter 3, caution must always be exercised. It is remarkably easy for external expressions of the brand to excite and simultaneously communicate completely irrelevant messages. To underscore this point, consider this: The very edifice upon which much of Asian business is being built is being daily undermined by the regressive practice by many key decision makers of moving—without hesitation—directly to this phase, in the absence of much of the preparatory groundwork and effort that is the subject of most of the preceding chapters in this book. This is a fundamental brutal truth that characterizes a seriously misguided industry practice that must be remedied if Asia is rightfully to claim the title of "the world's business engine" in the near and long-term future.

The external expression process, like everything else in the company, is heavily dependent on the brand blueprint for relevance and salience. The blueprint must never be overlooked, misinterpreted, or altogether ignored. It forms the frame of reference, as well as the foundation, for all external expressions.

External expressions cover a wide variety of activities and media. A selection of the more common drivers is identified in Figure 7.3. It is at this stage that the company is finally in the best position to review its corporate identity and, where relevant, its packaging or retail store designs. It is at this point that the company has collected sufficient

Figure 7.3 Common drivers of external expression

(a) Corporate identity (brand name, logo, color, typeface, signage)	(d) Graphic standards manual	(g) Customer experience
(b) Packaging design	(e) Corporate video	(h) Brand architecture
(c) Literature/collaterals design	(f) Website development and design	(i) External briefing sessions: ➤ Advertising ➤ Promotions ➤ Public relations

knowledge during the branding project to determine whether its visual identity simply needs to be refreshed, modernized, or changed altogether. The brand blueprint provides all the necessary cues to make this important decision and serves as the brief to design companies.

While the corporate identity visually illustrates the company, other visual elements also play separate but complementary and vital roles: product and packaging design, while specific to the product, will (depending on the brand architecture strategy) reveal consistencies with the corporate (or master) brand; collaterals will reflect the corporate identity in different measures depending on the individual roles of each; and the same will apply to the website design and even its desired user-experience. All these elements will use the graphic standards manual as an inviolate source of reference for all decisions that relate to application and regulations. Everything, and especially the graphic standards manual, will be created relative to the brand blueprint.

For many service and retail businesses—particularly those that sell branded products belonging to other companies, such as department stores—price and customer service are often the two main elements that drive business strategy. While a price strategy (widely used) provides very little room for sustainable growth, customer service is rarely exploited for the advantages that it is capable of providing. The real strengths of customer service lie in the expression of its more sophisticated iteration: customer experience. Customer experience goes beyond courtesy training and aims to deliver a branded customer experience that reflects the brand's positioning or an interpretation of that positioning. The more unique and compelling the experience, the more likely customers are to loyally align themselves with the brand. Customer experience cannot, therefore, be created in the absence of a brand blueprint. It is only at the external expressions phase—after the branding project is completed—that this important strategic dimension can be formulated.

Brand positioning and repositioning projects have a way of redefining or simply fine-tuning business strategy as a bonus deliverable. A clear business strategy coupled to a newly defined brand positioning for the master corporate brand or product brand provides a sound basis for brand architecture decisions. Again, this can only be possible at the post-branding project external expressions phase, and not before or in the absence of it.

The final deliverable of external expressions is arguably one of the most consequential. It provides for the briefing of the company's strategic partners: its advertising agency, its promotions agency, and its public relations agency—among other partners responsible for customer communications. The key understanding that all participants—company and partners—must share is that the information transfer must anchor all communications that are created moving forward. The briefings should not be ad hoc; nor should they be entrusted to junior executives. They should be formal, structured, comprehensive sessions that communicate a clear message to agency partners: "Stay on-brand." Theoretically, the information imparted at these sessions should be enthusiastically welcomed by agency partners who recognize the elimination from the mix of much unnecessary and potentially damaging guesswork (which takes place in the absence of information transfer), allowing them to get on with creating effective work that is relevant.

Re-launch

Sooner or later, the company with its revised brand blueprint must make its public debut. When the time is right, the company needs to announce what it values, what it aims to deliver to different stakeholders, and where it aims to go in the immediate and near-term future. A re-launch sends the appropriate signals to the two most important company audiences—employees and customers—that the company is invigorated and heading in a new and exciting direction.

The company's ability to make its re-launch convincing lies, in large part, in the amount of activity invested in the internal alignment and external expressions phases. If the measures and efforts taken have been consistent with the company's needs to deliver on its declared goals, then employees will have reason to support it and management will have confidence that customers will in time begin to "believe." Without these two preceding phases, the re-launch effort is likely doomed to failure.

How a re-launch is rolled out depends on the size and circumstances of the company and its geographical footprint. If the company is small, operating in one or a few markets, the effort will obviously be more modest than that of a multinational company with thousands of employees and multiple brands. Several tools are available, depending on need and budget. On the one hand are formal events complete with presentations, corporate videos, and prepared announcements to guests that include clients, opinion leaders, public officials, and media representatives. On the other hand is the option of going directly to market with media communications: advertising, promotions, and PR. Still other companies opt for a stealth approach that makes no effort to communicate formally any changes or new news—at least initially. Instead, they rely on customers noticing the change on their own as they experience the new offering.

Be careful what you promise. Regardless of what approach companies choose, the one common denominator they all need to have is operational readiness. Rushing to market without the proper processes and systems in place, or without employees being clear about and aligned to the new brand blueprint, and assigned to the right (often, restructured) roles that allow them to deliver, risks causing untold damage by failing to deliver on one's promises.

Brand Measurement

Consider the athlete who competes to win: What is the point of training to run faster or jump higher if no measurement of incremental progress is made? What benchmark does the athlete have against which to measure how well (or not) she is performing or what part of her training regimen works well and what part does not? In short, without a measurement process that employs relevant metrics, no athlete has the means to improve their performance—much less excel. The same applies to companies doing business where competition is a constant. For all of the obvious benefits that measurement in general and brand measurement in particular delivers, the practice continues to be carried out only rarely by companies in Asia.

To invoke an expression that is thoroughly overused but no less relevant: "What is not measured is not managed." If a brand isn't measured, on an ongoing basis, it won't deliver targeted outcomes. Once again, it is important to remember that everything in branding is *connected*. All of the development work invested in a branding project will be for naught if internal alignment and external expression efforts are not carried out. And these efforts, in turn, will disperse in random directions with minimal impact and effect unless brand measurement monitors, manages, and fine-tunes the brand as it is disseminated internally and takes shape externally in the field.

Measuring the brand requires selecting the right metrics from a long list of possible alternatives. Here, more is definitely not better. Adopting too many metrics that are not directly aligned with specific company objectives risks generating an avalanche of data that creates confusion and invites regression, rather than forward momentum. Separating the "nice-to-have" from the "must-haves" emerges as a critical imperative. The Business and Branding Flowchart introduced in Chapter 4 illustrates the role business goals and business objectives play within the larger, multi-phase process that translates a business idea into a customer relationship. For those relationships to materialize in the manner intended, relevant metrics that measure internal change and external customer engagement need to be activated.

Internal metrics

Internal metrics measure essentially three things: (a) the efficiency of operational processes and systems; (b) how strongly employees embrace the brand; and (c) the brand-centricity of functional departments.

The process that encourages employees to support and embrace the brand is not instantaneous and doesn't happen in a vacuum. That it is going to take time should be a consideration accepted and accounted for by management. Time is a facilitator common to the four phases employees typically need to experience in an internal alignment process: awareness, relevance, credibility, and inspiration (see Figure 7.4).

Awareness: Sharing with employees the new brand blueprint, as well as the strategic goals and plans the company has moving forward, contributes to awareness. These are typically covered during the internal alignment phase discussed earlier in this chapter. A combination of seminars and workshops provides the means to impart this information. The important consideration in this level is that all employees take part.

Relevance: But awareness alone is not sufficient. The awareness effort will reveal, among other things, some of the specific changes the company will need to implement in order to facilitate its ability to deliver the overall promise that it hopes to make to all stakeholders (internal as well as external). These will include revisions and, in some cases, significant changes to the role and job definitions of certain employees. The aim of this phase is to align—to make relevant—the jobs and

Figure 7.4 The internal adoption process

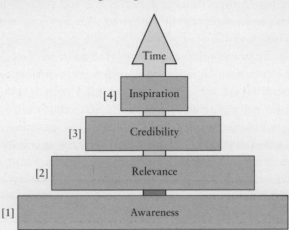

expectations employees have with the goals of the company so that synergies take place instead of friction.

Credibility usually sets in when employees see tangible proof that real changes are taking place and, more crucially, when the strategic pillars are seen to be actually implemented. This is all about walking the talk. Leading this effort should be the brand ambassadors—most importantly, the CEO in his capacity as the brand champion, supported by senior management. Credibility goes a long way in delivering consistent outcomes, be it quality at the assembly line or good customer service in the field.

Nevertheless, companies should always aim for *inspiration*. The level of difficulty of delivering this is only matched by the enormity of the benefit: engaged employees who embrace the brand, who love their jobs and are even defined by them. When this level is reached, the incidence of more employees becoming positive brand ambassadors on their own begins to increase to the point that an internal community emerges. This level of the adoption process is more commonly found in some of the more iconic companies. One of its more visible characteristics is the presence of a strong culture. A strong culture will be built over time if the company is true to its core values and its declared mission. Central to this happening is the commitment made by the CEO.

Internal brand metrics are, in a sense, the ongoing extension of the internal alignment process. They are the checks and balances that manage and reinforce the characteristics of the brand blueprint to all employees. Different types of metrics are available to management to measure progress relative to desired goals. The goals, themselves, mostly dictate which metrics are most relevant and useful.

Dozens, if not hundreds, of different metrics that relate to operational efficiencies or target specific purposes are available. These are generally implemented when specific needs emerge or problems arise. On the other hand, brand saliency, engagement by employees, and brand-centricity require a different set of metrics that need to be implemented on a regular basis to track meaningful trends for fine-tuning and other remedial measures. Both quantitative as well as qualitative research can be used. While the former provides statistical measurements better suited for comparisons, the latter provides valuable insights that help provide context to the data. Among the metrics most commonly used are typically those that measure ongoing understanding, credibility, and "stickiness" of the brand blueprint and engagement among employees:

- What are our core benefits?
- Are core benefits being consistently delivered?
- What are our core values?
- Do we demonstrate genuine belief?
- What is the mission of our company?
- Are we always true to that mission?
- What motivates our employees?

External metrics

The absence of external metrics renders a company blind, which is fine for companies that don't know where they are heading and are content to do business by reacting to market forces. This, of course, is dangerous, as it removes control from the company and makes it vulnerable to all market dynamics—those that may be predictable, but mostly to those that are volatile. For those companies that have established a destination (through vision or well-articulated business goals), the business strategy created to help the company get there will require the tracking of key metrics.

Central to the most frequently used measurements are those of customer awareness and brand recall. But these alone provide little to no benefit in the business landscape of most categories characterized by well-informed and savvy consumers and increasingly sophisticated competitors. Much more is needed. Among the metrics many companies find relevant and useful are those that relate to brand understanding, brand consideration, brand preference, and brand advocacy:

- *Brand understanding:* How clear is the message being communicated to consumers? Are elements of the brand blueprint clear and understandable?

- *Brand consideration:* To what degree does our brand blueprint resonate with consumers? Are there some elements that resonate more than others? Which and why?

- *Brand preference:* Beyond resonating, are the elements of our brand blueprint sufficiently strong to create preference? Which and why?

- *Brand advocacy:* Has the entire customer relationship with our brand been satisfactory enough to compel the customer to recommend it to others?

SUMMARY

Companies are effectively held hostage by their employees. If employees don't want to deliver, they simply won't and often in ways that are difficult to detect immediately and become apparent only after lasting damage has already occurred. By that time, it is often too late.

The ability of any company to make products and deliver services at a level that is expected and consistent depends entirely on its ability to engage employees and make them want to do better and be better. Internal culture—the value of which is woefully underestimated in most Asian companies—plays an integral role in creating engagement.

Good internal culture is not a product of wishful thinking. It evolves out of corporate environments that demonstrate a meeting between words and action: what management promises, and the tangible steps it actively takes to help make those promises materialize. The injunction "Be careful what you promise" applies as much to employees as it does to customers.

A brand implementation program brings the brand alive. This infers that its absence results in brands that end up moribund, or worse. Good internal culture is also the end-result of a consciously planned and executed program that aims to make the company more effective and more efficient. In a brand-centric company, effectiveness lies in properly implementing the brand internally, so that its external expression is what it aims to be, and in doing this consistently.

To help ensure that a brand lives up to its promise, CEOs need to recognize the importance of tracking them. The right metrics provide the vital intelligence needed to ensure that the brand is continually being communicated in the right manner to the right people at the right time and under the right circumstances. This delivers control to the company and places it in charge of its own destiny. Brand measurement effectively converts internal alignment into internal branding—which is an ongoing process. It is the complementing element of the all-important follow-through that telegraphs a company's conviction internally as well as externally.

NOTES

1. Roger Malone, "Remaking a Government-Owned Giant: An Interview with the Chairman of the State Bank of India," *McKinsey Quarterly*, April 2009.
2. Employee comment, BrandAsian Brand Education Seminar to Singapore Yellow Pages, October 6, 2006.

8

CONCLUSION

THE FUTURE IS HERE

"The trouble with our times is that the future is not what it used to be." This observation was made by Paul Valery, a French critic and poet who lived between 1871 and 1945. The comment is as relevant today as it was then—and probably even more so. Change is taking place in a manner that defies predictability and at an exponential rate that is inspired by Moore's Law. And like the effect of compound interest over years, the sheer volume and pace of change today, while incomparable to any other time, is all but likely to be dwarfed by what lies in the near and longer-term future. Looking ahead, Ray Kurzweil predicts that there will be a thousand times more technological change in the 21st century than there was in the 20th century.[1]

The confluence of globalization and technological development has created unprecedented and momentous disruption over the past 20 years, with the spectacular ascents of China and (to a lesser degree) India emerging as two of its most significant manifestations. Now joined by these two emerging juggernauts, most of Asia (which began its modernization drive more than a decade before China and India) has transformed itself and transitioned from a Third World region into one with a critical mass capable of shifting economic power and influence away from the West—what Kishore Mahbubani describes as "the irresistible shift of global power to the East."[2]

The Asian/Chinese Century is not a possibility; it is an inevitability. It is not a question of "if," but of "when." But contrary to the exuberant conviction of Mr. Mahbubani, the signs are pointing to later rather than sooner, mostly because Asian business has been slow to recognize (and exploit) the daily changing landscape and the role it must play in helping to make this paradigm change materialize. In Asia the velocity and magnitude of change that is taking place is so vast and overpowering that, instead of triggering a sense of urgent action among Asian CEOs, it is doing something else altogether curious, if not a little strange: It is crowding the clarity out of the picture. In other words, the amount of change taking place is so overwhelming that it has become all but invisible to these important decision makers.

It is like standing in the middle of a giant crop circle. At ground level, it is almost impossible to recognize it. What is disturbing, however, is the suspicion that even if the pattern were visible, most CEOs would still take little action.

CAUGHT UP IN A GOOD THING

The past two decades of change have delivered a boon to hundreds of thousands of Asian companies across the region, and especially in mainland China. Change has, among many other things, created the circumstances for the "China engine" to roar into life and distribute a great deal of wealth to a great number of people over a relatively short period. That engine is the "China price." High-volume, low-cost production of virtually everything consumed and used on the planet has not only powered Chinese companies, but a not insignificant number of non-Japanese Asian companies as well. The "low cost = high consumer demand" formula has created a momentum that has lasted some 20 years. Many Asian CEOs consider business during that time as having been good, and they see no reason to change their business "philosophy." But the times are changing. That early-model engine, while still powering much of the region, is beginning to feel stretched and tired, and seems visibly out of place on the superhighways that are increasingly replacing the old roads.

Change has not only created the means for Asian business to rise; it has also profoundly impacted the consumer landscape. The desires, needs, and expectations of Asian consumers have changed dramatically over these same years, creating another paradigm shift of its own.

With increasing affluence, Asians have dramatically improved their quality of life—certainly in the metropolitan centers of Singapore, Kuala Lumpur, Seoul, Taipei, Hong Kong, Beijing, and Shanghai. With basic needs satisfied, many have developed desires that are more sophisticated. And very much like consumers in the United States and Europe, they are simultaneously developing higher expectations not only of the brands they buy, but also of the companies that produce them. They are newly empowered and liberated from the financial constraints that formerly limited their consumption choices to only essentials.

A fundamental disconnect is steadily emerging between evolving Asian consumers and virtually inert Asian companies. Instead of closing the gap not only as a matter of good business practice, but also in recognition of an elementary opportunity, Asian companies are, instead, distancing themselves from evolving Asian consumers. While this is not the product of conscious self-destruction, it might as well be. Asian CEOs are not paying attention and are failing to notice that things are different. Some are unwittingly oblivious to the changing landscape, while others just don't want to know. This less-than-desirable picture reflects anachronistic management philosophies, dysfunctional organizational structures, and—amongst many, if not all, CEOs—a streak of hubris that not only prompts them to close themselves off from advice, but also precludes others from providing it out of a fear of being verbally dismissed or physically terminated from their jobs.

THE ASIAN/CHINESE CENTURY

Whether it is referred to as the "Asian/Chinese Century," or the "Asian Century," or the "Chinese Century," or even—as some of the more enthusiastic and bullish Indians (and India admirers) are doing—as the "Indian Century," there clearly exists popular agreement in both Asia and the West that the balance of power is inexorably shifting away from the West. The endless discussions and predictions by economic analysts on global television networks, as well as the profusion of books that either directly debate the subject or refer to it in some measure, all use the same definition of "power": economic might. And for good reason; the evidence is clearly compelling.

> . . . the more compelling brands will also emerge as metaphors for all things that define people.

So, the idea that this shift might soon hit a glass wall would, no doubt, be resisted by many and be dismissed entirely by others who see it as enjoying massive, even unstoppable momentum. This would be a mistake. Looking at the transfer of power uniquely through an economic prism is somewhat myopic. As always, and as with everything, clarity is most visible through a multidimensional view. There is one missing dimension that may appear too subtle to some, but which, in practice, will provide the glue that will cement the great paradigm shift that this and future generations will experience. That dimension, this book argues, is the cultural impact that Asian brands will make on the social fabric of everyday life—everywhere. Presently, this dimension is being underestimated and sidelined because conventional thinking by Asian CEOs confines the role of brand exclusively to business and commerce. This, also, is a mistake. It narrows the construct's universe and perverts the broader appreciation of what brands are in fact capable of achieving. At the center of what is most misunderstood or is poorly understood is the capability of brands to define people.

The unwillingness of many Asian CEOs to recognize the implications of the unprecedented scale of global change, combined with an across-the-board inability to understand and appreciate the fundamental role that brands play as building blocks of great and enduring companies, makes Asian firms especially vulnerable in the present business climate.

EVERYTHING IS CONNECTED; THE REST IS CONCEPTUAL

Understanding and accepting the critical power that brands are capable of harnessing goes hand in hand with the need to accept the central role the branding process needs to play within the internal ebb and flow of companies. This means recognizing a very fundamental construct: *Everything is connected.* Most Asian CEOs make the mistake of treating branding as an isolated function that needs to be addressed individually alongside a laundry list of other operational imperatives. This is not only wrong, but also dangerous. Where brand essentially amounts to the proposition made to stakeholders, branding is the interconnected process that enables it. The reality is that "branding" amounts to one major jigsaw puzzle, with the "brand" at its center influencing everything else (see Figure 8.1). Miss out on one piece of the puzzle and the picture (the company) risks losing clarity and relevance.

Ultimately, the idea that brand-centric companies are best suited to deliver a customer promise successfully and consistently is an operational one that requires not much more than common sense. The more conceptual dimension of brands that Asian CEOs will find more challenging to embrace is the notion that brands are capable of defining people.

Central to creating great Asian and, specifically, great Chinese brands will be the jettisoning of the ingrained collective practice that creates and markets products and services that offer no visible differentiation and, instead, provide consumers with generic attributes and features

Figure 8.1 Branding is like a jigsaw puzzle: Everything is connected; every piece counts

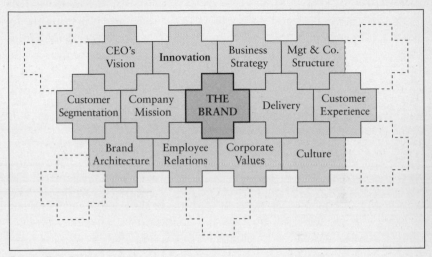

Source: BrandAsian.

that they simply take for granted. This practice—which is almost always anchored by "price"—dominates not just tactical marketing efforts but the very business strategies of many Asian companies. This is not sustainable. Replacing this will require a leap of faith from many CEOs: the confidence to rely on intangibles to create bonding relationships with consumers. The leading-edge driver of intangibles lies within the emotional dimensions of brands.

For the rise of China and the rest of Asia to be sustainable, nothing less than genuinely great Chinese and Asian brands will need to rise alongside. Beyond the profound economic impact this will create, this is going to be crucial, because the more successful brands will be those that emerge as metaphors for all things that define people. And herein lies the formidable power of the brand: The more compelling we find a brand, the more that brand is likely to enter the orbit of our everyday lives alongside other great brands that collectively create a mosaic of associations, values, and beliefs that define who we are (to ourselves as much as others). With many, this begins with brands that help deliver a measure of self-actualization found in religions and (to some) ideologies, which travels down the chain to the personal brands of special people we trust or admire or relate to, and seamlessly crosses over into the commercial canton to brands we enjoy simply because they make us feel good or because they empower us.

> The emotional dimensions of brands . . . will define the DNA of the great Asian brands of the future.

The emotional dimensions of brands—not functional attributes and features—will not only create powerful and compelling Asian brands that will define new generations of consumers around the world; they will also substantiate the DNA of the great Asian brands of the future.

In a corporate context, emotional dimensions are most strongly found in areas that are routinely overlooked or underestimated by decision makers: brand values, brand personality, and the mission to which a company dedicates itself to. Yet, these are the very drivers that provide what people search for the most: validation. In the present environment of rapid change, these will increasingly dictate the alignment that customers externally have with brands, as well as the extent of motivation employees develop internally. As a consequence, the widespread present management attitude that considers these as "nice to have" will need to be replaced with a "must have" commitment.

Creating values and purpose for a company, or generating the right kind of brand personality, is not easily or quickly accomplished; nor are these the sorts of things that can be farmed out to professional third parties. The starting point lies in believing. The CEO must sincerely believe it is worthwhile to want to build a great company for a host of reasons other than just making money; that developing an enduring bond with customers based on trust and relationships matters; that there is an inherent good worthwhile pursuing in providing a reason for employees to feel good about the work they do, the company they work for, and, ultimately, themselves.

> While Asia is rising, the next level up in the value chain beckons.

So, yes, without a doubt, Asia *is* rising. But the next level up the value chain beckons. The undeniable reality is that the region is awash with big and successful companies. While "big" is a relatively objective notion, "successful" lends itself to more subjectivity. "Successful" would almost certainly equate to "good companies." The region is, therefore, overflowing with good companies (with good brands). There is, however, a monumental paucity of great Asian brands: category leaders capable of creating global benchmarks. This, in itself, would not necessarily be remarkable if it were not for the fact that the world is in the midst of a great transition. Great Asian brands are the essential missing ingredients that will trigger the sustainability of the Asian/Chinese Century era.

Beyond CEOs, at least two other parties of interest will play significant roles in helping Asian brands develop qualities of greatness that will help usher in the Asian/Chinese Century: government agencies and advertising agencies.

Government agencies have a huge stake in the business of creating strong brands, for a variety of reasons. Foremost among these is national image and pride—at least, this is how it is mostly interpreted by government bureaucrats all the way up to ministers. To this end, several countries have set up dedicated agencies mandated to help indigenous companies "brand" themselves. The idea is that successful companies will not only contribute to the national economy but will also emerge as valuable national ambassadors. It stands to reason that government agencies are motivated to help companies not only to operate more efficiently, but also to create positive perceptions with customers and "observers" all over the world. The milk melamine scandal in China in 2008 is a case in point. The reprehensible behavior of several Chinese milk companies that resulted in the deaths of at least four children and made more than 50,000 others ill did a great deal of damage to Brand China. It also fueled the popular perception in many corners of the world that Made in China products are either shoddy or deadly. This incident and others like it are major setbacks to Asian government efforts at nation branding. And because everything is connected, commercial brands suffer when national country brands are compromised. If the efforts of government agencies charged with helping indigenous companies create strong brands are to be successful, its officers are going to need to do something that has eluded business executives: fundamentally understand the branding construct themselves. This will achieve at least two important outcomes: (a) the millions of taxpayers' dollars granted to companies will be invested more effectively; and (b) genuinely strong brands will (in time) begin to emerge that (in time) will contribute to positive national perceptions. In most cases, this will require a fundamental restructuring of the way the relevant agencies operate and the conditions upon which assistance and grants are provided. Only great brands have the capability to position their countries of origin in a desirable light. Conversely, "rogue" companies are capable of dispro-portionately damaging the image of a country by creating the perception that other companies are tarred with the same brush.

The role that advertising agencies and other communications com-panies play in creating and building strong brands cannot be overem-phasized. The end-product of their efforts is the most visible expression of brands that consumers see and experience. It is essential, therefore, that the messages created by advertising be as equally on-brand as they are creatively compelling. Right now, the balance is decidedly favoring the latter. Over the past two decades the advertising industry has been rocked by major challenges from within that have given rise to spirited debate over its relevance and future. Nevertheless, its role remains legiti-mate and its importance to the global corporate community, essential. It has the resources to address and overcome these challenges. In Asia the momentum that is empowering Asian companies is providing an addi-tional huge incentive to the better agencies to match their resources to will. Those that come out ahead will be those that manage to do two things: (1) figure out a new breakout strategy that will reposition Asian, but especially Chinese, brands as desirable and emotionally compel-ling companions to global consumers; and (2) demonstrate professional integrity. This will involve recruiting better human resources, then train-ing them to be even better, as well as having the professional fortitude to tell clients what they need to hear.

SUMMARY: TOMORROW'S ASIAN CEO TODAY

Everything starts (or does not) with the Asian CEO. Mahbubani identi-fied Asians' "hierarchical view of the human universe"[3] as one of the reasons contributing to Asia's slow adoption of free market economics.[4] It also happens to be a key contributor to the paralysis that handicaps many Asian companies from moving up the value chain. An alterna-tive management approach that is more open, more inclusive, and more meritorious will be an essential characteristic of the more effective and successful Asian companies of the future.

Secondly, Asian CEOs determined to create great global brands will need to reconsider the very purpose that drives them and anchors their companies. The goal of "making money" as a pure end in and of itself will need to be replaced by a broader commitment to create something that delivers enduring value and benefits multiple groups of people (and not just the brand owner). While this mindset has always been an effective approach for building strong companies, present global circumstances now make it an imperative. Environmental concerns, coupled with economic volatility and political instability, are making consumers the world over both more anxious and more demanding. As governments fail to address the growing list of problems and challenges, the onus is increasingly falling on global companies to step into the breach. For Asia, this creates a unique opportunity. By reinventing themselves, many Asian—and particularly Chinese—category leaders will rediscover the value of purpose as a strategic driver of growth and expansion and, in the process, not only create effective differentiation for their brands, but also capture the imagination of tomorrow's new customers.

Enlightened Asian CEOs will require a not insignificant measure of courage, as well as vision—the ability to see crop circles, as it were. The willingness to see beyond the short term, and the ability to create a comprehensive snapshot of a coherent and plausible heroic future that the company is capable of delivering, will provide critically important direction to companies determined to reach specific destinations. Supported by a meaningful purpose, these companies will redefine the image of Asia not just to Asians but to people around the world. It is these companies that will create great brands.

> *"I think in terms of traders and builders. There are those who are in the market because they see that they can buy something at a high price and flip it around for even higher. That's a trader mentality. Then there are the builders, who realize this is a real strong market that's coming up, and it's a real inflection point in the history of the world. And they are building, despite the ups and downs, they're building for the future."*
>
> Peng T. Ong[5]

The eventual desire of Asians (and, soon, non-Asians) for great Asian brands (like their present desire for great Western brands) will trigger more than a transfer of economic clout to Asia; it will signal the beginning of a more profound change in the world order in cultural terms. It will signal the beginning of the era of global citizens defining themselves via Asian cultural icons and Asian brands.

There is greatness in Asian brands. But for the most part, and for the present, it lies dormant; an untapped fountain waiting to be discovered—not by Asian or Western consumers, but by Asian CEOs. Over the past decade, Westerners have shown a great interest in things Asian. At a time when entire communities in corners across North America and Europe are struggling with social inequalities, the disintegration of familial ties, ethnic tensions, and the corroding effects of drugs and other societal challenges, alternative paradigms are being increasingly explored. Much of that attention is being directed toward Asia. Having the capability of being vehicles to impart new perspectives—even new values—Asian brands are perfectly placed to rise and be embraced by whole new generations of individuals geared, ready, and looking for change.

But, as always, everything starts with the Asian CEO. And there is reason to be decidedly optimistic. Among the legions of competent, but nonetheless conceptually challenged Asian CEOs managing Asia's companies, there exist the exceptions: the mavericks, the risk takers, the visionaries. These exceptional business leaders demonstrate no reverence for tradition and actively seek out new, better, more innovative ways of doing things. They are driven by the desire to create something of enduring value—something that aspires to greatness. These individuals—the equivalent of early adopters—embrace the idea that, for brands to become "great," they must achieve three things: (1) they must be created holistically; (2) they must deliver genuine consumer relationships that tap into human emotions; and (3) they must be a force for good in a world characterized by great and unpredictable change, which is increasingly translating into concern for the environment and anxiety over personal security.

Beyond how these exceptional leaders will lead, is the crucial role they will play as catalysts for other Asian companies. Though presently few in number, they will lead the way and provide inspiring examples for others to follow. Critical mass will be that point when Asian Apples and Asian Nikes and Asian BMWs emerge and capture the imagination not only of Asians, but Westerners as well. When these great indigenous Asian brands emerge, they will likely impact the consumer landscape around the world in much the same way American brands did over the past half century and trigger a new era of momentous social disruption on a scale not seen since the period following the end of the Second World War. To these leaders, the vision is clear, spectacular, and worthy of the risks that come with thinking differently. And when this change happens, it will not only anchor the rise of the Asian/Chinese Century, but will sustain it.

At a time when "Western societies seem to be losing their optimism"[6] and are looking in new directions for renewed inspiration, Asian brands will emerge as new and very seductive benchmarks for ready and receptive audiences the world over. Whether they will share the stage with existing great Western brands or completely dislodge them remains to be seen. According to Kishore Mahbubani, "Asia wants to replicate, not dominate the West."[7] Ultimately, it is consumers who will decide.

NOTES

1. Ray Kurzweil, "The Law of Accelerating Returns," KurzweilAI.net, 2001.
2. Kishore Mahbubani, *The New Asian Hemisphere: The Irresistible Shift of Global Power to the East* (PublicAffairs, 2008), jacket copy.
3. Ibid., p. 57.
4. Ibid., p. 52.
5. Theresa L. Urist, "Creating a Soulful Company: Peng T. Ong's Personal Mantras for Startup Success," *Eyemine*, www.voxunity.com/eyemine/magazine/articles/interwoven.htm.
6. Mahbubani, *The New Asian Hemisphere*, op. cit., p. 3.
7. Mahbubani, *The New Asian Hemisphere*, op. cit., jacket copy.

INDEX